praise for
the accidental millionaire

"Gary's book is a true source of inspiration, while also very engaging and entertaining. Through his journey of life, he demonstrates that opportunities are everywhere—you just have to seize them. He also is living proof that success is not just about numbers but more the fun and excitement of every day. When you are done reading you will be ready for the sequel!"

—JEN GROOVER, author of *What If? and Why Not?*, creator of Launchers Café

"Gary Fong is a world-renowned photographer, inventor, and entrepreneur who has made multiple fortunes and lived a life far more colorful than any of his photos. From his inauspicious beginnings in a tiny, hairspray-saturated apartment that doubled as his parents' wig studio, he went on to become, at a very young age, one of the world's most successful wedding photographers. After making millions in an industry traditionally reserved for small businessmen, he practically stumbled upon serial successes in the photo printing, software, real estate, and camera accessory industries by making intuitive decisions based on his own quirky impulses.

Gary Fong is not a traditional businessman and his story is not a traditional rags-to-riches tale. Known to make important life choices on the flip of a coin, he has followed the whims of fate and instinct to create a life of astounding prosperity and adventure.

Sometimes hilarious, sometimes touching, *The Accidental Millionaire* is a series of 'snapshots' from key periods of Gary's life. When strung together, they form a rich mosaic of a life fully lived and an adventure that is still unfolding."

—ANDY WOLFENDON, story editor for *Chicken Soup for the Soul*

the
accidental
millionaire

how to succeed in life

without really trying

———————

a memoir by

gary fong

BenBella Books, Inc.
Dallas, Texas

Some of the events described in this book happened as related;
others were expanded and changed. Some of the individuals portrayed
are composites of more than one person and many names and identifying
characteristics have been changed as well.

BENBELLA

BenBella Books, Inc.
6440 N. Central Expressway
Suite 503
Dallas, TX 75206
www.benbellabooks.com
Send feedback to feedback@benbellabooks.com

Printed in the United States of America
10 9 8 7 6 5 4 3 2

Library of Congress Cataloging-in-Publication Data is available for this title.
978-1933771-91-5

Proofreading by Erica Lovett and Gregory Teague
Cover design by Michael Fusco
Text design and composition by Yara Abuata
Printed by Bang Printing

Distributed by Perseus Distribution: perseusdistribution.com
To place orders through Perseus Distribution:
Tel: 800-343-4499
Fax: 800-351-5073
E-mail: orderentry@perseusbooks.com

Significant discounts for bulk sales are available. Please contact Glenn Yeffeth
at glenn@benbellabooks.com or (214) 750-3628.

table of contents

the plan

My life has not gone according to "The Plan."

The Plan was for me to go to medical school and eventually pull down a respectable salary of about $150,000 a year.

Had I gone with The Plan, by this point in my life (I'm in my mid-forties) I probably would have just finished paying off my student loans and would be eyeing that thirty-two-foot Catalina sailboat with the FOR SALE sign that I passed every night on my way home from the clinic. I'd be settled into a comfortable home in the 'burbs, with my wife of twenty years and my 2.3 kids, driving a Lexus sedan. And living the life of my dreams.

Well, my *parents'* dreams.

Which I tried, for a time, to convince myself were my dreams too.

Following The Plan made me cry a lot. Eventually I found myself with a literal gun to my own head. That's when I ran from The Plan and began an adventure into uncharted territory.

Uncharted territory goes completely against the grain of my upbringing.

My parents were first-generation Asian immigrants. Their lives' territory was *very* well charted. And they'd charted mine too. My destiny was determined before I was born, and I had absolutely no say in it. My parents didn't know (or particularly care) if I was going to be gay or blind or a violent psychopath. All they knew was that I was going to be a doctor. Secondarily to that, of course, I would be married at a young age to a nice Chinese girl whom my mother endorsed, and I would deliver my mother numerous grandchildren for her to spoil. ASAP.

While I was growing up, my family suffered through sobering bouts of poverty. My parents sacrificed everything to ensure that I could get a good education. All they wanted was for me to not have to face the same financial struggles that they had. As a side benefit, they also weren't going to mind the privilege of saying, "My son, the doctor."

I didn't want to live in poverty either, so I gave The Plan a go for many years. I even got a degree in pharmacology in my attempt to become a physician.

I failed.

And what did I do instead? I became a wedding photographer.

You can imagine the songs of joy this caused to leap from my parents' hearts.

And yet, spring-boarding from that career, which began with moving back into my parents' apartment and shooting weddings for $150 each, I became a multi-millionaire within a fairly short period of time. And it happened due to one improbable accident after another.

I use the word *accident* because I never set out to be rich. I am really not all that gung-ho ambitious, as you'll discern from the pages of this book. I guess ambition is a relative thing. I certainly don't fit the mold of the inspirational characters I've read about. And this book does not contain conventional wisdom about getting rich. Becoming wealthy was never the dream for me. The dream was simply to get as far away as possible from the brutal struggles my parents had gone through.

It wasn't their modest lifestyle that troubled me. I could have lived with that. It wasn't the lack of money either. What got to me was the constant panic on my parents' faces as they sweated out how they were going to survive another day, another week, another month. To me, that look was hell itself. I still have nightmares about it. It's probably something I'll take to my grave.

I credit two very small events in my life, separated by many years, with changing my life. The first occurred when I was ten years old. I wrote in my journal, with oddly grown-up clarity, that I was going to become my own parent. I was no longer going to derive my sense of safety and well-being from Mom and Dad. I simply realized that they would never be able to provide it. This journal entry became a mandate for me to take complete responsibility for my life's direction.

The second event occurred when, as a grown man, I glanced at a bumper sticker on a car. Yes, a bumper sticker.

I was stuck in heavy L.A. traffic, feeling utterly frustrated with the fact that my life was not going according to The Plan, mired in the depths of apathy and frustration, when I saw nine little words on the rear window of a Subaru wagon. Instantly—and I do mean *instantly*—my perspective changed.

The bumper sticker said: SINCE I GAVE UP HOPE, I FEEL MUCH BETTER. I read it, laughed myself sick, and immediately felt the proverbial weight of the world lift from my shoulders.

In that one instant, I gave up all my focus on things going the way I wanted them to. *Ever.* I surrendered all my goals, my visions, my fantasies, my expectations. My Plans. I was suddenly knocked from my inner railroad tracks and felt my perspective opening up like a morning glory in the sun.

That bumper sticker gave me my freedom.

chapter one

My Mom, the Guinea Pig

I'm convinced that an only child has formative experiences that are vastly different from those of a child with siblings. First of all, only children spend most of their time around adults, adults who lack the curiosity and sense of wonder that children have. Adults find the everyday world humdrum and mundane, whereas everything is fascinating to a fledgling human. When an adult and a child are constant companions, the child matures faster—and the adult is reduced to blithering infancy.

As the mother of an only child, part of my mom's job description was to be my primary playmate. She was a great sport about it. We would play army games for hours, wearing salad bowls on our heads as helmets or sitting under a laundry hamper and pretending I was in a car with a mesh cage. She was fun, and she never gave me the "Okay, that's enough" too soon. She played for as long as I wanted.

Little did she know, even after she fell asleep, she continued to be a great source of fun and experimentation.

We would take midday naps, and hers always lasted longer than mine. I would lie patiently beside her, waiting for her to wake up so we could play more games. Lying still in bed and waiting for her to awaken got old fast, and I would quickly run out of things within easy reach to play with. All I could get my hands on was this pebbly blanket covered with tiny sweater balls from the washing machine. I soon discovered that these sweater balls could be easily plucked off, and that there was an endless supply of them. No matter how many I plucked, I could not make a dent in the pebble population.

"When is Mom going to wake up?" I would wonder, as the sun streamed through the windows. I'd be hyper-bored and anxious to play. Mom's loud breathing through her nostrils would make a wheezing sound that was terribly distracting. Wind would rush in and out through those two air holes. In, out. In, out. Like the tide. So much wind! A veritable natural resource. What a shame it couldn't be harnessed . . .

A light bulb ignited over my head.

I wondered what would happen if I held one of those tiny little sweater balls near her nostrils when the air was going in. Determined to find out, I harvested the perfect sweater-ball specimen—not too big, not too small. Pink and full-bodied. Holding it gently between my finger and thumb, my head cocked at a curious angle, I timed the release of the tiny fabric pellet to one of the "in" cycles of Mom's nostril wheezing.

me and mom
sharing a milkshake

Zoop! Like magic, the little ball was gone! Yay!

I plucked another ball, brought it up to her nostril and *Bing!* Just like magic, it, too, was gone! Now I was hoping Mom *wouldn't* wake up. I felt like a magician with a new disappearing act. The Vanishing Sweater Ball Trick became my secret ritual. It was endlessly fascinating. I would watch intently as each ball disappeared, wondering if I could predict its direction and velocity as it left my fingertips.

Years later, when I was studying quantum physics and learning about the Heisenberg Uncertainty Principle (which says that you can't simultaneously measure both the location and momentum of a subatomic particle), I was able to absorb that confusing bit of theory by visualizing the sweater balls disappearing into my mom's sinus cavities.

Oh, the science I learned! One nostril invariably had more suction than the other, and from day to day they would switch roles. Would this be a right-nostril day or a left-nostril day? I couldn't wait to find out. The game just never grew old.

Eventually Mom developed sinus headaches. I remember her blowing her nose furiously and peeling back the Kleenex with a concerned expression when she saw her nasal output was so pink.

Poor Mom was an inexhaustible laboratory.

I can vividly remember back to when I was about nineteen months old. I know this because one day when we were in Seattle I pointed to an apartment building that I thought looked familiar. Dad said that we had moved out of there when I was nineteen months old. Yet I clearly remembered it. I also remembered that this was where I had discovered another ageless scientific principle: When you are in the shower with Mom and you turn the chrome lever to the left, it makes her scream.

When I was very young, Mom would sometimes take me in the shower with her as a matter of efficiency. I liked it better than being bathed. I liked watching her operate the shiny chrome lever. After careful study, I concluded that a turn to the left produced warmer water and right produced colder. Incremental changes in the angle of the lever would change the water temperature proportionately. This was fascinating to me. Of course Mom, being a grown-up, had lost all sense of fascination and scientific inquiry. She never tested the limits. That was *my* job. So one day while she was washing me, I waited until I was safely out of the stream of water and cranked the lever hard left. A full one-eighty.

"*Ayyyyy Da Ka Daaa!!!!*" shrieked Mom at an ear-piercing volume. This was the first Korean phrase I had heard in my life. I still don't know what it means, but I suspect it may be something like, "Do I look like a fucking lobster to you?!!" I remember being juggled wildly about in a flurry of fleshy motion, hot steam filling the room and Mom's skin turning pink. Eventually she got control of the knob and returned it to its boring old predictable position. She didn't even get mad. I tell you, they ought to give out medals.

What's Behind the Mysterious Window?

My habit of testing the extremes got me sent to a special school for gifted children when I was in third grade. Their mistake was telling me I was going to a school for smart kids. Not being particularly well socialized, I proudly announced to all of my classmates that I was going to Genius School and bid them a civil adieu.

The new school was weird. At first I was put in a room alone with a nice man named Mr. Lynne. I remember his name because he looked like Paul Lynde on *Hollywood Squares*. During our sessions, his eyes would always wander toward a mirror on the wall. Something was really strange about that mirror—it was darker than any mirror I'd ever seen. One day I scooted out of my chair, marched up to the mirror, cupped my hands around my eyes to block out the ambient light, and saw two people wearing headphones.

These people were spying on me from another room! I confronted Mr. Lynne about it and he was forced to sheepishly acknowledge the two-way mirror to me. Evidently I was "under observation." This violation of my sense of privacy gave me two-way mirror paranoia for a long time. For years, I would go into bathrooms and cup my hands to check out the mirrors. The thought still crosses my mind occasionally.

At home, I started to have behavioral problems. Like when I told my mom the story of the "see-through" mirror and she said she had never heard of such a thing. I responded, "Well, I'd explain it to you, but you're too stupid to understand because you don't go to genius school!"

That endearing attitude kept getting worse until one day everybody agreed that while the school for gifted kids was stimulating my intellect, the risks of my developing a socially disastrous superiority complex far outweighed the benefits. So they sent me back to public school.

"Ha ha ha! Look at the Genius School dropout!"

"Did you flunk out of smarty-pants school?"

After one day of such treatment, I lost my superiority complex pretty much forever. I never mentioned anything about being smart again. I settled into being a quiet and happy member of the pack.

Then, when I was eight years old, I got yanked out of this comfort zone without warning. My dad was an electrical engineer for Boeing and they had no job for him anymore due to the loss of a major contract. So we had to leave our comfortable house and move to a small courtyard apartment in Los Angeles.

Hairspray

My family's little two-bedroom apartment—six hundred square feet of concentrated paradise—always had a thick odor of sticky, semi-dried hairspray. My mom sold wigs, and you can't just sell wigs straight from the manufacturer. Wigs need work. Mom bought them un-styled, then mounted each one on a gray pincushion head, combed it into a style, doused it with hairspray, then plopped it on a broomstick stuck into a plywood table.

The pincushion heads were cartoonish, with painted eyes and lipstick and fake eyelashes. It was very eerie whenever

my mom fitting a customer with a wig at the wigstore

Mom completed a style job. She'd just take the head and stick it on a pole, where it would sit among a forest of others, looking like the severed heads of the French aristocracy.

Then she'd start in on another one.

Halloweens were good for business because people bought lots of rainbow-colored afro wigs. They looked like furry snow cones, with assorted neon colors sprayed into a rainbow pattern. Very stylish.

Since we sold wigs at the Compton swap meet, most of our customers were black women. Accordingly, those rainbow afro wigs were always mounted on black mannequin heads. Some with blue eyes. Some with blue eyes and fake eyelashes. And all of them thick with the acrid smell of lacquer hairspray that permeated everything in the house.

Our food tasted like hairspray. My fingers smelled like hairspray. When I put on sunglasses, it was like looking out of a windshield after the wipers have smeared it with bug juice. To make matters worse, the glasses would stick to my hair. They were plastic, and believe me, *nothing* could remove that lacquer from plastic.

I often wondered: If everything in the house was coated with lacquer, what was happening to our lungs? I blew my nose and smelled lacquer. All of our dishes were filmed with lacquer. The chopsticks. The toothbrushes. Even the television set had a dull and uneven surface that made *I Love Lucy* look faintly brown and ripply.

We lived on the third floor of a courtyard apartment complex. The building was basically a trapezoidal three-story building surrounding a kidney-shaped pool. The sign that permanently read WARNING: NO LIFEGUARD ON DUTY made me feel lonely whenever I walked by it. For some reason the Beatles' song "Revolution" was always playing in one of the apartments, and you could hear it throughout the courtyard. The name of the building was depressingly misleading: Palace Court.

On the rare occasions that I would invite friends over, nobody said anything about our living conditions. Dozens of lifeless heads frozen in lifeless shock, staring like a jury of C3PO's peers. The acrid smell of plastic and lacquer everywhere. My mom's desk with its adjustable roller-ball headstand where she would tease furiously and joylessly at wig heads, for a styling charge of $6 per crispy hair-hat.

Friends wouldn't say anything, but the next time we'd get together, we'd always meet at *their* house.

Declaration of Independence

Eventually other kids' homes became my home because I basically forced their families to adopt me. I was the kid who came too often, stayed too long, and invited himself to dinner. Oh, and by the way, can I spend the night? Thanks—I brought my sleeping bag. Don't worry about breakfast; I'll help myself to the cookie jar.

I spent so much time at the Ciaobella household, I became fluent in Spanish. They were an Argentinean family whose grandmother lived with them and spoke no English. So the entire household spoke Spanish. As a self-adopted member of their family, I did as the Argentineans did.

As a result, I don't speak Chinese or Korean, the languages of *my* parents. I grew up speaking Spanish with a Castilian dialect.

My parents grew up in two very different cultures. Although both were Asian, and to the untrained eye they looked as if they were from the same country, there is a world of difference between the Korean and Chinese cultures. Language, for instance. When they got married, neither could speak a word of the other's native tongue. While some might see this as a marriage made in heaven, others might point out the obvious impracticalities. How did they get around it? By using the small pool of broken English they shared.

But language was the least of the problems in my parents' house.

Whenever I was home, I felt like I couldn't breathe. There was no real space for a kid. My parents had their hands full with their own concerns. My mom often had health problems and would spend long periods of time in the hospital. When she wasn't sick, she was flailing at the wigs. My dad struggled with unemployment as an electrical engineer and worried. Tension and financial concerns filled the air like hairspray fumes.

I felt despair for my future and fretted about it constantly.

I've kept a journal for as far back as I can remember. (That's where all these stories come from.) One day, when I was ten years old, I wrote an entry called "My Declaration of Independence." It had become abundantly clear to me that my folks had their hands so full with life's struggles that I could no longer entrust my care to them. It was too risky a proposition. I realized that under their emotional umbrella I would forever be unable to relax and grow into the person I needed to be.

So on that fateful day, I resolved that I, Gary Fong, being of sound mind and body, would become the commander-in-chief of my own destiny. I elected myself to the position of self-parent. I became my own custodian. *I* would keep me off drugs. *I* would ensure that *I* would study hard, get enough sleep, and use self-discipline to make myself not only a survivor, but an achiever. I would be responsible for realizing my full potential. Everything—I repeat, *everything*—was to be completely up to me from that day forward.

After writing my declaration, I felt liberated. I had issued myself a daunting challenge, but now I was in control. At least of my internal world.

As a ten-year-old child, of course, my external world was still very much under the control of my parents. But now I knew that it was up to me to take care of inner business and make sure I was always getting what I needed.

That was when I started living a dual existence—always doing what my parents required of me, but also finding ways to do what *I* required of me. This continued until manhood.

Zen and Karate

When our country declared itself free and independent, it took steps to insure domestic tranquility and provide for the common defense. Likewise, as soon as I wrote my own Declaration of Independence, I began to make plans for my own self-defense and survival. How? I decided to take up karate.

There were many different karate schools in the Yellow Pages to choose from. One ad in particular caught the eye of this independent, self-empowered ten-year-old. It was from a studio that taught the *Zendoryu* style of Karate. *Zen-do-ryu* literally translates into "The Zen Method." Of karate.

Putting the silent art of Zen together with the cinder-block-smashing art of karate might seem an odd pairing at first glance. Kind of like the SPCA hosting cock-fighting tournaments. Of course, I would learn that it wasn't very odd at all.

The ad for this particular school said, "Offers solutions for childhood bullies." How wonderfully ambiguous. Did that mean it was designed to help bullies kick even more ass? Or was it a self-defense *against* bullies? Or did it give students the inner calm and self-confidence they needed to quell all desire to fight? Needless to say, reason number one held all the appeal for me.

I was a childhood bully, of sorts. Not that I picked on helpless kids per se, but I did buy into pack behavior. Our school was very into meeting at the flagpole at 3:05. Rather than pick fights on the playground and risk suspension, we would *declare* a fight, and fighters and spectators alike would meet at the flagpole, then migrate to a fighting ring outside of the school's direct jurisdiction, usually some vacant lot or alley. We'd have to rotate the fight venue often because we didn't want to get busted.

I was the new kid in town. Being a complete unknown evokes a lot of mystery, which is heady stuff to a ten-year-old. I'd also had an early growing spurt, so I was 5'5" in fifth grade. If I was going to play up this mystery thing, I wanted to be Bruce Lee. Being the biggest kid *and* knowing karate was my one-way ticket to becoming the new alpha male.

The karate school had a different idea. Their basic message was "walk away." Walk away from confrontation. Walk away? I had to pay $29 a month to learn *that*?

Yup. Every week my karate class received very profound, very Eastern-sounding lectures on why the karate way was to disengage and invite peace. I shut my brain off during these lectures. I wanted to win fights and be an ass-kicking master.

Part of the training required sitting in lotus position for long periods of time, on a hardwood floor, making and hearing no sound whatsoever. The lotus position is more than just sitting cross-legged; you also have to cross your ankles in your lap. This renders you 100 percent immobile when attacked. How this made sense for kicking ass on the playground was beyond me. But the head instructor was a very serious guy, and he had a way of making you listen.

He made us do Zen meditation. We'd start every session with thirty seconds of complete silence. The idea was to completely clear your mind, like a still pool of water. Zen is called the Art of Nothingness, he explained. "Then why are we here?" was the first question that came to mind. Again, it seemed I could get all the nothingness I wanted for free, without shelling out $29 a month.

To make the meditation pass more quickly, I would daydream in vivid detail. I got really, really good at it. It's probably similar to the way people create multiple personality disorder when life is too unbearable to face on normal terms. My escape was daydreaming. Of course, that wasn't the purpose of Zen meditation. The purpose was to be at one—with nothingness.

Eventually I ran out of things to daydream about, and the "nothingness" began to creep in. The reason Zen meditation is great for a fighting art is because it stills the mind. So often when we get into a fistfight, all we picture is popping the other guy in the jaw. But it doesn't work out that way most of the time. Mike Tyson once said, "Everybody's got a plan until they get hit." The moment we're struck or threatened, what typically happens is that the mind becomes frantic, primitive, and extremely stupid. Perception shuts down, balance evaporates, and we become adrenalin-poisoned, lizard-brained, fist-swinging imbeciles.

Zen meditation trains your mind to be still. And a still mind sees clearly. It makes the clearest, fastest possible choice in every moment. Even in a fight.

Of course, what ended up sticking with me from my years of Zen karate training was not the kick-snaps, the karate chops, or the board-smashing, it was this practice of mental stillness. With increased time on the floor in lotus position, the skill of nothingness—and it *is* a skill, believe me, especially for TV-addicted modern Westerners—became more and more accessible to me. In short, Zen meditation is training on how to zone out, how to stop thinking and be in Flow.

It can't really be described in words. It took a long time to learn. After a year, I was able to do forty-five minutes on the floor, in lotus position, completely free of thoughts about how much my legs hurt, or how my butt was falling asleep, or when this was going to be over. They made you do it for so long that you had no choice but to tune out, even if you were a congenitally caffeinated ten-year-old.

Recently, I tried to explain my Zen training to my wife Melissa. She tried it staring out the window of my beach house, gazing into the water with great frustration. She explained, "Even when I'm trying to think of nothing, I'm *thinking* of trying to think of nothing." Believe me, I know. That's the way it works for the first several weeks or months, until effort finally dissolves. Meditation is not about struggling or trying, it's about allowing, letting go.

Melissa thinks I am one of the most patient people she has ever met. My Zen training was definitely instrumental in honing this attribute. Zen is not really about *patience*, though, because when you're patient, you're still secretly waiting for the outcome. Zen is about the process, not the outcome. I learned that when you focus on the outcome rather than the process, you can easily miss the target by ignoring all the little clues along the way that point you in the right direction. The signs are subtle and nearly silent and can only be perceived when there is a lack of distractions.

The biggest distraction of all is focusing too intently on the goal. And the skill of "defocusing" became a skill that would pay off handsomely for me in the future in unexpected ways.

Manny's Mudsuckers

Not long after my Declaration of Independence, I discovered a passion for bicycle motocross. For those of you unfamiliar with BMX, this organized suicide attempt involves flinging specially modified bicycles with knobby tires and small wheels (with your body attached) around a series of dirt hills and rocky outcroppings, making occasional bone-shuddering contact with the ground.

My BMX career came about because all the kids in my neighborhood would hang out in empty lots on our little Schwinn Stingray bikes. Bored to tears, we eventually built bike jumps. Then we would light fires below the jumps so we would be able to jump through fire. When this was deemed not dangerous enough, we would lie, side-by-side, like cordwood, below the jumps and take turns trying to "clear" longer and longer lines of bodies.

You didn't want to be at the end of the line when the limit was reached.

We came up with all kinds of genital-destroying games to play on our bikes. One day I decided to try to get in the *Guinness Book of World Records* for the furthest-ever jump off a ramp. I penciled a design for a jump ramp that would enable me (in my dreams) to fly hundreds of feet before landing in the marina harbor. This idea came to a screeching halt when I learned that landing in water from a high drop was every bit as violent as landing on concrete. So I cancelled my plans for the big jump. But that didn't squelch my desire to fly around rocks and dirt on a little self-powered bike.

Eventually our suicidal cravings gave way to organized races. In fact, I can honestly say that I was there when the whole bicycle moto-cross phenomenon started. It began at Palm's Park in Santa Monica, under the guidance of Ron Mackler, a neat guy in his twenties who genuinely cared about kids. He made this small bicycle motocross track that started off in a sandbox, wrapped around a tree or two, went up a hill, and then ended in a flat area. Some of the kids added some bumps and berms. BMX has since grown into a serious sport (it was even an event at the Beijing 2008 Olympics), but at the beginning it was just a bunch of kids racing around sandboxes.

My parents, of course, would have none of it. They wanted me to study all the time, so extracurricular activities didn't make sense to them. Why spend time playing sports when I could be studying to get even better grades?

This was obvious to them, but not to me. As CEO of my own life, I knew that BMX racing was important, even if I didn't know exactly why. So I kept doing it every chance I got.

One day, completely out of the blue, my parents said they'd noticed I was getting little bowlegged. My dad informed me that he had thrown my BMX bikes in the dumpster. Well, this was an issue, especially since one of the bikes belonged to my sponsors. An executive decision needed to be made. I called up my friends and asked them to rescue my bikes from the dumpster and hide them in various locations.

Being expressly forbidden to ride BMX bikes made it even more enticing. I could feel the competitive pulse pumping through my veins whenever I thought about racing. But I now had a dilemma to solve: my parents had forbidden it.

But they hadn't forbade fishing. Maybe because it produced fish, and fish could be eaten. So, working with the options I had at hand, I devised a scheme that would allow me to race bikes and keep my parents happy at the same time.

I went fishing.

Every Saturday there would be motocross races at Lemon Tree Mall. I had become such a strong rider that I was invited to join a BMX team for a local bike shop called Manny's Cyclery.

Manny was a terrific bike mechanic. His custom-welded frames were painted only in primer. The color was between rust and mud, like something you'd see in Santa Fe. These bikes were rough and rugged-looking and came to be known as "Manny's mudsuckers."

Having made my way on to the team, I was entrusted with one of these coveted bikes. Of course, I couldn't bring it home. It had to be hidden at my friend's house.

Here's how the scam worked. On Saturdays I would wake up at 4:30 A.M., even though the race day didn't start until around 1:00 P.M. I would grab my fishing pole, bucket, and tackle box and walk a mile and a half to my friend Kevo's house, where my bike was hidden. I'd pull my bike out from behind a shrub, remove the tarp, climb on, and ride down to Fisherman's Village in Marina del Rey.

There I would fish for about an hour. A salty old fisherman taught me this cool technique of filleting live anchovy bait that practically guaranteed one fish caught per every cast. It was a formula for success that went hand-in-hand with my motocross scheme. It gave me my alibi.

After I had bagged three or four fish, I would throw them into my bucket and pedal back to Kevo's house. I would deposit my catch in his fridge, pedal five miles to Manny's Cyclery, and join my teammates for a day at the races. At the end of the day, I'd come home with fish.

I always won trophies. Those never went home with me, which made me sad. But they did stay on display at Manny's shop, where I would visit them and marvel at my growing collection.

Then one day, Manny's shop was gone, and so were my trophies.

You can only control so much.

A couple of years later, Dad ended up getting laid off for a full nineteen months, and that's when things really started getting dicey.

A Night Under the Stairs

At twelve years old, I became terrified that we were going to become homeless. The strain of my dad's unemployment was not lost on me.

If we got kicked out of our little apartment, I doubted that my parents would be prepared for surviving on the streets. As was my custom, I decided to take matters into my own hands.

While browsing through a magazine, I happened on an ad for a Desert Survival Kit. The ad said, "Includes a Space Blanket—fits in your pocket!" Back in the 1960s and '70s, you just used the word *space* in front of anything you wanted to hawk as cool and high-tech—like "Space Energy Drink." The survival kit was of particular interest to me because of my impending sense that my family might soon be out on the streets.

The Space Blanket, let me tell you, was some kind of futuristic stuff. It was, as I mentioned, part of the Desert Survival Kit, which included a can of Sterno, a cheap radio, some freeze-dried bars that stayed freeze-dried even after you bit into them, some kind of brownish jerky-substance, waterproof matches, a flare, a plastic mirror (to signal planes in case your flares ran out), a plastic compass with a randomly circling needle, and three eight-ounce containers of "potable" water—not *fresh* water, mind you, just "potable."

The centerpiece, though, was the Space Blanket, a thin sheet of Mylar that indeed fit into a little pouch—that part was true. Calling it a blanket, though, would be like calling your mailbox an apartment—it was an absurdly crinkly piece of micro-thin plastic that crackled whenever you moved.

A handy feature when one is trying to sleep.

The Desert Survival Kit cost $12. But it guaranteed that you could live for up to three days with no other supplies. I honestly thought, "Well, if my family's going to be homeless, I might as well practice and get used to the idea." So I shelled out the $12—pretty much my entire life savings—and decided to give the homeless thing a whirl.

I wanted to face my fears. I wanted to embrace homelessness, squeeze every bit of romance and adventure out of it. Like Steinbeck or Kerouac. After all, I figured homelessness was inevitable because my dad seemed to be chronically unemployed. It wasn't his fault; he was an electrical engineer for defense contractors, and in those years when the Cold War had really cooled off, there was no work.

My dad tried to keep his anxiety to himself, but come on. We were selling wigs at weekend swap meets and delivering newspapers. It was obvious we were not among the Hollywood elite. We were one sheetrock wall away from the streets.

So I was determined to face down the inevitable. One afternoon, armed with my freshly purchased Desert Survival Kit, I hopped on my BMX bike and rode down from Playa del Rey, across the spectacular oceanfront bike path to Marina del Rey's Fisherman's Village, a quaint-ish seaside village with boutique shops and fancy restaurants on a boardwalk.

At the entrance to the village sits the Marina del Rey sheriff's station. I quickly spied the perfect place to be homeless: underneath the stairs. It was dark and dry and away from foot traffic. All in all, a pretty cherry piece of real estate for a hobo in training.

It was about 3:00 P.M. on a weekday. I parked and locked my bike, then ducked under the sheriff's station stairs.

Step 1: make camp. This meant laying out the Space Blanket.

Did I mention how loud the Space Blanket was? It was louder than the Emergency Radio that came in the Desert Survival Kit. In fact, the two items sounded remarkable similar—scratchy, ear-stabbing static. I actually thought the Space Blanket was going to blow my cover before I even had a chance to settle in. Everyone in Marina del Rey must have been able to hear that thing! I swear, it took me a full twenty minutes to unfurl it on the ground, because I had to proceed in quick little fits and starts. CRINKLE—pause—CRACKLE—pause—RUS-TLE—pause—CRACKLE—pause . . .

I finally managed to unfold the whole Space Blanket, but how I was going to actually sleep on it without drawing down the entire sheriff's department with weapons at the ready, I had no idea. For now, though, there was a more pressing concern: I had no pillow.

I actually considered going through the dumpsters to look for a discarded beach towel to rest my head on. Instead I went into the public lavatory and grabbed two rolls of toilet paper. Those and the Space Blanket would have to do for my underside, but what would keep my topside warm at night? All I had was a hooded sweatshirt. I was quickly discovering the limitations of the Desert Survival Kit.

I lay down on the Space Blanket, hugged myself with the hooded sweatshirt, re-formed the toilet paper rolls with my head and neck, and settled into my little fort-home.

Okay, now what? This was as far as I'd thought things out. What did one do when homeless? How did one spend one's leisure time?

I decided to begin with a little reconnaissance work. I scoped out my environs. There was the public restroom, plus a drinking fountain, so I could really make my "potable" water supply last.

Then I took inventory. I didn't have any money, but I had my can of Sterno (with nothing to cook or keep warm), my unidentified jerky substance, and my energy bars. Plus, of course, the "potable" water, in case I had to really go to ground.

I decided to wait until I was ravenously hungry before tapping into my rations. My strategy was to fill myself up with a large volume of water to displace the hunger. I tried to nap from time to time, but the stentorian sound of the Space Blanket eliminated all hope of that. I played with the waterproof matches. I tested out the Sterno. Yup, it burned. I wondered if it was provided for cooking a fresh kill, but the Desert Survival Kit offered no weapons. Evidently it was designed for gatherers rather than hunters.

I pretended I was a missing P.O.W. in the jungles of 'Nam. Turning on the Emergency Radio to KNX 1070 Traffic News and Sports quickly shattered that illusion.

I was discovering a decidedly unromantic and non-Steinbeckian fact about homelessness: It was boring.

I spent one night of fitful sleep under that staircase. I remember awaking in the pre-dawn hours with no recollection of where I was or how I'd gotten there, followed by the groggy realization that I had chosen to sleep under a staircase. A sheriff's station staircase. A nearby sodium vapor light was casting a beam into my hole. I covered my eyes with my forearms and fitfully dozed to the sound of horn blasts, swearing fishermen, police radios, and sidewalks being hosed down by merchants.

Come morning, I made an executive decision: I had learned all I needed to learn about homelessness in one night. I didn't really need to complete my research study after all. Two more nights weren't going to teach me anything I didn't already know. Besides, if I had to take another bite of that jerky-matter, I might just contract scurvy, and that would mess up my life for months into the future. So I put my unbelievably loud Space Blanket back in its pouch and headed off on my bike.

When I got home, I went to my room and realized it wasn't very different from my under-the-staircase fort. Not much bigger, and, really, not much nicer. Then something strange happened. I let go of all my fear. I realized that living homeless versus living in my bedroom was not much of a leap after all. I lay down on my bed and slept like a baby.

Thankfully, we never became homeless. But to this day I've never forgotten the fear. In fact, what has driven me for much of my life is not so much the desire to be rich as the desire to distance myself from poverty as much as possible.

But I still have nightmares.

Swap Meets and Filet Mignon

On Friday nights my family would load up our old sky-blue and white Dodge van in preparation for the Saturday swap meet. The engine compartment actually sat in a metal box inside the van, between the passenger's and driver's seats. Good design decision. That meant the smell of gas fumes constantly filled the van, whether it was running or not. Gas fumes and hairspray. That was my weekends.

My dad was clever in transporting our "wig-wam" to the swap meets. One table was made out of plywood and had those do-it-yourself table legs on the bottom and a bevy of broomsticks screwed into the top. These were set up amphitheater-style, with the wig heads arranged in tiers for optimal viewing. Another table fit perfectly underneath, with the wig-head poles pointed downward. An array of numbered plumbing pipes would clang about the cargo floor of the van, along with a box of plumbing connectors and giant clips. We also brought along a large sheet of canvas.

We would drive forty-five minutes to the Compton Swap Meet before sunrise—right after we finished delivering newspapers—and line up in what looked like a gypsy caravan to await entry to the swap meet. These swap meets were held in drive-in theaters during daylight hours. We would pay our daily "display" rent fee, they'd let us into the lot, and we would speed to our preassigned sales space.

I don't know what the hurry was, but all of the cars would bob crazily up and down through that bumpy lot. Sort of like motocross bikes going through whoop-de-doos. Everywhere you looked you'd see gypsy-like families flying around the cabins of their vehicles as if they were product-testing a new line of pogo sticks.

Once we got to our spot, the silent ritual began. Dad would lay out a pattern of lead pipes. I would get the corner-fitting pieces and we would screw the pipes into the corners. We would then use the large clips to attach the canvas, and up would go our tent like an Amish barn-raising. The goal was to create a shady shopping area for wig-browsers. This was a competitive advantage and definitely worth the effort. Within half an hour, we would have our swap meet "wig store" up, complete with a WIG − SALE! sign and tiered rows of heads watching the crowd like a silent, decapitated choir.

All I was really needed for was the setup. Once that was done, I had absolutely nothing to do until closing time at 3:30. There was nowhere to lie down, so I would sit in the passenger seat of the truck and daydream among the gas fumes. Through the flat, square windshield I looked out on a massive empty cinema screen, chalky white and bulky in the midday sun. Nothing says "no fun" as succinctly as a blank movie screen.

For Christmas one year, we got a Sony 12-inch black-and-white TV. It was great because it had rechargeable batteries. It gave you about ninety minutes of TV with the best signal you can crank out of a pair of rabbit ears encircled by a sheet-metal van. That meant I could watch some bad TV for a little while—before the sound went silent, the signal snowed out, and the screen turned black. Well, lacquer brown. Once the batteries were spent, it was naptime. The fumes always made me drowsy.

Noon would roll around and my mom would open a gooey pot of rice. Inside a Tupperware bin, she would have Korean barbequed short ribs. While it all had a tinge of hairspray flavor mixed with the smell of gasoline, it was delicious. I would eat loads of rice because I knew if I got full, I would fall asleep for another couple of hours, leaving me fewer hours to wait before we had to dismantle the tent and load the mannequin choir (what was left of it) back into the van for our forty-five-minute drive home.

There was one amazing side benefit to doing the swap meets: We feasted on filet mignon steaks every evening. That's right. See, there was a meat vendor at the swap meet who sold filet mignons in vacuum-sealed pouches. A big box of filet mignons was really cheap, and one box was a week of dinners, so we ate filet mignon literally every night of the week, despite the fact that we were on the verge of financial ruin.

Funny thing, though. Today I can afford to order the finest meals at the world's finest restaurants. And you know what? I never order filet mignon.

From $75 a Month to $75 an Hour

As a teenager, all I wanted to do was play tennis and chase girls, but "fun" was not on the Fong family agenda. I had to study whenever I wasn't in school or working. And I was pretty much *always* in school or working. When I was in high school I needed to wake up at 3:15 every morning to deliver newspapers with my father. Throwing papers was the only way we knew to diversify our wig-selling business.

The daily delivery of a newspaper to your home requires a lot of work. From some very low-paid people. Most of the folks delivering papers are like my dad and me were: struggling, barely making rent. (Keep that in mind when Christmas tip time comes around!) Paper hurlers are like the undocumented aliens washing dishes in our favorite restaurant—we don't want to know they're there; we just want to keep paying $8.95 for the Burger Plate.

Every morning—and I mean *every* morning, no days off—we'd haul our station wagon to a parking lot, where automated newspaper-folding machines waited next to an impossibly huge pile of papers in our assigned parking stall.

We'd back up to the pile, rain or shine, and fire up the automated string machine. The reason you need to fold and string the paper is because if you throw a paper without binding it, it will, of course, blow open all over the yard. This causes a lot of unnecessary swearing during the wee morning hours. So each paper has to be folded and tied with string.

Everyone who confronts the string machine first puts their hand in it and watches with amazement as a super-taut string instantly snaps over their wrist, with a pre-measured amount of slack—and it doesn't even hurt. I always used to know who slung papers for a living—it was the person with string around their wrist. We were like a secret society.

I could string as fast as I could fold. Dad and I would stand side by side, throwing papers into the back of our station wagon with the rear hatch suspended. Other people had pickup trucks. We felt sorry for them, because a station wagon would at least allow the thrower in the back—me—to stay warm and dry on rainy days. What we didn't count on was the dizzying effect of three hours of inhaling exhaust fumes in an enclosed space. In those days, it seems, the only time I *wasn't* inhaling noxious fumes was when I was in school.

Your first day of throwing papers is a washout. You have to get papers to people's homes before they leave for work or else they phone in a complaint. Trying to navigate your map assignment on day one is absurd. We took a wrong turn on about every third block, and sometimes we'd miss the address, so I would have to walk around in the cold and dark, dodging snarling carnivores, looking for the right house number.

That first day, many of our papers didn't get delivered until 8:30 A.M., a woeful five hours after we started folding. Phones were ringing off the hook at the newspaper dispatcher's office.

If there's a worse way to make money than newspaper delivery, it is a classified secret. You have to pay for your own gas and your own vehicle's wear and tear. And to make it work with anything resembling efficiency, you need two people, because you can't throw and drive at the same time. Once you've mastered your route, you can get through it in maybe three hours. That's seven days a week. In the middle of the night. For a whopping $75 or $85 a month.

God help you on Sundays when your (always ancient) vehicle's suspension system is thoroughly overwhelmed by a massive cargo-load of Sunday papers. On Sundays, we would tool around the neighborhood at speeds of up to 40 mph. No seatbelt, of course. And every time we'd hit a bump, sparks would fly from the dragging tailpipe and down would come the hatch!

Our route, once we perfected it, became a robotic ritual. Dad and I wouldn't talk much, and the radio always played Top 40. Whenever I hear "Rock the Boat" by the Hues Corporation, I find myself right back in the trunk of that station wagon.

We would usually get home by 6:30 A.M., which meant I could sleep for another hour before I had to go to school. Man, I hated that. I had to go to bed by 7:30 every night to get enough sleep to do the paper route. The few hours I had left to myself every day were apportioned to homework.

It dawned on me one day, with stunning clarity, that hard labor made absolutely no sense as an economic model. How could my time be worth only a few dollars per hour? I mean, just in terms of caloric value, the energy I spent hauling newspapers around ten square miles of L.A. suburbs would need to be replenished by at least one McDonald's Big Mac combo, which cost almost exactly what I had earned.

Therefore, this was an activity that resulted in zero net gain. That meant I could just as profitably stay at home and sleep, not work up an appetite, and thus not need the money that only went into feeding myself.

How this money model made any sense at all to my dad I couldn't understand. I figured he must know something I didn't. All I knew was that I had to find a way out of this labor trap.

Then one day Dad discovered subcontracting. While the benefits and job security weren't there for these short-term jobs, the hourly rate was astonishingly high. He was an engineer and made $75 an hour—about what we made in a month of delivering the paper. So that zombie ritual ended.

Dad started working in Malibu, right on the Pacific Coast Highway. He used to have a funny saying: "Chicken one day and feathers the next." These, supposedly, were our chicken days.

So everything changed, right?

Nothing changed.

Nothing Changes

Dad saved every dollar he could hang on to. On one level I could understand it. Every hour's wage he squirreled away meant a month of not having to throw papers again. But on the other hand, what was the point of earning more money if you couldn't live a little? The fact was, nothing changed in our lives except for occasional dinners at the Malibu Sea Lion. (We always had to order the least expensive items on the menu, but at least we could watch the waves crash at the windows.)

For some reason, I was keenly aware of Dad's savings. Eventually he had over $20,000 put away. He made a few good buys on the stock market, too. One day, we went to an affluent coastal suburb of Los Angeles called Palos Verdes Estates. My dad had a friend there who'd come from China with him. His name was Kuey Fong, and he lived in a spectacular ocean-view house. We were living in the Palace Court apartments, but this place was a *real* palace. It had a grand staircase that reminded me of the Brady Bunch house. It smelled of new carpet and fresh paint, not hairspray. And it was huge. I mean, we were living in about six hundred square feet, and this house had to be five times that. Not being big on social etiquette back then, I asked Kuey Fong what a house like that had set him back.

me and dad "shaving."
I actually didn't start shaving until I was
thirty years old

Sixty-eight thousand dollars. I was shocked. That was a lot of money to me. But I also knew that my dad, in a fairly short time, had accumulated enough for a healthy down payment on a house in the same neighborhood. And what a neighborhood it was! Great schools, spacious ranch-style homes with California-signature terra cotta roofs, and the roar of the ocean. It felt like it was my destiny. It seemed like a no-brainer. And real estate was going up. We needed to buy!

Dad's favorite phrase was "next year." I think it came from so many disappointments. Would this be a chicken year or a feathers year? He never knew, so he didn't want to risk losing a house. He'd sold his house in Seattle during a market downturn and had made just a little more than he paid for it. Had he hung on a couple years more, the price would have quadrupled.

So he said "next year" to a Palos Verdes house. I kept looking at the real estate ads. Next year, the same house had doubled to $150,000. I would show my dad the ads: "See, you could've doubled your money!"

He said no, real estate was a bad investment.

Do kids do things subconsciously to settle the score for their parents' misguided judgments? Kind of like how G.W. went after Saddam Hussein after his father backed off? Maybe. All I know is that when I see a nice piece of real estate in my adult life, if it's a good deal and fits within my investing profile, I buy without hesitation. I've bought homes over the internet, sight unseen. I've made good money in real estate, but my dad never believed in it. He knows I've done great, but he says that it's because I'm lucky.

He never said why he thought real estate was a bad investment. I guess he felt he had some special inside information that the rest of the financial world didn't know.

The next year the same Palos Verdes house was over $400,000. Dad kept saying, "Nobody is going to pay that." But prices kept going up. Every Sunday I would see the ads. Now $800,000. Now $1,100,000. For a house he could have snagged for $75k a few years back.

I think it made Dad angry when I would say, "Look what you missed!" But hell, I was angry too. We were still living in the cramped Palace Court apartment when we could have been living in an ocean-front palace.

That was when the veil started to lift for me about the mysteries of adulthood. I was beginning to see the wizard behind the curtain, and he was not so mystical after all. Up until then I had thought that maybe adults had some secret knowledge unavailable to kids. That belief had pushed me through slinging newspapers and selling wigs, even though it made no sense to me.

Now I saw, starkly, that it just wasn't true. It slowly became obvious to me that decision-making is actually quite simple. In any situation there are three possible outcomes, and two of them are winners. (1) You can gain, which is obviously a winner. (2) You can lose, which is also a winner, because in the process of losing, you learn what not to do next time. Or (3) you can choose to do nothing and stay exactly where you were before. Option three was the only real loser.

To advance in life, you needed to *do* something, I realized. Do anything, but don't try to preserve your position. In a world of endless change, that's the one position that guarantees failure.

Where I used to think there was some hidden formula that prevented my dad from taking action, I started to realize that this formula didn't exist anywhere but within the steel clamps of fear that shackled him. I realized that Dad and I saw our worlds differently. He didn't want to lose what he already had; I didn't want to lose opportunity when it arose.

Both my dad and my mom grew up in wartime. They had lived feral lives in a hostile Asian environment. Like wild dogs, prowling about, ducking for cover, and scavenging for food. That experience changes you. I would not know what it was like to live in a country under attack until well into my adulthood.

When you grow up during a war or in an economic depression, you tend to see the world through a very different lens than those of us who are privileged to grow up in relative stability. Opportunity seems like too much to ask; all you want to do is hold on to what you already have. All you want is for the world to stop clobbering you so you can appreciate the simple things.

My dad came to the United States at age eighteen and met his father for the first time. My grandfather had departed for the States shortly after my father was born. He'd gotten work as a cook and eventually become a US citizen. My dad grew up during the second Sino-Japanese war. Most of his young life, he just wanted to get away. That was his prime motivation—to be somewhere other than where he was. Finally he got his chance to come to America, the land of promise, the land his father had adopted. After a three-week boat trip, he arrived on our shores, a naturalized US citizen. At last his life could begin!

No sooner had he unpacked his suitcase than he was drafted and sent back to Korea. He was back on the boat before he had a chance to see his first full moon over Malibu.

It's bad enough to worry about putting a roof over your head; it's worse still to worry about the roof over your head being blown off. Dad just wanted the shelling to stop. He and I simply had different agendas. As I was becoming more action-oriented, he was becoming more risk-averse. I started to see this objectively and no longer felt frustration or anger toward him.

Looking back, I think all Mom and Dad wanted was to never have to sell wigs at a swap meet or sling newspapers again. But when Dad's $75-an-hour gig ended, where did he invest his money? He bought a wig shop in Compton, California. My mom, he reasoned, had the experience to earn $6 per hour!

So they bought the store right in the heart of Crips and Bloods country. And I dreamed of ocean waves.

But I did make a resolution. I resolved never to pass on a piece of real estate I liked that was a good deal. I also resolved to never ever *EVER* use the phrase "next year" for anything I was pondering. I would either do it immediately or let it pass, but I sure as hell wasn't going to wait one year to act. Watching the value of that oceanfront real estate increase tenfold while I choked on hairspray fumes changed my philosophy on life. And I've never looked back.

Surviving in Compton

Our Compton wig store was called Sasco Wigs. The store was about thirty feet wide. When closed, it was protected by a steel cage that we rolled in front like a sideways garage door. Inside, the noxious gas of acrylic hairspray was everywhere, just like at home. Wig heads too. At night we would have to turn the lights off in the back before exiting by the front door, creating an eerie gallery of ghostly mannequins in the dark, whose eyes seemed to follow us out the door. I hated that.

The city of Compton borders Watts (ground zero for at least two massive race riots) and is smack in the middle of South Central L.A. The area is solidly black and the militarized zone for the Crips vs. Bloods gang war. Back then, gang members carried jacked-up tape players called "boom boxes" on their shoulders. These boxes were something like 4' x 1' x 1', quite heavy, and had flashing lights and about four million batteries to blast the bass as far and wide as possible.

On the adjacent corner were a Savings and Loan building and a dentist you could pay on credit who specialized in dispensing sodium pentothal. Painless dentistry reached new heights in his hands. We would often see the familiar brown vans from the L.A. Coroner's office pull up and haul off another body lost to too much anesthesia. Black body bags on gurneys and hushed conversations were a common sight at the back entrance of the credit dentist. We all wondered why he was never closed down, and mused that if the victims had been white, the place would have been history.

Next to our store was an oddly out-of-place, stylish haberdashery owned my Mr. and Mrs. Jones. They were a lovely older black couple with an air about them that reminded me of *The Cosby Show*. With short-cropped salt-and-pepper hair, Mr. Jones always showed up at his humble but elegant store wearing a suit. Mrs. Jones always looked like she was just returning from the opera. In all my time there, I honestly never saw them with a customer, but their gracious manners always made me sit up at attention whenever they would stop by to say hello.

There was an oddly insular, cozy feel about having a little store in Compton in the heat of summer. Our shop was air-conditioned. When it was blazing hot outside, we remained semi-comfy inside, sitting on ratty old cloth couches.

The back room was where I spent a majority of my time, watching TV or waiting until the next meal.

Those meals would be ordered at the counter of the nearby burger joint. The owner's name was Bruce. He was a nice middle-aged black man who worked the counter and the cash register, and made the greasy burgers and fries that he offered with thousand-island dressing or chili. I loved his food because it made me groggy enough to doze off and kill a few hours.

There was absolutely nothing to do in the back room of Sasco Wigs. It was beyond me why my folks mandated that I spend my summer days in that store. I guess it was for my own safety, but I would have taken my chances anywhere else on the planet.

We had a wig stylist named Consuelo. Consuelo was a Latin *muchacha* in her early thirties. She was extra busty and overweight, and the shape of her jeans resembled a two-fingered latex glove filled by a fire hose. Her over-processed hair looked exactly like a dyed-orange floor mop. The thought of touching it gave me the heebie jeebies. But I knew she had kids, so somebody must have touched it at some point.

Consuelo believed in her heart of hearts that she was smoking hot. She smoked a lot, too, so secondhand smoke blended with the smog of hairspray to further intensify my daily pounding headaches. She wore wedge-y platform heels called *famolares*, which were all the rage in the '80s and so ugly that I'm sure they're back in style now. Her shoes were always too small, which made her toes grip the edges like monkey fingers. Her extra-long toenails would usually be painted black or bright yellow, giving them the appearance of parrot claws. One time she wore tan nylons and her toenails poked through them; this didn't make her the least bit self-conscious.

For some reason—and this is true of many women—her conviction that she was drop-dead sexy seemed to work. Men would constantly visit the shop and hit on Consuelo. She would always reject them, but would glow from the attention, feigning exasperation with a cigarette dangling from her lips.

I was completely mystified as to how she induced sexual thoughts in anyone.

Black men can be extremely funny when they hit on women. They don't try to be courteous and indirect like white guys. They put it right out there: "Come on, baby! Let's you and me get married, only let's skip the marriage part and go straight to the honeymoon!" Or smooth lines like, "Oooh, my, my, my, I want some of that! Come on, baby!" It was hilarious to see their unabashed pleas followed by sassy rejection. Consuelo loved it, and I enjoyed watching it.

Consuelo probably saved our lives.

One gentleman caller of hers was a security guard at the Savings and Loan building next door on the other side. He was always armed and he was always coming over. He would bring Consuelo a flower in a little vase or some chocolate. He really liked her. She would say, "Honey, you know you're too old for me!" Or other harsh thumps like, "I like my men tall, and gooooood looking."

Still, this guy was pride-free and undeterred and would regularly visit our shop for five, ten, fifteen minutes at a time. You never knew when he was going to show up.

One day Mr. and Mrs. Jones were killed, execution-style, on their knees in their lovingly decorated men's clothing store. Later my friend Bruce, the burger guy, was gunned down in the same manner.

Both of our neighbors, killed in robberies. We mused at why we hadn't been hit. Probably because that armed security guard had a jones for Consuelo.

You would think we'd have hightailed it out of Dodge after the murders. But no, we just got even more numb. There's a slow, glacial tide of apathy that washes over every aspect of your life when you work in Compton. I understand why people become stuck in the ghetto. You just accept the cards you've been handed and you carry on.

Premeditated

The apathy stuck with my folks, but not me. I didn't want to be a quiet victim. I would watch movies about the Holocaust and see this herd of people waiting in line to get a bullet in the back and fall into an open burial pit. I always wondered why these folks, if they were going to die anyway, didn't at least go after one of the guards.

I always imagined I would be the one who snapped back, and snapped back hard.

One day in the Compton wig store, after Bruce and the Joneses had perished on their knees, I concocted a scheme. I decided I would mount Dad's .38, containing one hollow-point bullet, on a clamp behind the register. I would then loop fishing line around the trigger and thread it through an elaborate trail of eyehooks leading to the back room. There I would build a red "oh shit" lever, which, when yanked, would pull the trigger of the gun and blow the would-be robber's groin all over the shop before he finished saying, "Yo, down on your knees!"

I made careful diagrams of where I wanted the fishing line to go (it had to be foolproof, lest we blow away one of our loyal wig customers by accident).

Then a friend of my parents who worked in law enforcement told me that if I did take down a robber, even if it was self-defense, the fact that this contraption had been made in advance of the killing would make it premeditated. In other words, Murder One.

So we just sat there, waiting to die.

Hope is the first thing to perish. Mom and Dad actually started looking at apartments in the dreadful inner-city neighborhood of Bellflower. Bellflower borders Compton and is equally scary. We were going to move from our seaside community of Playa del Rey to the inner city. I would be the only Asian American in an all-black school. I tried to look at the positive side: Near our apartment building was a motorcycle shop that sold cool accessories. I envisioned going to the store after school every day and browsing through all of the gadgets I would never be able to buy.

That bubble popped when my folks decided to sell the Compton store. I still don't know what event pushed them over the edge, when the murders of both of our neighbors had failed to do so. But I was glad—SO glad—that we found a buyer for Sasco Wigs and I would not have to make the hour-long drive to the inner city anymore.

How Not to Run a Business

We purchased a larger—but equally unprofitable—wig store near LAX airport. It was a corner store (it's now a Blockbuster video), it was large, and it grossed $85,000 a year. Rent was about a third of that, and gross margins about half. In other words, it constantly lost money.

We had one of those door-dinging things. My mom would nap on a sofa in the back until a customer walked in. Then, groggily, she would help them with their purchase. She gave everybody a 20 percent discount at the register.

There went the profit margins.

"Mom, why do you give people twenty percent off when they come to the register?" I'd ask. "The deal is closed, they've got their wallets out, and they're ready to pay full price. You're giving them a discount *after* the purchase decision has been made! Wouldn't it be smarter to put up signs offering 20 percent off everything in the store, so that people would be incentivized to buy impulse items?"

These words were lost on my mom. I feel confident that money-making ability is not inherited, it's learned.

Further busting the "acorn doesn't falls far from the tree" theory was my dad's marketing prowess. Here was his get-rich scheme: He would go to the nearby racetracks on "free windbreaker" day. He would purchase a general admission ticket, get the free windbreaker, go to his car, put it in the trunk, and then go through the turnstile again. He would do this at least a dozen times, making a circuitous route through the general admission gate, to the free windbreaker station, and back to the car trunk. He'd do the same thing on "free visor" day. Soon our apartment would be full of Santa Anita logo wear, umbrellas, and key chains. I asked him what he was doing.

"I'm going to sell them at the wig store. We're right next to the airport, so tourists can come in and get some souvenirs before they fly out," he said, proudly. He thought it was a great idea because he'd gotten this merchandise for free and so if he sold it, it would be all profit. But he completely failed to account for the admission price he paid to get each and every item. He also failed to account for the fact that people don't typically go into wig stores for racetrack souvenirs. Anyway, his profit theory was never tested because the "free" junk stayed in the apartment until it was eventually thrown away.

While we had physically gotten away from apathy of the inner-city environment, I don't think my parents ever shook it off.

One day I heard a crash through the ceiling of our store. A cloud of dust went up in the back room as a young black guy landed on a pile of boxes, waving his limbs like a turtle flipped on its back. The thief and I looked at each other with panicked faces and I ran.

Mom and Dad were in the front. I yelled, "Get out! Get out! We're being burglarized! There's a man back there!" and, without looking back, I dashed to the fabric store across the street to call 911. "Please!

Please!" I begged, "I need to use the phone, we're being robbed!" I called the police and frantically explained the situation. The few customers in the fabric store were peering out the window, murmuring things like, "I don't think there's really a robbery…" I was confused as to why they would doubt me. Surely my fear and excitement were convincing. But as I looked across the street, I could see, in my parents' store, my mom sitting listlessly on a stool and my dad mechanically sweeping our carpeted floor. I was bewildered.

Within minutes, four black-and-white units whipped into view, and parked in dramatic fashion at haphazard angles. Cops stormed out, guns drawn. They charged past my mom and dad and into the back room. As they emerged with the perpetrator cuffed, my parents just shrugged impassively. I stood in amazement. My parents hadn't moved one bit—even as the officers directed the suspect into the back seat of the patrol car with the oddly courteous warning to watch his head. (I've always wondered why cops do that. After a deadly armed confrontation with a robber, wouldn't you feel a little better watching him bang his head on the door?)

Later I asked my dad why they hadn't moved. He said, "I don't know. We just froze."

Not me, baby. I do not freeze. That for sure is not genetic.

Now, I reasoned that if the perp got into the store just before closing time, it was probably a Trojan Horse move. The plan was probably for him to hide inside until an accomplice arrived after hours, at which point he would open the door and they could empty the store together. A *wig* store, of all things.

So, after perp #1 was taken away, I stayed in the parking lot for the next few hours waiting for the getaway vehicle. Sure enough, a van showed up and waited by the back door of our store. And waited. I called the police and watched with great satisfaction as they hauled the two guys from the van away as well.

While it wasn't as satisfying as being the hero who blew the nuts off of a would-be murderer from the safety of the back room, I had settled my personal score against apathy and gotten a little bit of revenge against the kind of violent criminals who had probably killed the Joneses and Bruce the burger guy.

I recently read an interview with an emergency room physician who was asked, "How do you handle stress?" He replied, "Rather than focus on the outcome, I focus on the process."

That describes the awareness that was emerging for me at that time in my life. It wasn't so much the outcome that interested me, it was the doing.

I've never focused on becoming rich, nor was it ever *really* my intention to blow the nuts off of some would-be wig store burglar. The part that pushed all my buttons was the strategizing. As a teenager, I began to see life as a game filled with creative strategies. Once I uncoupled my mind from the box of self-imposed limitations (otherwise known as "rules"), I started to realize that there were unlimited possibilities for achieving anything I desired.

And once I started to be open to anything, the game of life began to be ridiculously fun. I was entering the "amusement park" period of my life. Of course, my parents could not relate to this, because *they* sure weren't having any fun. But I was not going to let that stand in my way.

chapter two

I Start a Career in Pictures

Our local theater in Marina del Rey was an awesome place for a six-teen-year-old to work. First of all, we had this cool and likeable general manager named Hanson Copeland. He was a dashing, debonair guy in his late twenties who bore a striking resemblance to Apollo Creed. Hanson Copeland had a black belt in karate and a charisma level right up there with Martin Luther King, Jr. He was a true leader, a guy's guy, a girl's guy. He was a lot of fun to work for, but we also genuinely respected him. He always encouraged us to work as a team and to be boldly experimental. Our running goal was to be the best and most profitable theater in the chain.

Working at the Cineplex was like being at summer camp. The staff was friendly, entrepreneurial, and highly motivated. We sold more tickets by far than any other local theater. When the movie *Superman* (starring the late Christopher Reeve) was screening at our theater, the Superman licensing franchise erupted like Mount St. Helens in our lobby. We sold Superman cups, Superman popcorn tubs, and a seriously idiotic Superman "fan pin." You could put this miniature monstrosity on your vest or stick it on your fishing hat to show the world how much you loved Superman.

Because every psychologically healthy adult wants to be pegged at a distance as a Superman fan, right?

I had no idea why anybody would pay a dollar for this eye-offending chunk of cheesy plastic. I mean, I could see it as a prize inside a box of Cracker Jacks, but I couldn't understand how it could be pitched as a retail item. Who would buy it?

No one, it turned out. The Superman pin was a complete flop. We had hundreds of them in the back room, boxed up to be shipped back to the factory. For some reason, though, this little item intrigued me. Probably because it was so boldly lacking in any perceivable worth from any angle whatsoever.

It got my gamer blood boiling.

I knew that if I could create an aura of value around this product, I would be able to sell it at a premium. So I presented Mr. Copeland with a proposition: If I could sell the pin for more than its retail price, could we split the profits? Mr. Copeland said sure, but I think he was paying more attention to the barf crisis in Theater 3 when he agreed.

I, on the other hand, was dead serious. I went home and devised my strategy. When I arrived for my next shift, I brought out a small card table, covered it with black velvet, cordoned off a perimeter around it with red velvet ropes, and got the two burliest ushers available to stand guard near my table. I found a little display stand from an old merchandise promotion and placed a Superman pin on it, surrounded by oceans of velvet. As you entered the lobby, it looked like a display of a rare Fabergé Egg. With my well-dressed security detail, Teague and C.J., guarding the exhibit to the left and right, I set my bullhorn to a dignified volume and announced to the incoming 7:00 P.M. Superman crowd that at the conclusion of the show there would be an open auction for one of the last remaining Superman pins available anywhere.

The show let out around 9:20. I was surprised when about a dozen people exited the show early to stand around and wait for the auction. The movie, after all, had one of those great, not-to-be-missed endings.

At about 9:30, the entire lobby was filled with moviegoers crowding around my elaborate homage to a ridiculous, one-dollar, red-white-and-blue plastic Superman pin. I had created an event.

Standing very perkily at the front of the crowd was my friend Christina. She had this proud "I know the auctioneer" look on her face that immediately told me she was not there to serve as my shill—she was there to *win*. Oh no. I tried to shoot her a look that said, "Get lost, this is all crap," but it's hard to do that effectively when a hundred people are staring expectantly at your face. She just shot me this big, competitive grin that said, "Roll the dice, monkey boy."

What could I do?

I started the bidding.

Teague and Hanson stood there like Roman centurions in business suits, at full attention, aloof yet ready to take a bullet for that precious piece of plastic.

"Do I hear one dollar?" I said. A hand popped up. Christina, of course.

The bidding war had started. "Do I hear ten?"

"Ten!" Christina again.

On and on the bidding went. I remember feeling the room start to spin in a dizzy whirl of disbelief. Offers were flooding in to purchase this three-cent piece of plastic that I'd given an entirely fictitious value. I began to feel physically ill. Though my hypothesis about the power of presentation and perceived value was being boldly proven, I wasn't feeling very proud of myself. Especially as my hypothesis was having its greatest effect on one of my best friends.

Bidding ended at $72, and as the large crowd dispersed, one person remained, clasping the Superman pin with both hands, holding it close to her heart. Who but Christina, of course?

What could I say but congratulations? The boss shook his head in amazement and with no hesitation snatched the $72, telling me that we would settle up my half later.

He looked pleased, and a bit uneasy, as he split our haul.

I sheepishly pocketed my share and treated Christina to the most expensive lunch on the menu at Bob's Big Boy to celebrate her "victory." It helped ease my guilt.

With the momentum of that success, though, I began to treat the movie theater as my marketing laboratory. Having proven the inarguable link between perceived value and presentation, I was about to embark on my next study, the complex financial concept of "derivatives." At the theater, we introduced, for the first time in history, the concept of selling movie tickets on margin. And it worked really well for a while. We wound up selling so many tickets that we had people standing in the aisles.

Which, from a customer point of view, is not necessarily a good thing.

Let me explain. There was a girl who worked at the ticket counter named Amber. Of all the ticket sellers, she was the most personable, but also the most peppy. I would later find out she had a massive cocaine habit, but at the time I just thought she was seriously chipper.

One day she came to me with a proposition. She described a "business concept" she'd worked out, which she assured me was completely safe. "Completely safe," I have since discovered, is always synonymous with "extremely dangerous and criminal." At sixteen, I knew there was a difference between right and wrong, but I thought of it more as a shaded continuum than a binary concept.

Amber proposed: If a smiling couple comes into the theater and orders a pair of tickets for, say, *Midnight Express*, Amber would sell them the tickets. The smiling couple would then bring those two tickets to the smiling usher at the door, me. I would take one ticket and tear it in half, giving the couple back two halves of the same ticket. This would leave me with one intact ticket, which could then be re-introduced into the local economy.

I was in. At varying intervals throughout the evening, I would take a small number of these low-mileage, pre-owned tickets, saunter up to the ticket counter, and slip them to Amber as if we were characters in *The French Connection*. She would then resell them, but, of course, pocket the proceeds, which she would later split with her cohort.

There were six screening rooms at the Cineplex, each with a seating capacity of two hundred, and tickets were $6 apiece in those days. So if Amber resold, say, four tickets per line, that meant $24 per showing per theater. It usually meant about $100 extra per evening for each of us.

You can't keep a good business idea quiet. Eventually lots of ticket girls and lots of ushers were starting their own side businesses. Anybody who worked at this movie theater in those days had the coolest clothes, the flashiest ski gear, the sickest skateboards.

Game theory says that each individual will do what benefits them the most in a Nash equilibrium, taking into account all perceivable risks and benefits, which results in the greatest good for all. Our movie theater was a stunning example of game theory gone wrong. Soon customers were standing in the aisles because shows were alarmingly oversold. This, of course, would not have been possible if we were hewing to the tired, conventional business model of selling seats only once.

We organized secret meetings about the overcrowding crisis. We all agreed that we would moderate our activities and enforce a limit as to the number of scam tickets per show. But it never really stuck because everyone thought *somebody else* was going to be the one to moderate. Greed got the better of all of us. We proved, for the nine trillionth time in history, that human beings, while able to employ reason as individuals, are absolutely incapable of behaving intelligently as a group.

One evening there must have been at least fifty extremely pissed-off customers storming about the lobby, wondering why they'd shelled out six bucks for the privilege of buying a tub of bad popcorn and eating it in the men's room. I got a sick feeling as I realized this thing had officially gotten out of control. The bloated genie was not going back in the bottle. The scam was going to explode in our faces and there was absolutely nothing any of us could do to stop it.

I went home and spent the night in sick dread. It dawned on me that the activity I'd been engaged in had a cute little nickname in the law enforcement community: felonious larceny. We were going to get caught. My parents would disown me. I would never work again. I would be destitute and penniless forever.

Woe was me.

A few days later a "special staff meeting" was called. We all knew the ax was going to fall.

Everyone got fired.

Cracking Down

Lest you think my life was all fun and games at this time, let me correct that impression. I was still running on two separate tracks, my own and my parents'. My track was fun; my parents' wasn't.

In my junior year of high school, my folks decided to really crack down on those "my son the doctor" dreams. It was decided, with no input from me, that I was going to enter UCLA's pre-med program. In this way, my parents reasoned, I could continue to live at home during college and Mom would be able to supervise my studying from 6:00 P.M. to 11:00 P.M. every night and on weekends.

Thus did I find myself, at seventeen years of age, standing in a massive hall at UCLA on registration day, about to become a single spermatozoa among a million others swimming toward that glowing, beautiful, perfect egg called an M.D. Problem was, I had absolutely no personal yearning to reach that egg. But I was thrown into the messy ejaculate and commanded to swim fast, swim hard, and win this battle.

"*You* want to be a doctor, Gary. Right? You *want* to be a doctor." This was repeated to me so often and with such conviction that for a while I came to believe it.

I spent my first two years of college at UCLA. I entered as a sophomore because I had done my first year of university concurrently with my last year of high school.

UCLA, it would turn out, was my last real attempt to live my life for my parents.

To tell you the truth, the only two things I found appealing about a career in medicine were (1) you got to carry a pager (yup, you read that right), and (2) you could buy a BMW 630 CSI. My dad had a BMW 320i. That was the bottom of the line, and the 630 was the top of the line. We would go to the BMW dealership and I would look at the CSIs and then I would look at their price tags and become dizzy. Literally. I figured the only way I could afford one was if I became a doctor.

I have a new 650ci convertible now, which is weird because I didn't think about how much I had wanted one until I wrote that last paragraph. It's a fine car, but not worth going to medical school for. I also have a couple of Range Rovers, a Lexus, a Porsche, a Prowler, and a Mercedes. If you had told me back then that this would be the reward for choosing to become a wedding photographer instead of a doctor, I probably would have referred you to the nearest AA meeting.

Anyway, I had great grades, so I entered the pre-med program. I also entered what was called the Pre-Med Mentor Program, where you were assigned to a physician at the UCLA medical school. I worked with the medical photographer doing autopsy photos and fun things like that. Cameras just seemed to want to land in my hand.

I took on quite a course load. Those first two years were strange and lonely. The campus was so large that there was no way to meet anyone. When you're a freshman, your classes often have at least two hundred people in them. Heather Locklear was in my psychology class, but I only glimpsed her every once in awhile. The classes were so large it was like spotting someone at a concert.

So life was hard and lonely. I commuted from my parents' house. Anytime I didn't do great on one of my midterms, Mom and Dad clamped down. I would come home from school at 7:00, Mom would make me dinner and then watch me study. She would literally sit there for hours and watch me. I just accepted it—studying in the evenings with my mom silently watching.

I studied so much I was nauseated. Competition was nuts because UCLA grades on a curve, which means that only 15 percent of the class can possibly get an A, no matter how well the class did as a whole. And you really needed As to get into medical school. In addition, some of the students were taking the class a second time in order to try for a better grade, which UCLA allowed you to do. So in a class of four hundred, only sixty would get an A, and half of them would be class repeaters who had an unfair advantage.

The weeding-out process was insanely stressful. People were dying. Literally. There were suicide prevention hotline notices posted everywhere. What a place.

I remember one day walking by Buenche Hall, which had an observation deck, and seeing the police chalk outline of a body. *The Daily Bruin*, the campus newspaper, reported that a student had jumped to his death. I found out he'd been in one of my smaller classes, Mandarin Chinese. It was creepy seeing that empty chair for the rest of the semester. Little did I know, the suicide thing was going to hit even closer to home.

UCLA Can Be Deadly

One of my best friends from high school, Roger, also got into the UCLA pre-med program. He had introduced me to racquetball and sushi, among other things. We'd often gone skiing together with a group of friends. Everyone was a much better skier than I was, and Roger would stay behind and ski with me so I wouldn't be alone. He was just a kind, sensitive person. Incredibly funny too.

About a dozen of us from high school ended up at UCLA. We would often meet at the Campus Corner, this little outdoor lunch spot. Roger was too much of a fun-lover to take studying very seriously, but he wanted to be like the rest of us.

One day, he rode in to school with his best friend Jill, who was also in our group. All through the drive he kept saying things like, "Jill, I want you to know that you have always been wonderful to me." "I just want you to know that I love you very much." "Someday you're going to be a great mom." "You are so special." It scared Jill. She started crying and asking him what was going on.

She was worried that he was going to do something drastic, so she followed him around the campus that morning, missing her own class.

Roger went into the men's gym, which Jill wasn't allowed to enter. She was freaked out, but all she could do was wait outside for him. A few minutes later she heard this loud bang from the other side of the building and just knew it was Roger. She ran around the building and there, on the lawn in front of the Campus Corner, she saw the bloody scene. Roger had shot himself in the chest with a shotgun. Jill was devastated.

What had made Roger kill himself? He got a C- on a psychology midterm.

Roger's story hit me hard. I saw myself as the ghost rising from his lifeless body. In so many ways he was me. Roger had no desire to be a physician. He was a funny guy, the class clown, our own John Belushi. Can you imagine John Belushi trying to get through medical school?

In organic chemistry, Roger would be the one looking at you cross-eyed as the professor described benzene rings or SN2 reactions.

Had Roger been true to himself, he'd probably be a fat, successful insurance salesman today, chuckling with goofy amazement at the silly little miracles of life, and following his toddlers around Westchester Park. Instead, he forced himself to measure his own self-worth against unrealistic expectations. His goal was so incongruous that it literally killed him.

I knew then that if I didn't wake up and take a good hard look at the lie I was living, I would be the next chalk outline on the UCLA turf. Roger's death was a bright red warning to me: *Get out.* Get out now at all costs.

One-Hour Photo Snapshot #1: Thumbs Down

The last real job I ever had was as a printer at a one-hour photo lab. A *series* of one-hour photo labs, truth be told. Alas, I had this trouble-some habit of getting fired.

Being a one-hour-photo tech was an okay job for a young guy for one main reason: porn photos. You see, the big labs had a policy of not printing any nudity or pornography. The small shop I worked in had no such policy, so word got around that we were the cool place to bring the kinky stuff. It was only a small part of our work, but we definitely had a little X-rated cottage industry going.

Whenever we would get some particularly frolicsome shots, in-volving Gumby dolls or rolling pins—I didn't start this custom, mind you—we would always print an extra copy for our pin-up board in the back room. There were sexual practices displayed on that board that the *National Enquirer* would pay good money to see.

The days of the one-hour-photo shack are pretty much gone now, as today couples can print and view all sorts of digital antics behind closed doors on a Mac or PC. Back then, though, it was party time for us one-hour-photo guys.

The funny thing is, when one-hour photos first came out, it was such a novelty that we would position our conveyer belt next to the storefront window so people could see the images emerging from the print drying machine. We were probably breaking about twelve local obscenity statutes by doing this. I can remember this one fourteen-year-old kid who used to skateboard by twice an hour, religiously, every day. (Actually, I don't think religion had much to do with it.)

Maybe these adventurous couples (or single white males with

inflatable dates) who brought their negatives to us were into the whole exhibitionist thing. Because they knew for sure that the prints would make their rounds past the storefront window. After all, they'd had to pass our little Adult Cinema to enter the store!

Now, as I believe I mentioned, I got fired from pretty much every one-hour photo I worked for. Here's how I recycled this one particular job position back into the public domain.

When you load the machine, there is a special tape made of thin plastic that you attach to a long card, which pulls the film through the machine. The tape has to be a consistent length, so there was a special tape-dispensing machine that would spit out a set length of tape for you to tear off. Our tape machine was getting so worn, though, that when you tried to tear the tape it would un-spool an extra foot of it, uncut. This was terribly frustrating. It was like trying to work all day on a computer that keeps randomly shutting itself off every few minutes. It was enough to drive a person insane.

Well, consider me driven.

I found a single-edged razor blade and taped it to the bottom of the dispenser to give it a clean cutting surface. It worked beautifully! Now, rather than having to laboriously "zip" the tape, using two hands, I could just gently tug on it with one hand. Awesome! That one little razor blade improved my working life by 500 percent.

One thing I learned from this experience is that employees are motivated by good tools more than by raises or job titles. It was so demoralizing to have to work with that crappy tape dispenser, and so energizing to have it fixed and working right! I would take this lesson to heart in the future when I had my own photo lab.

Anyway, the tape machine with the new razor-edge was making everybody happy.

Everybody except my boss Pong. The tape dispenser did not make Pong happy.

One day I was in the back room taking one of my numerous "mental health" breaks, when I heard a bloodcurdling scream from the front of the shop. I ran out to see what happened, and I swear the scene that met my eyes looked like something straight out of *Dexter*. Pong was grasping his bloody hand and shrieking like a goat impaled on a fencepost. His face was as white as a sheet of photo paper, and there was blood spattered from wall to wall. All over the floor, all over his lab coat. The place looked like a carnival spin-art machine that had run out of blue and yellow.

And where did the trail of gore lead? Three guesses.

Right back to the tape dispenser, of course. On the counter in front of the dispenser lay a flesh-colored almond. Upon closer examination, it turned out to be a thumbprint. Pong had sliced his thumbprint completely off! Apparently he was used to the dull cutting edge, and had adapted to it by using a lot of force with his thumb. Little did he know, there was now a razor blade protruding into his swipe path.

I had to act fast.

"Oh my *God*!" I shrieked. "Some idiot put a razor blade in the tape dispenser!" (Luckily, I had not yet taken formal credit for my masterful innovation.) "What kind of moron would do such an *idiotic* thing?" I was making such a scene that they didn't know right away that it was me. I guess it's like when you fart and say "Wow, that stinks," everybody knows you did it, but if you get completely hysterical about it, they don't know what to think.

Anyway, they didn't seem to suspect me—in fact, they thought I was being very helpful in finding his thumb and packing it in a nice, clean baggie to take to the hospital.

I never saw Pong again after they wheeled him off in a gurney. Gosh, he looked sad. The last thing I remember saying to him as they opened the ambulance doors was, "Don't forget your thumb!"

I don't remember the exact explanation as to why there was a pink slip with my name on it tacked to the porn board the next time I came in to work. But I do remember noticing a little reddish smudge at the bottom of the paper. I'm pretty sure it was a thumbprint. With scars.

One-Hour Photo Snapshot #2: Barbra Streisand Didn't Get It

So I went down the street to Speedy One-Hour Photo and filled out an application. In those days, one-hour photo booths were sprouting up like kudzu after a Georgia rainstorm. Getting hired wasn't tough. (*Remaining* hired, that was another story.)

Working in Westwood was a trip. Lots of famous people came in with their photos. One time Barbra Streisand parked behind our store. I was so excited that I ran out of the booth and up to the black-tinted window of her Mercedes and started pounding on it with my fist!

This was right after John Lennon got shot, so I'm sure if cell phones had been invented then, I would have spent a lovely weekend in a hospital filled with soft music and cushy walls. I have no idea why she rolled down her window and simply said, "Yes?" But that's what she did.

Now that I had her attention, I needed to come up with something worthy to say. I recognized her boyfriend Jon Peter's son from paparazzi photos. He was in the passenger seat looking utterly freaked out, but she was calmly staring at me over the top of her sunglasses, as if I was her dry-cleaning guy, asking me what I wanted.

What did I want? What did I want? Think, think, *THINK*! All I knew was that here was an opportunity, and unlike my father, I was not going to be one to let opportunity pass by without taking action. I had this one in a million chance to have an audience with Ms. Streisand, and I was going to jump at it.

Here's what came tumbling out of my mouth: "Ms. Streisand, I really loved your *Superman* album. I'm a songwriter and I wonder if you would listen to my demo tape?"

She just stared at me and said, "Well, do you have it?"

I said, "No, it's over in Lot 32, but I would love to get it for you."

To which she tendered the most unlikely response in the history of mankind: "Okay, get it."

I said the only words that fit: "I'll be right back."

If you are familiar with UCLA, Lot 32 is about four blocks from the top of Westwood Boulevard, where the store was, so I had to run eight blocks round-trip to get a cassette tape from my car. It was about 85 degrees that day. It ended up being about a fifteen-minute jaunt, and I know you'll have trouble believing me, but Barbra Streisand was waiting for me when I got back. I could hardly believe my eyes. I ran to the car. "Ms. Streisand, Ms. Streisand," I said between gulps of air, "thank you so much for waiting!" By the way, I've since learned that celebrities typically like being called by their first names. It's much more comfortable for them. Anyway:

On this cassette was a single song called "I Don't Get It." It was a song I wrote about a guitar that I had purchased, a Gibson Dove acoustic that was really expensive but didn't sound good. I didn't get it. It was very midrange-y and stupid, and I hated it so much I wrote a song about it. Here are some of the lyrics:

I DON'T GET IT
MUSIC AND LYRICS BY GARY FONG

Oooh ooh, my my
I can never seem to reach you on the telephone line
Oooh ooh, my my
It's a mess, I'm in bed, and I can't get ahead
Oooh baby, I don't get it
Five o'clock in the morning
The doorbell rings, it's time to make the bed
Like it came without warning
Spotted doggie, hook and ladder, yet . . .

Yes, I gave *THAT* song to Barbra Streisand. I handed her the tape, she said she would listen to it in her car, and where would she like me to return it? I wrote down my address and phone number.

Can you believe the gonads? This whole transaction took something like thirty minutes in the hot California sun!

After I said goodbye to her, with profuse thanks, I walked back to the photo lab and saw four of my coworkers pressed up against the glass door. When I walked back in, one said, "Dude, did you just give Barbra Streisand your autograph?"

"Yes," I replied. "Yes, I did."

I never did get anything in the mail from her. She didn't call, and she didn't send my tape back. Yeah, the song sucked, but there was an infinitesimal chance that it may have had a brilliance that only a superstar like Streisand would recognize. I took the chance and I don't regret that I made a fool of myself. I did learn a valuable lesson from this stunt: If you're going to make a great pitch, have a great product to back it up. My tape probably wound up somewhere on the Pacific Coast Highway heading toward Malibu.

One-Hour Photo Snapshot #3: Oxy/Moron

Fast forward to my next one-hour photo stint. This sweet old man used to come into the shop pretty often. He would always have tons of film. I only knew him as "Oxy," because that's what the photo envelope said. Oxy was the lord high master of the underexposed image. He brought in hundreds of them, many featuring a big airplane with Oxy on the back, and a bunch of kids. All of them underexposed.

No Ansel Adams, this guy.

I would watch this humble old man eagerly tear open envelope after envelope, then scan his 4 x 6 disasters with crushing disappointment. So one day I said, "You know, you should try using fill flash to improve your photos." They were just way too underexposed, and this would be a simple, quick fix. (No "flash" of destiny went off, telling me that I would one day become one of the world's largest flash accessories manufacturers.) Oxy seemed as if he had all the time in the world to listen to me telling him how to improve his photographs. But the funny thing was, I was not even a photographer yet. I knew very little. But I did know what an underexposed negative looked like, and I did know that he needed more light. When he shot the inside of his private jet, all you could see was the little rectangular windows.

He started using a flash, and he was *so* excited. He would proudly show me his new photos. I congratulated him on the vastly improved images, and we shared an easy rapport. I had no idea in the world who he was.

Well, I found out he was one of the most famous investors the world has ever produced. His name was Dr. Armand Hammer. He was Chairman and CEO of Occidental Petroleum, and he came into my dinky little one-hour photo lab to ask me how to improve his photos. Wow.

One day he offered me a job as his personal photographer. He was financing some schools in South America and he wanted photos. He needed a photographer and he wanted to know if I was interested. I told him I was pre-med at UCLA and in school full-time. He told me he was a physician, too, but had never practiced medicine a day in his life. He was a horn player. I told him I was a guitarist. He said, "See?"

He asked if I would take a quarter-year off and go to South America with him. I told him I would ask my dad.

I asked my dad, and he said no. My dad was concerned that this old guy might be a weirdo with something other than a telephoto lens in his pocket, and of course my dad also didn't want anything to distract me from my studies. Not exactly a "follow your bliss" type, my dad. At least not back then.

I wonder what direction my life would've taken if I'd flown off in a private jet with the good doctor. I wonder if I would have ended up in the same place, here at this beautiful horse ranch in British Columbia.

I told Dr. Hammer the answer was no, and I resumed my thrilling part-time career in the "film business." I'm not a big one for regrets, but I've regretted that decision more than once. I should've stuck to my Declaration of Independence. I should have overridden my parents' decisions. But there was always that lingering doubt that they might be speaking from deep wisdom and experience. (Naw, it was just fear of taking risks. They passed that fear on to me, and I paid an unknown price.)

But the experience wasn't for naught. It reinforced my resolve to stick to my guns and to own each and every important decision fully and independently.

One-Hour Photo Snapshot #4: Chill, Dude

I eventually—big surprise here—got fired from that lab. There were a couple of basic concepts I couldn't wrap my head around, like credit card slips. Back in those days we had those clunky machines where you put the card in and slid this thing back and forth to imprint a carbon copy onto two receipt slips. Slip one was the customer's copy, slip two was the store's copy.

Our job was to give slip one to the customer and put slip two in a drawer. I'm not talking superstring theory here, folks.

Whenever my shift ended, the store was always really low in revenue, by some huge percentage. So the owner stayed one day to watch me at the counter. I would complete the sale, thank the customer, and cheerfully hand over *both* copies of the credit card slips.

"Aha!" he shouted, his face turning red with rage. "Look what you're doing! You're giving away both slips!"

My response was probably, "Chill, dude," or something equally non-alarmist. That's when he explained to me that giving them both copies of the receipt was throwing money away. Each time I did this, the store would not get paid, because it had no copy of the transaction to turn in to the bank.

It started to sink in why he was so irked. I say "started to," because on the next sale, some five minutes later, the girl had really pretty legs and I became distracted. With a goofy grin smeared across my face, I handed her both credit card slips. I instantly felt a pair of hands grasp my shoulders, turn my body away from the counter, and physically march me out the door.

Sigh. Fired again.

Santa Barbara Bound

A couple of my friends were attending UC Santa Barbara, and I went up to visit them for a weekend. I could not believe how lovely the area was. Rugged cliffs, ocean waves, bushes laden with bright flowers.

Everybody was riding bicycles, laughing, and having a wonderful time. The green grass and sunlight sparkled like magic. It was such an attractive place, I knew I had to be there. Without telling my dad, I transferred from UCLA to UC Santa Barbara, even though I knew my expenses would go up. I was determined to do whatever it took to get the money together.

The campus was jaw-droppingly beautiful. Right on the beach, with an on-campus lagoon where teachers' aides would have office hours. A far cry from Suicide Alley, the UCLA campus.

I had good enough grades that I was accepted into a demanding program called Bachelor of Science, Pharmacology. This pre-med course was limited to only thirteen students per year because it was so expensive to run. We had high-end gear like ultracentrifuges and

SDS gel electrophoresis equipment. We were performing surgeries on cats.

The school claimed it cost $38,000 per year to put a student through this program. In the course catalogue it said that in all the years the program had been running, they'd had 100 percent placement of graduates in accredited medical schools.

Until I graduated.

Now when you look at the course catalogue, it says *virtually* 100 percent of graduates have been placed in accredited medical schools. Why? Because of the one person who didn't go. Me. I became a wedding photographer instead.

College life in Santa Barbara meant freedom because I no longer lived with my parents. I didn't have Mom watching over me while I studied. I could stay up as late as I wanted, buy my own groceries, and do all those other things that give you a sense of grown-up autonomy.

I immediately joined a band called Teaser. We were all flash and no content. I think we knew six songs. We built a drum riser, and our singer would do these Rod Stewart–like leaps off it. He always wore colorful scarves that he would fling at girls, who would show no interest in the sweaty things. We were all talented musicians individually, but we never developed much of a taste for practicing. Whenever we went on gigs, we would play the same six songs over and over again.

College life at Santa Barbara was an odd mix of studying super hard and then cutting loose on the guitar. I shared a tiny dorm room. The only way for my girlfriend Annette and me to get any privacy was to nail some sheets up around the bed, just like those drapes in the emergency room at the hospital. I could go inside my little fort and nobody could see me.

I lost my virginity at twenty-one inside that little tent, with my roommate sitting just a few feet away on the next bed. We had to be silent because I didn't want him to know we were in there and I *really* didn't want him to peek.

Two Jeffs

When I think back on life at UCSB, two Jeffs come to mind.

Downstairs was Jeff Gold. He was—get this—sixteen years old, and he drove a Nissan 280ZX, an expensive sports car at the time. Jeff was considered a "generational genius." Some people, it seems, have very high IQs, and others are so incredibly off the charts they come around only once in a generation. Jeff was one of those.

We'd see him on the cover of *Newsweek* and *USA Today*, or on *The Phil Donahue Show*, then we'd run into him in the hallways.

Jeff had created a computer program called Rubik's Cube Unlocked. It's hard enough for normal mortals to figure out how to *solve* the Rubik's cube. Jeff's brain was so far into the stratosphere he actually *designed a software program* that taught you how to solve your Rubik's cube in the fewest number of steps. You would input whatever colors were facing you on the cube, and the software would walk you through the simplest solution. He sold a lot of these programs and made a fortune. He was something of a celebrity at the time.

Jeff was always coming up with nascent ideas that would never get finished because he would get distracted and move onto something new. He came up with this amazing device, for instance, called the Benjamin Microphone, which recorded sound three-dimensionally. He would use the mike to record, say, a plane flying overhead. Then when you played the recording back, using just two speakers on a wall in front of you, you could hear the plane flying over your head and then behind you.

I asked him how he was able to accomplish such a remarkable feat. He said, "Well, your head has two holes for sound and they're on the sides. It's easy to understand how you recognize sounds coming from the left or right, but how do you know if something's over your head or behind your head?" He said that the secret lay in the shape of the ear. The ear has various folds and creases, so that when a sound comes into the ear from, say, above, it reflects off a particular fold of skin and creates a particular sound, equalization-wise. So the innards of the speaker replicated the shape of a human ear.

He could have made a fortune on this, but he got distracted and moved on to his next big thing. And here's where his genius truly shone, at least to me. What did Jeff do? Did he invent the hydrogen engine? Design a flying car? No, he started a massage service for sorority houses. He would set up a table and massage hot sorority girls all day long. (He shared with me that the Phi Delta sorority had the hottest girls.) You've got to respect that kind of ingenuity. Jeff Gold was an inspiration to me because he followed his muse and did whatever he wanted. He made millions of dollars on some of the first game software titles for Apple Computers, then lost all of it. Then he made millions selling computers to school districts, and then lost that. Then he made another fortune buying and selling internet domain names, such as go.com and q.com. Soon after, he was broke again.

He made and lost several fortunes over the years, but it didn't faze him. He always knew he could make another million or two any time he wanted. So each time he got his hands on some money, he'd blow it right away. Though I've built several great businesses, I've always saved as much as I could from the proceeds because there is never a guarantee that any business is going to stay profitable.

Jeff #2 was my roommate. Jeff #2 was not a generational genius. He was a guitar performance major, and every night while I was trying to study enzyme reactions and kinetics, he would play finger scales to a metronome.

While I was able to relate more easily to Metronome Jeff, with his endless, monotonous scale-playing, I truly envied the carefree aplomb of Entrepreneur Jeff. There was no mystery to Metronome Jeff (except why he had chosen guitar performance as his major when he was terrified of playing in public). He was, in his predictably nonconformist way, very much a conformist. Everybody understands conformists and everybody expected me to be one too.

Yet here was this flashy, exciting, spectacular Entrepreneur Jeff who paved the way for me to envision the possibilities of a limitless life.

I didn't want to be tied to a metronome. I wanted to be more like the Jeff who once flew his entire staff to Denmark because he wanted them to have a taste from his favorite pizzeria. *That* was the kind of life I wanted to live.

One-Hour Photo Snapshot #5: Firing Myself

With my training in operating one-hour-photo minilabs, I knew that I would immediately be given an apron and a decent hourly rate at any minilab anywhere. We were little money machines back then. So I snagged a job at the Santa Barbara one-hour photo.

Those unsullied, fresh-faced Santa Barbara folks had never put up a "porn board," of course, so I had to educate them. Santa Barbara didn't get as much crazy stuff as the West Hollywood store, but when we did, it was *real* crazy. A couple of those shots still haunt my dreams.

You might be shocked to learn that I eventually got fired from that store too. But this time I had to fire myself.

See, I had a midterm and had spent the entire night studying. So by the time I came into work, I was walking into walls, closing drawers on my knuckles, etc. I concluded that I would be a far better employee if I was more alert, so I did the only responsible thing: told my coworkers I was going to get a little shuteye and to wake me up if it got busy.

I assembled three chairs into a makeshift cot: one for my head, one for my butt, one for my feet. You frequent flyers know all about the three-chair insta-cot. In about twelve seconds I was out cold.

My "professional attitude rejuvenation procedure" was rudely interrupted, some hours later, by the sound of the cash register opening and closing, the ripping sound of tags being printed on the dot matrix printer, and the constant little jingle of the front door. I rubbed my eyes, looked out, and saw that we were swamped.

But, lo, I also saw that it was 5:00 P.M., the end of my shift. So I got ready to go home.

I strolled out of that overwhelmingly busy store without even offering to help stem the crowd. I had to go home and take a nap, after all. I was still sleepy.

The next day I got a phone call from my boss' wife Sandy. She was a schoolteacher, but her grandmother had bought her and her husband this one-hour-photo lab. They didn't know how to manage a business. Thus, they had never fired anybody. She said, "Wait, my husband wants to talk to you."

Poor guy, he worked so hard to spit the words out. "Well, we've been kind of talking things over . . . you know, in general . . . about things . . . you know, around the shop . . . and . . . So how are you doing today? Did you get enough sleep? So anyway . . . er . . ."

I decided to make it easy and talk him through the process.

I told him I understood that he needed to let me go, that if I were in his situation, I would do the same thing. I comforted him, consoled him, told him that I knew it was coming, that it was no surprise, that I was okay and had no hard feelings. When we hung up the phone, I felt so bad for the guy, I thought *I* had fired *him*.

I began to sense a pattern emerging. I was starting to get the feeling that I was unemployable, and to a person who is deathly afraid of being broke, that is a very, very bad feeling.

After so many firings (eight in a row), the employee route seemed to be drilled dry for me, and the decision to go into business for myself became an obvious one. I put my thinking cap on and tried to come up with ways to make money without the obstacle of having to please a boss.

The school year was coming to an end, and I noticed we all were taking photos of each other as keepsakes. These photos were uniformly poorly lit, out of focus, and lacking the tops of their subjects' heads. That's when it hit me. The students at UC Santa Barbara needed a special Photo Night at their dorms, where a photographer with a professional lighting setup would take quality images of their departing friends. It was a no-brainer.

End-of-the-Year Photo Night

I did the math with my Texas Instruments calculator and came up with projections that blew me away. There were twenty-one thousand students. Each student had friends they were going to miss over the summer (or longer, if they were in the graduating class). If I did a little tour of each dorm building with my portable studio setup, I could shoot these groups of kids together and sell them copies as keepsakes. There were a dozen dormitory buildings at UCSB. All I had to do was secure a small mention in the campus paper with a sample photo and an itinerary for "End-of-the-Year Photo Night."

But of course—surprise, surprise—there were obstacles, the chief of which was this: No one was allowed to make money on campus without a sponsoring organization and a charity as a benefactor. So I had to do pitch meetings to the sponsoring organization, which turned out to be the Phi Delta sorority, because a friend of mine was the head of it. Phi Delta was involved with the Foundation for the Visually Impaired.

In my pitch meetings, I waxed rhapsodic about the astonishing upside of this photo venture. Consider this, I proposed: There were twenty-one thousand students. If each student bought $75 worth of stuff, then we (well, mostly me) would make $1.6 million in one short week of hard work. I didn't think about breaking it down to number of students per hour, scalability, throughput, etc. Never once did it cross my mind how long it would in fact take to physically photograph twenty-one thousand students. But no matter, I didn't need *all* of them. I really was naïve enough to think that if I got even *half* of them, it would be amazing. Never mind that not all the students lived in dorms, and that typically the response for promotions is measured in "basis points" (i.e., *fractions* of a percent) rather than majority percentages.

I have no idea how I was able to get everybody so excited about the potential earnings for this thing. Somebody could easily have brought me back to earth by introducing even the faintest measure of logic, but no one did. I got the Foundation for the Visually Impaired so excited that they scheduled a check-presentation ceremony for the Monday after the dorm tour. I promised the FVI 10 percent of my net earnings.

One of the most awkward moments of my entire life occurred when they sent over a photographer from the college newspaper for the check-presentation ceremony. The check was valued at a little over thirteen bucks. That's right.

I netted $130 for two weeks of carrying a rented portable photography studio around to over a dozen dorm buildings. What would happen was, kids would walk up, see that nobody was participating and that we were sitting there looking baldly desperate, and they would tell everybody else in the dorm that Photo Night was a wipeout.

Word got around and everybody made it look like such a stupid idea, *nobody* came. And so it became a self-fulfilling prophecy. A total and complete bust.

On the third night, some beer-saturated moron snuck behind my paper background and peed on it. I actually started to cry.

On one of the last nights, I finally remembered the lesson I had learned from my huge success selling the plastic Superman pin at the movie theater: People are drawn to a spectacle. Why I hadn't planned that into my original marketing strategy is beyond me.

I suddenly remembered that I had a full house of preppy Phi Delta girls. All I had to do was offer *them* free photos and pizza! That would draw a crowd.

That evening, there was a big crowd of girls all hamming it up in front of my camera, and when word got around (finally) that Photo Night was a fun thing to do, I started to do some very brisk business. The last few evenings of the project were a relatively big success, which put us into profitability. Up until then, I'd been hemorrhaging money I didn't have! Now at least I had *something* to give to the foundation. The thirteen dollars plus change wasn't even enough to cover the fuel cost for the president of the society to drive up to Santa Barbara for the ceremony, but at least there was a check presented, instead of a bunch of blind kids owing *me* money.

The check was given in a sealed envelope, of course, not to be opened until I left the room.

Had I staged the event better from day one, by filling the room with people, it would have been a financial success in the mid four to low five figures. But I did get a taste of success, I re-learned an earlier lesson, and, worst of all, I was now encouraged to try more crazy crap in the future.

Life Magazine Changes My Life

I spent two years in Santa Barbara studying my ass off, playing in bands, and experimenting with being in a relationship with Annette.

One day I was telling her about this guy I'd known when I was a kid. His name was Rocky Gunn and he was a friend of my mother's. He sang and played the guitar, and my mom said that he was really good. He was one of those guys who seem to be good at everything.

As an older child I'd run into him again at my karate school where he was a guest instructor teaching kung fu. Rocky was also in the *Kung Fu* television series, playing the prince that David Carradine, the star, had killed.

I had last seen Rocky when I was fourteen years old. At that time I had asked him what he was up to and he said, "Oh, actually, I've started a photography studio."

At Santa Barbara, I had been playing more and more with photography. I was taking a course on black-and-white darkroom work and enjoying it. Like Rocky, I had played in bands and had also spent much of my childhood in martial arts. I was telling Annette about how I'd always felt this guy Rocky and I were so much alike.

As we were talking, I was flipping through the pages of the June 1982 issue of *Life* magazine. "I wonder what he's doing now," I mused aloud.

Just as I said the word *now*, in front of my eyes was a two-page spread with the title NOBODY SHOOTS WEDDINGS LIKE ROCKY GUNN. Talk about destiny biting you in the ass!

I raced through the article and confirmed that this was indeed the same person I'd just been talking about. The same Rocky Gunn. It said he was a musician and TV performer and martial arts instructor. It went on to explain that the forty-two-year-old Gunn was now a famous wedding photographer.

Here's the quote that hit me between the eyes: "He earns over a million dollars annually shooting weddings." A wedding photographer who makes over a million dollars a year? They had to be joking.

Here was another guy who, like Genius Jeff, was living a big, splashy life by boldly doing what he wanted.

The idea wouldn't let go of me.

Rocky Gunn

Turning that magazine page was way too freaky. I'm not someone who sees signs and messages everywhere, but I do believe that when the universe picks up a megaphone and screams in your ear, you ought to listen to what it's saying.

That article had arrived right on cue. I couldn't ignore it. Plus, I was curious about Rocky. Last I had seen him, he was teaching kung fu at my karate school, and now he was this world-famous photographer who drew massive crowds by teaching—of all things—wedding photography.

So I wrote him a letter. This was before the internet, so you had to write letters and send them by postal carrier, which caused a lengthy delay in response time of at least a week.

© Brian Lewis

the legendary Rocky Gunn inspiring a group of photographers to "shoot from the heart"

In the letter I told him all about my freaky little experience with the magazine article. As I look back now, from the perspective of someone who receives letters from tons of people I don't know, I'm sure my letter to Rocky was written off as psycho fan mail. I should've just said "Hi, I'm Mrs. Fong's son—remember me from the Korean restaurant? Remember me from the karate school?" But no, I wrote all about the universe showing me his two-page spread in *Life* magazine.

How do you respond to a letter like that?

So I waited, but there was no word. I figured it was just like the Barbra Streisand thing. I started to wonder if I had some kind of hidden stalker tendencies I should be dealing with in therapy, but I was busy with school and music, and quickly forgot about it.

Then one morning I got a phone call from Rocky's sister, who was also his personal manager. She said that Mr. Gunn had received my letter, was glad to hear from me, and wished me well. In other words, "Thank you and goodbye." Should have been the end of the story.

But two weeks later, I was in a Westwood camera store with Annette, buying some batteries. She picked up this *How to Shoot Weddings* book by none other than Rocky Gunn. As I added the book to my purchase, the guy at the counter said he knew Rocky.

Fate knocking again?

"What's he like?" I asked.

The guy said Rocky was a super nice, friendly person (as opposed to the "Mr. Gunn" of his sister's phone call), and that he enjoyed meeting new photographers. The guy went on to explain that Rocky had meetings every Thursday night. He had one of Rocky's business cards on him, gave me the phone number, and told me to call the studio manager, Jack, to see if I could attend the next one.

I called Jack, told him that I knew Rocky and that I was in town. He was much friendlier than Rocky's sister and invited me to the meeting that Thursday. I was so excited.

I showed up at the appointed time and place. Of course, I brought my calling card along—my acoustic guitar.

Not in Kansas Anymore

You know that scene where Dorothy first steps out of her house into the Land of Oz? That's what it felt like entering Rocky's studio. I knew nothing about wedding photography and had been to only two weddings in my life. Suddenly I was immersed in this make-believe world of lacy invitations, champagne glasses, and fake baby's breath. I saw wall-sized images of brides and grooms standing on rocks with seagulls flying overhead in perfect threes. There was even a photo of a bizarrely posed bride standing in the snow, holding a bouquet, squinting as the snowflakes flurried around her.

The feeling of being in Oz was not dispelled by the Munchkin-like voice of Rocky Gunn. He waited until everybody had gathered, then made a late entrance like Donald Trump does in the boardroom. As he headed straight for me, he said, "Hi, I'm Rocky Gunn." I couldn't help but notice that his voice sounded exactly like a tape machine sped up.

"Hi, I'm Gary Fong!" I said, then plunked myself down in his little group of about a dozen photographers.

The main purpose of these meetings was for Rocky to critique everyone's work. He would ask each photographer to report on his most recent wedding, share his images with his fellow shooters, and discuss whatever lesson had been learned in doing the job. He would also give great tips on improving the images.

Some of the first guy's images were downright hilarious. Most of them had a snapshot quality, but there were a few where the bride was artificially posed as if she were a waterfall, her limbs, fingers, and toes cascading down from the top of the head, gracefully sculpted into place by photographers trying to be like Rocky.

And Rocky was all about the refinements.

"Fan the fingers out gracefully! Don't have her make a fist—you'll never score a merit with a bride making a fist." (What was a merit? I wondered.) "Here! Let me show you how to pose a hand. Pull the knuckles back at the wrist, and position the fingers just like this." Rocky proceeded to take an older man's rough and masculine hand and pose it as if it belonged to a princess. The man held his hand in place for at least five minutes, staring at it intently.

I noticed everyone in the room doing the same thing with their own hands. I found myself doing it too, until I snapped out of the trance. Rocky was very persuasive. And he knew it.

When another photographer's image was on display, Rocky said, "Now, you see this image, John? This is exactly why soldiers get killed at war. They just can't make it up the next hill." Everybody in the room nodded in unison. I had absolutely no idea what he was talking about.

After the meeting, Rocky approached me and asked how my mom was and what I was up to these days. I said that I was a musician and that I did a little photography. He didn't seem to remember my letter, so I figured his staff had weeded it out. (Maybe that was for the best.)

We talked more about music than photography. I told him I was writing some original songs and doing a lot of recording. He fondly reminisced about his musician days, and I told him I had brought my guitar. He immediately perked up. We went to my car to get it and he said, "Let's go out on the Redondo Beach Pier," which was about three blocks away.

He closed up shop, grabbed his camera bag, and out we went to the pier. We just sat there, playing swap the guitar. He sang mostly old songs, like "Leaving on a Jet Plane," and when I harmonized with him, he smiled and we sang even louder. A lady walking by dropped a dollar bill in his open camera bag. We laughed.

"We could make a living as a duo!" he said. "Let's get a donut with our earnings."

And that was the beginning of our friendship. This was no longer the famous photographer featured in *Life* magazine, or the Mr. Gunn who wanted to thank me for my letter. Rocky was now my friend. Just like that.

Before we said goodnight, the talk circled back to photography. He asked me what kind of camera I had. Desperately wanting to make a good impression, I blurted out, "A Hasselblad." What a lie! A Hasselblad was the finest camera in the world at that time and cost as much as a good used car. Hardly something a student could afford. Rocky proposed that if I was that committed to photography I should come to a wedding and see what it was all about.

Well, fate had led me this far. I figured I'd better explore Rocky's world and see what it was all about.

But I knew I'd better not tell my folks about it. Not yet, anyway. No, I thought, I'll play this one cagily. Like the fishing and motocross days. Pre-med was soon to become the phony Saturday morning fishing excursions I did to satisfy my parents, while photography turned into my new motocross.

chapter three

A Rocky Start

The first time I assisted Rocky, he told me to meet him at his home in Van Nuys and we would go to the wedding from there.

I arrived at his home, which was a surprisingly modest place, about a thousand square feet, in a not-so-nice neighborhood. I was shocked, as the magazine article had said he was a world-famous wedding photographer with a million-dollar-a-year business.

When I later learned about his business model, it made more sense. He ran a low-price, high-volume operation, sort of the opposite of what you'd expect in this line of work. He had about a dozen photographers in Southern California shooting for him. Yes, his business took in a million a year, but he kept his fees low and had a lot of people under him, which meant short margins and small profits.

In short, Rocky Gunn did not make a lot of money.

Anyway, it was quite a surprise to see his house. But there were weirder surprises to come. I went to a side garage door, as he'd instructed, and knocked. Rocky invited me in. He had turned the garage into an office/living room/bedroom/kitchen/warehouse. Stuff was piled everywhere. This couldn't be the headquarters of a world famous photographer!

We sat on the couch and talked about music while Rocky downed an entire half-gallon of vanilla ice cream. As a side-dish, he rolled up long, flat strips of raw bacon and popped them into his mouth, eventually finishing the entire package. This guy had the most atrocious eating habits I had ever witnessed (which might explain why he died of a heart attack at age forty-two).

About six thousand calories later we left for the first wedding. We get into Rocky's old Ford Econoline van, which reminded me of the crummy old van my dad used to drive to the swap meets. Rocky's van was really beat up, and each time we turned a corner I could hear things rolling around and crashing in the back, just like the lead pipes that would clang around my family's van on the way to the swap meet. But this time, the clanging was several very expensive camera lenses being knocked around. Rocky never put them in camera bags, he just threw them into the truck.

So we pulled up in front of the church in this rusty old van. Rocky was wearing a pair of baggy jeans and a t-shirt with a silk-screened cartoon character on it (Hamm's "Beer Man," as I recall), which was half-covered by a frayed sweater-vest. His jeans were so loose we all could see his butt crack each time he bent over, and he was constantly hoisting them up.

It didn't matter how he dressed, though; Rocky had charisma that instantly excited people. They would literally applaud when we walked in the door, and he would humbly say, "I'm just here to take a couple of photographs."

Hooked

The moment we arrived at this first wedding, the groom came charging out of the church. He shouted in a happy and excited voice, "Rocky Gunn is here and we're going to take some pictures!" He then spun around and ran back into the church. It seemed a little odd.

Rocky took me and another assistant, Albert Gianelli, aside and told us to listen very closely. We needed to work very quickly today, he said, and whenever we spoke we needed to do so in hushed tones. This was imperative.

We responded: "Whatever you say, Rock."

So we began tiptoeing around, doing anything and everything Rocky asked of us. At one point he tossed me a roll of film and asked me to load it for him, having remembered that I'd claimed to own a Hasselblad. What I didn't know at the time was that learning how to roll a Hasselblad takes a solid day of practice. There are three different mechanisms that you have to click and . . . well, basically it's a very complicated process.

I stared at the film as if it were a component from an alien ray gun. Rocky looked at me kind of like Morgan Freeman does in *Bruce Almighty*, gave a chuckle, and raised his eyebrows. It was a look that said, "You are full of shit and I'm on to you." Now he knew damn well I didn't own a Hasselblad. I felt exposed.

He grabbed the film, started rolling it, smiled at me with a wink and a nod, and went on his way, shooting the wedding.

Despite how excited the groom had acted when Rocky arrived, it was a very solemn wedding. The energy was low, the behavior bizarre. Muffled tears rather than laughter. I couldn't figure it out.

After the wedding, Rocky was shooting the family group photos at the front of the altar and we heard the groom's sister Julie say, "I don't care what the photographer says, I'm not going to move."

Rocky heard her comment, but he didn't react. Instead he started looking back and forth from her to the family. Finally he said, "Oh my goodness, do you see how the light is hitting Julie?" He subtly gestured for us to agree with him.

"It's the most beautiful lighting I've seen in my life," Albert played along, laying it on really thick. I didn't know a lot about photography then, but I did know we were in a very ordinary church, with florescent, classroom-style lighting. The light hitting Julie was far from striking. In fact, it was pretty dismal.

Rocky told Julie not to move a muscle and asked the whole family to gather around her. He took a picture with Julie in the middle, and before ten seconds had passed she was wearing this big old shit-eating grin. Rocky then suggested they take some more photos at the altar and asked everyone to move again. With that big smile still plastered to her mug, Julie picked up her bouquet and marched to the altar.

Just before the reception, Albert and I learned that the groom's mother had been killed in a car accident the night before. Suddenly the family's behavior started to make sense. They had decided to carry on with the wedding and mourn the loss of the groom's mother later. People were trying as hard as they could to have a good time, but the wedding was a catastrophe.

During the reception we asked Rocky whether he'd known that the groom's mother had been killed the previous night. After all, he had told us to move quickly and speak in hushed voices. Rocky said that he hadn't known the specifics, but that he was sure the groom was grieving the moment he saw him.

"But he seemed so happy and animated," Albert said.

Rocky replied, "Yes, but if you looked carefully, there was a rage in his eyes. That's when I knew."

I was hooked. If this was the sort of human insight needed to be a great wedding photographer, then I wanted in. I thought about the way Rocky had handled Julie, too. Not pushing her, respecting her mood, yet knowing that some day in the future, the family would appreciate having these important photographs, and doing what was necessary to make them great.

We went to five more weddings that day, all of them much happier affairs than that first. Everywhere we went, people were smiling and shedding tears of joy. I thought, *This is exactly what I've been looking for*.

At that time I was already struggling with the idea of going to medical school. I had spent a lot of time working in hospitals, and I knew it just wasn't for me. The patients always wanted something—change *my* bedpan, clean *my* gunshot wound—it was always me, me, me. I'm joking, of course, but the truth was, I really don't enjoy needy people. I'm someone who feeds off the positive energies of people around me. I wanted to be involved in something where I'd be surrounded by happy people. Being a musician had that element, but I knew that, as a profession, music was a really tough go.

I wanted something that would challenge me to grow and surround me with cheerful, energetic people. I didn't know for sure if wedding photography was the answer, but when Rocky asked me to assist him for the summer, I leaped at the opportunity.

Rocky Horror Picture Show, Snapshot #1

Fate had handed me an opportunity to work with this world-famous photographer. I was excited, but I still thought of myself primarily as a musician, and I didn't know what I wanted to do with my life. As a summer gig, though, working on the "Rocky Horror Picture Show" was quite a trip.

One day I was with Rocky shooting at Le Vendome, a beautiful location in Palos Verdes for garden weddings. It's a very peaceful place with an ocean view. We were photographing the bride when someone came up to her and gave her some news she obviously didn't appreciate. She started to swear and freak out. She threw her bouquet on the ground and began stomping on it and jumping up and down, her face turning red. I mean, she was losing it big time.

I stood there with no clue what to do. It was as if a herd of wild horses had just burst from their stalls in front of me—this was a problem beyond my repertoire. I looked at Rocky, and he did the oddest thing. He laid his camera down on the grass and slowly walked up to the bride, cracking his knuckles. He then drew back his fist and punched her in the stomach. *Hard.*

I couldn't believe my eyes. There were four other people watching this. I stood there paralyzed, just waiting for one of them to call the cops. But they were too shocked to move.

The bride was doubled over, her mouth open and a little string of drool dangling off her lower lip. She was gasping for breath like a beached salmon, and her eyes were as wide as coasters.

Rocky came up to her from behind, put his left hand at the base of her back, held her shoulder with his right hand, and said (in a very deep, calm voice that reminded me instantly of Barry White), "I would like you to straighten up now." The bride obliged. "Yes, straighten up all the way, just like that. Relax and start to breathe. In. Out. In. Out."

I waited for her to regain her voice so she could threaten him with assault charges, but when she was finally able to speak, all she said was, "Rocky, thank you so, so much."

She was now ready for more pictures.

Rocky Horror Picture Show, Snapshot #2

One afternoon I went to Rocky's studio. As soon as I walked in the door, I heard his unmistakable high-pitched voice shouting, "And you can tell your daughter the little scam didn't work!" A woman was crying, hysterical. She whizzed by me as I stepped into Rocky's office.

Rocky filled me in on what had just happened. This mom had come into his office to discuss the photographs he'd taken for her daughter's wedding. She said she wasn't happy with them, although she couldn't say what was wrong. She made a few lame criticisms, such as that her smile was crooked in one shot. Rocky had been down this road before. He knew what she really wanted was a discount.

Rocky's response was that if she wasn't happy with his work, he didn't want to charge her anything for it. He got out his checkbook and wrote a check to her for the entire amount of the wedding fees. She said she didn't want the whole check, she just wanted some type of discount. He was insistent, saying that he couldn't charge her knowing that the photographs would upset her now and in the years to come.

Rocky then proceeded to cut the negatives in half right in front of her face! The mom cried out like a wounded water buffalo, then screamed, "Stop! What are you doing?!"

"If you're not happy with the photos, I don't want you to have them."

"Why did you *DO* that?!" she demanded. "I promised my daughter I would get a discount on the photographs, not destroy them!"

Rocky answered, "Did you think you would get a discount by insulting my work? I'm giving you all of your money back and now you can never have any of the wedding photographs. And you can tell your daughter the little scam didn't work!"

Rocky Horror Picture Show, Snapshot #3

I remember another time I was at the studio with one of Rocky's top photographers, a hotheaded guy with a notorious temper, and we got a call from a frantic bride. It seemed the studio had sent a trainee photographer to her wedding and he froze. Panicked. Blew a piston.

We had to go rescue him.

We sped to the bride's house and found the new photographer standing there stiff, eyes glazed, practically catatonic. This is going to sound really crazy, but it's true. The boss photographer opened a closet, shoved the stunned photographer inside, and shut the door.

He then proceeded to do the pre-wedding shots himself, with the trainee still in the closet.

This guy wasn't Rocky himself, but this was something Rocky would have done. I wondered, is this what they learn at the photographers' meetings? What to do under critical circumstances? Here it turned out to be the perfect response. The new photographer had been overwhelmed by the responsibility of shooting his first wedding and needed an opportunity to get his equilibrium back.

We finished the pre-wedding photographs and went on to the church. Eventually we got a call from the frozen photographer saying that he was ready to resume; he had just needed to shake the fear from his system.

The guy came back as if nothing had happened and shot the rest of the wedding.

The Coin Toss of Destiny

After those first few weddings, I decided I could have a good time at this. It was a lot of fun. If I'd been shooting funerals or liposuction procedures, I might not have felt that way, but weddings were such emotional, high-energy events. And I could see that people valued the contribution you made as the guy who captured it all on film.

But I was still being pulled two ways: I wasn't sure if I should stick to music or do photography. I knew that I couldn't do both, not with any seriousness of purpose. I had to make a commitment to one or the other. Either way, though, I felt I would be happy.

So how did I handle it? The coin toss of destiny.

This may sound strange, especially to those who think that because I've been successful at a number of different businesses, I must use some kind of secret, high-powered executive-decision-making process that only the Elite Few know. But many of my life's biggest decisions have been made by a coin toss.

I find a coin toss particularly useful when I feel I'll be equally happy with either choice but don't know which fork in the road to take. I guess it's because I think the human mind is pretty limited at making big decisions. It never has all of the information; it only thinks it does. Let's say you get a job offer. You do your research and decide that the company looks perfect on paper. So you say yes. What you don't know is that a crazed mailroom worker is planning to blow the place up with a shoe bomb next Monday morning. If you had that one, small, crucial piece of information, you would make a very different decision.

Life is full of crazed mailroom workers with shoe bombs—metaphorically speaking, I mean. Small but crucial things you can't anticipate, but that make all the difference.

The way I see it, whatever intelligence is running this universe knows a lot more than I do, so I like to give it a chance to weigh in. Is it so odd to imagine that destiny might exert some influence on the way the coin lands? To me, it's more ridiculous to think that the human mind can figure out the best answers.

So, as I have done many times in my life, I placed my entire fate on the single toss of a coin. No two out of three. That's for sissies.

I said something mystical like, "Behold the power of the coin!" and decided that heads meant photography and tails meant music.

I tossed the coin and it came up heads. Photography. And you know what? I was content with it. With the decision-making part behind me, I knew exactly what to do. I was going to commit myself 100 percent to photography and put music on hold. I figured if I did well enough in wedding photography, I could save enough money to buy some really cool music equipment. It would happen a lot faster that way than by working for years at one-hour-photo shacks.

As I survey my life now, I realize that I do have quite a collection of rare guitars and pianos. I didn't really plan it; it just sort of happened as time went on.

I Take the Plunge

Since the coin toss had come up heads, I had to buy some photo equipment. I didn't even own a camera, so I sold my little portable recording studio and one of my guitars and bought my very first Hasselblad. For real this time. Hasselblad was the fancy camera the high-end pros used at the time. Owning a Hasselblad marked the line between amateur and professional.

Where I used to sit in front of the TV and practice guitar chords, I now sat and practiced loading film faster and faster, like the DeNiro character in *Taxi Driver* with his sliding handgun contraption up his sleeve. I wanted to get good at it in case Rocky ever asked me again.

I went through John Hedgecoe's book of photography. I read all of Rocky's books and basically gave myself a crash course in wedding photography. I memorized the shot list, the types of poses to use to make people look good, tips on lighting, things like that. Within about three weeks I was shooting wedding receptions for Rocky.

We would have these photographers' meetings where everyone knew me only as an old friend of Rocky's son who was a musician. Then at this one meeting he was making a big deal about my photos, saying how incredible they were. It was embarrassing because I had just learned how to shoot. He said the photos had a musical balance, there was a rhythm to them, blah, blah, blah. I don't know why, but he thought they were really great, and the other photographers seemed to agree.

My problem was, I really didn't understand why they were good— I didn't know enough about photography to know the difference between okay and excellent. It's like when I go to a hockey game—I have no idea when to cheer. But I decided that I enjoyed wedding photography and I was going to leave school and work for Rocky full time.

This was when I was a junior at UC Santa Barbara. I told Rocky that I wanted to quit school, work for him, and learn as much as I could. Rocky's response hurt me at the time, but I've come to appreciate it.

He said no. He told me it would be a huge mistake to quit college with three years under my belt. One more year wasn't going to kill me. He also said that he didn't want me to spend much time learning from him. I thought he meant he didn't want me hanging around, but it turned out that he thought I had my own fresh approach to photography, which would be different from his. He didn't want me to copy him and learn his habits. He thought I would come up with more innovative ideas if I did it on my own. He did agree that when I finished school, he would help me figure out what to do with my own business, but he didn't want me to join his.

Getting College Out of the Way

So I spent my last year of college at UC Santa Barbara going through the motions. All of my extra time was spent brainstorming and writing down ideas for my soon-to-be wedding photography business.

I didn't want to end up in a garage in Van Nuys driving an old Ford Econoline van. I was determined to find ways to make wedding photography more profitable. During my last year of college, I spoke with a lot of photographers, seeing if I could intern with them.

That's when I ran into a guy in Santa Barbara named Clint Weisman.

Clint, like everyone else, knew of Rocky Gunn. When I told him I was an assistant for Rocky and finishing my last year of college, he gladly agreed to take me on as an apprentice and a friend. He let me shoot some events for him. The remarkable thing about Clint was that he was making good money. He was pulling down $100,000 a year, which in those days was big bucks, at least to me. He had a stylish studio on State Street and a retail location in Santa Barbara. He drove a Jaguar, had a fabulous apartment, and, most impressive of all, had tons of Hasselblad equipment. And he was still in his twenties!

Clint taught me a key concept for making money in wedding photography: the up-sell. I began to salivate about the possibilities. I whipped out a calculator (I loved whipping out a calculator in those days) and punched up some absurdly optimistic numbers. I reasoned that if I could get one hundred weddings in my first year for $1,000 each, I'd have myself a six-figure income in my first year out of college. I set that as my goal and was absolutely devastated, later, when I booked only forty-nine. I grossed a "meager" $64,190 (which I didn't even realize was more than most doctors fresh out of medical school were making).

When my schedule started taking shape and I wasn't doing two weddings per weekend, I was anxious and tense all the time. All I could think about was how I was missing my numbers, which I took as a sign of failure. I remember spending a lot of time in the swimming pool, trying to dull the pain of the non-ringing phone and maintaining my sanity by aggressively doing absolutely nothing. (I told you I don't fit the profile of the standard high-achiever.)

Since then, I have learned to set small goals as baby steps. I remember when I made my first website, for example, I decided that I was going to spend a weekend building the simplest website ever. One image, a little text, a link to another site, and an e-mail contact box. And that's what I did.

Within a year, I had one of the biggest digital photography websites/forums, with over a million page views per month. Had it been my goal from the start to build this mega-website, I would have given up before publishing that first splash page.

But I didn't know that then. All I knew was that maybe wedding photography would be my ticket to breaking out of the "trading labor for dollars" trap. Maybe this was a way to stop delivering newspapers out of the back of a car, once and for all.

Once Upon a Time (The Storybook Opens)

It didn't take me long to realize what was wrong with Rocky's profit picture. It was his merchandising. Rocky's prices were typically $500 to $750 per wedding. To my mind, with all the material and labor that went into it, that wasn't enough.

Rocky's main business model was to sell a standard package of twenty 8 x 10s. In a wedding, twenty 8 x 10s makes for a relatively small number of pretty large photos. When you go down the list of the twenty photos that the average customer might want, most are the "obligatory" choices: the bride, the groom, the bride and groom together, the wedding party, the bride's family, the groom's family, the cake cutting, etc. You've pretty much exhausted your twenty choices before you even get to the good stuff—the great spontaneous moment, the unexpected tear.

Average people are inexperienced with weddings, so they think the standard package of twenty 8 x 10s is enough. And Rocky's business made only a weak attempt to sell more.

Clint Weisman, on the other hand, charged a very low $150 to shoot a wedding, and everything afterward was à la carte. So for $150 he would shoot the wedding, but you wouldn't get any photographs. What you got was the right to purchase photographs at a certain price per print. He shot one hundred weddings per year, averaging $1,000 per wedding. This guy was not living in his garage, driving an Econoline. He drove a cool car. And no one had ever heard of him. I started to realize that if a no-name photographer in Santa Barbara can make this kind of money, this must be quite an amazing business.

With Clint's business model and the tutelage of the world's most famous wedding photographer, I figured I was in the right place at the right time. I became convinced of wedding photography's limitless possibilities. I instantly set sail for my do-or-die goal: to book one hundred weddings in my first year, for an average of $1,000 each.

I can thank Zig Ziglar for my frenetic zeal. Mr. Ziglar is a powerful motivational speaker, employed by major corporations to whip their sales forces into frenzies of positive thinking. Zig explained that goals have to be clearly set and committed to in writing, with a strict deadline. Then you must leverage against yourself to make them come true (meaning you have to set things up so that failure will personally cost you).

I wanted to be successful, and Mr. Ziglar was obviously a respected authority on the subject of success, so I swallowed the message hook, line, and sinker.

What I found was that his teachings are of dubious value. And for this simple reason: The more you set your narrow beam of focus on a singular outcome, the less you notice all of the juicy targets along the side of the road.

That, plus the fact that living single-mindedly is a gigantic bore.

But one thing Ziglar's influence did do was motivate me to take massive action. And so I spent countless hours with a notepad, formulating my strategy for unheard-of success as a wedding photographer.

I wanted to take great photos and sell a lot of them. Art and commerce joining hands. I realized, through Clint, that if a photographer retained the negatives, he retained the exclusive right to sell as many images to the bride and groom and their friends and families as he could persuade them to buy. With all of the hundreds of images that are taken on the wedding day, why were only twenty being selected? It just didn't make a lot of sense to me.

There had to be a way to sell more.

Have you ever noticed that when you buy a new car, all of a sudden you see that same make and model everywhere? It's not that more of those cars are suddenly appearing on the road; it's just that you never noticed them before.

Our brains filter out tons of information.

I once went to a Tony Robbins fire-walk seminar. I walked the hot coals twice, and it was great, a living metaphor for breaking through fears. But another exercise we did was of equal value to me. It was a demonstration of the power of selective focus.

He had us all look around the room for a ten count, making note of everything red. Then he asked us to close our eyes and picture the location of everything red. Then he asked us to picture the location of everything that was blue. Of course we couldn't do it, because we had filtered out all of the blue items when focusing on the red.

I harness this principle when I'm trying to find a solution to a problem. What I do is clearly define the problem at hand, then sit on it for a few days. Rather than miserably pound out a forced solution, I just keep the question percolating in my mind and let the world fill in the holes to the puzzle. My brain's filtering process does all the work; it unconsciously scans for answers that fit the "mold" of the question. Great ideas that I never would have conjured up on purpose come to me this way. This approach has been successful countless times in my life, and it continues to be so.

When I lock into thinking about a *problem*, rather than pushing for a solution, the answer lands in my lap. The reason is that I'm open to seeing it. I've set my filters to receive it.

By focusing on the question of how to sell more wedding photos, the answer was "delivered" to me in the upcoming story.

Charlie's Angels

Around that time, *Charlie's Angels* was filming near my parents' apartment in Marina del Rey, and they were fine with spectators watching the filming. What really got my attention was the "storyboard" standing on an easel near the set. This storyboard was an artist's sketch, frame by frame, of what was going to happen in the upcoming scene, complete with the dialogue. Looking at the storyboard, everyone involved in the movie was quickly able to see what was supposed to happen. The actress was going to jump over this rail, then she was going to run over to the car, then this person was going to say something and drive off.

Bells went off in my head. It was like the fateful meeting of chocolate and peanut butter. I was looking for a way to sell more wedding photos, and here was this great idea for showing story sequence.

I thought, why don't we take the photos that are shot in sequential order at a wedding and lay them out on a white board so that people can see how they relate to each other? Why not *tell a story* with the shots, rather than just sell a few isolated stock poses?

With that in mind, I came up with the idea and name for Storybook Weddings. It was a great name, I thought, friendly and memorable.

One of the issues I'd noticed at Rocky Gunn's studio was that he had eleven other photographers. Customers wouldn't understand why they didn't get Rocky Gunn himself shooting their wedding. They would feel vaguely ripped off. As if they'd paid full price for a Broadway show and seen the understudy rather than the star.

I thought, if I am going to create a company name, it probably shouldn't have my name attached to it. That way I could remain free to have associates shoot some or most of the weddings. Why make people feel cheated if they don't get Gary Fong? I'd rather lead with my concept than my name.

The idea of Storybook Weddings was that wedding albums should be like storybooks, with a photographic narrative. Instead of one photo of the bride cutting the cake, for example, we might have a cake-cutting sequence of *five shots* that told a story. Five shots instead of one. *Ka-ching!* I believed that if the storybooks were put together with any kind of creativity, I could entice couples to purchase many more photographs than the standard twenty, and make them much more satisfied and excited with the final product.

Nobody was using that approach. All wedding photographers were doing variations of what Rocky was doing—standard packages. They just used different names. You might get the Princess Petite for the small package, the Regency for the standard, and the Crown Royal for the premium package. But it was always the same basic concept: a set number of prints. With no real incentive to buy more.

I knew I would be doing something that had open-ended possibilities and had never been tried before.

I got a Rapidograph pen and sketched an open storybook with a big S, like the beginning of a chapter of a Dickens novel. I did my own artwork and business cards, and started to type out my own brochures. I couldn't wait to share the launching of my business with my mentor Rocky Gunn.

6.26
The Storybook Concept © 1986. Storybook Album planning: garter/cake-cutting combinations

in my Storybook concept of wedding photography,
I deliberately "staged" photos so that they would fit
together on a page layout. This style was big in the '80s.
Later I would design albums that were much less posed

I planned to spend my last year of college preparing for Storybook Weddings. I was going to create advertising pieces, make price lists and production schedules, open supplier accounts, get a business license . . . All of that would easily consume my non-school hours. I had pretty much decided that I was never going to use my degree in pharmacology, but I was so close to finishing up that it wouldn't have made sense not get it. Of course, it didn't make sense *to* get one either, so I compromised and worked on both in my final year of school.

There was only one little detail left to handle: telling my parents.

My Son, the Wedding Photographer

As I mentioned at the beginning of my book, as a child of Asian parents, you basically have two things to accomplish in life. One is to engage in an honorable and high-paying profession (doctor, lawyer, something like that). Two is produce grandchildren. As many as possible.

As I drove to my parents' apartment that morning, I thought back on all those hours my mom had watched me study and all of the sacrifices my parents had made to put me through college. Having to tell them that I was about to throw all that away to become a wedding photographer was not a pleasant proposition.

As far back as I could remember, my parents had referred to me as "my son, the future doctor." (Another favorite saying of my mom's was, "Don't even think about marrying a non-Asian." As a result, I have never dated an Asian girl. I've never even kissed one. I have married three white girls. Note to self for future parenting: Anything you mandate without a choice, your child is going to do pretty much the opposite.)

In Marina del Rey there used to be a local greasy spoon called Mr. D's, kind of like a Denny's. It was Sunday morning, so my parents and I went there for breakfast. The place was crowded and we had to wait a long time to get in.

Finally we got a table and sat down among the hungry mob. And that was the moment I chose to tell my parents I was going to be a wedding photographer.

My mom said, "Well, that's great because we sure could use some help paying for medical school."

I said, "You misunderstood. I am not going to medical school. I am going to be a wedding photographer."

She replied, "I know. That's really great. I am so glad that you are going to be a wedding photographer while you are going to medical school. That way, you can shoot weddings on the weekends and help us pay the school bills."

This wasn't going as I had pictured it. (Actually, it was going *exactly* as I had pictured it.) I said, "There's no medical school involved. I am going to photograph weddings."

"Photographing weddings seems like a lovely way to help us pay for medical school."

We must have gone around a dozen times. Mom was so stuck on the idea of my becoming a doctor, she literally could not hear me telling her the opposite. I hate to say it, but I think most of her concern had to do with what she was going to say to her Korean girlfriends. It wasn't about my happiness, it was about bragging rights.

Finally, I practically shouted, "Mom, listen to me!" The crowd at Mr. D's went silent. I waited until the noise resumed again, then continued in a quieter voice. "*I am not going to medical school*. I am *never* going to be a doctor. I am going to be a wedding photographer."

My mother said nothing for a very long time. I had no idea what she was going to do next. Finally she slammed her fist down on the table, clanging the dishes and silverware. The restaurant went silent again. She stood up and announced, in front of the entire Mr. D's breakfast crowd, "You are not my son. I raised my son to be a doctor! If you are not going to be a doctor, you are not going to be my son. You must leave my house!"

Um . . . check, please.

Rocky Dies

But nothing was going to change my mind. I was going to plow through my last year of college, then work for Rocky for a year or two to gain valuable experience, then break out on my own. I had it all planned out.

And as always, whenever I make a plan, the rug gets pulled out from under me.

I got a phone call that Rocky had died of a heart attack during a pickup basketball game with friends.

It hit me hard. I suddenly felt alone in the world. I was in Santa Barbara when I got the news, so I called my dad, long distance, collect. Long-distance calls were expensive in those days, but my dad never said a word about it. He just stayed on the phone with me for hours. I was crying and saying, "Dad, I feel like I've just lost a father." Probably not the words a father longs to hear. But he understood and stayed with me, and kept asking me if I was okay.

In my bed next to me was Annette. She had fallen asleep. It felt a little strange that I was going through this messy process of grieving with my father, not my lover. I remember the next day on the beach I was still crying. Annette and I were lying on a towel together. She looked over at me and said, "Are you done with this Rocky thing yet, or what?"

So much for helping me process my grief.

Rocky's memorial was held at Le Vendome at Palos Verdes. It was a surreal event. Le Vendome was Rocky's mainstay for wedding photography. He was their house photographer and offered a $184 special there.

Le Vendome was a high-volume operation, a virtual wedding factory. You had, like, three hours to conduct your ceremony and reception. The reception was limited to chicken wings, meatballs, and cheese cubes. You even had to throw the bouquet within a certain time limit. Shooting there was like a job on an assembly line.

It was very strange to be mourning Rocky there, instead of watching him snapping pictures and looking at his watch.

The service was attended by all these people from Art Leather Manufacturing, a company that made wedding albums. Mark Roberts, the son of the owner of Art Leather, gave the eulogy. I had no idea at the time, but in about a year and a half, I would be a well-known wedding photographer, traveling around the world giving seminars for Art Leather. All these people would become my friends and colleagues. And Le Vendome would wind up being the main catering venue for *my* wedding photography business.

But I knew none of this the day I bid Rocky goodbye. All I knew was that I had lost a friend and mentor, and an irreplaceable spirit.

I didn't have too much time to grieve, though, because pretty soon they had to move another wedding through.

On Parole

After Rocky died, I was back to square zero. There would be no studio to apprentice for, no mentor to shoot with. All of my future questions would go unanswered by Rocky. My guide, my path, my *plans* all disappeared, and I had to regroup and rebuild.

I assessed what I had left to work with, and all I had was Mom and Dad. The same mom who basically disowned me for deciding to become a wedding photographer was the person from whom I would need the most help.

At least I had sympathy on my side, as she'd been Rocky's friend too.

I proposed a deal: "Look, give me one year to prove myself. I just need room and board. You already put me through four years of college anyway. What's one more year of supporting me? I don't need anything other than free rent."

My mother finally thawed out and said, "Okay. You've got one year. After a year, if you don't make it big—and I mean in a way that's really impressive—then we're sending you to medical school."

"Deal," I said.

I had caught a small break, but I also knew there was no option to fail. It was do or die, sink or swim.

Rocky had once told me, "Never refuse help, Gary. Always run as far as you can with it. That's the best way you can show gratitude."

I took his words to heart.

The first thing I did for

this was my first photo studio—in a bedroom of my parents' apartment. I slept on a foam pad under my desk, and had a "Mastercard/Visa Welcome Here!" sticker on my door

my new business was throw away my bed. I had to make an office out of my bedroom. I bought this old student desk for about $200. It was huge and had a lot of drawers. Then I bought a foam cushion pad. I put a little sheet over it and that became my bed.

During the day I would roll this foam pad up and put it in the closet. At night I would unroll it. My head would actually go under the desk. I had myself a secure little fort. Kind of like the night underneath the stairs. Or my dorm-room bed.

So, within this 12 x 10 room, my humble wedding photography studio, Storybook Weddings Photography, was born.

My First Wedding Photography Assignment: Earn More Than a Doctor

With a strict one-year deadline to make it big in wedding photography (or be sent to the punitive dungeon of medical school), I had to get my calendar filled, and get it filled fast. I didn't have any money, except for the $254 I'd gotten from the Regents of the University of California as a refund for being a part-time student in my last year.

With no money to buy advertising, the decision not to advertise was a no-brainer. Plus I also knew that the way to get a lot of jobs was to have low prices. Odds were 120:1 against me making a living.

In my senior year of college, I had read a great book called *Marketing Without Advertising*. It revealed that many great, fast-growth businesses got to where they were without spending a dollar on advertising. For example, T.G.I. Friday's grew to some ridiculous size on word of mouth alone. That sounded good to me.

There were several reasons I was able to navigate around the costs of advertising. First, I was offering a service no one else was offering. Second, as I mentioned before, my shooting fees were low (I made my money on the prints). The third reason was something I'd learned from Rocky. He said, "Gary, the thing to remember is that you need to make friends with people. These people will refer you to their friends. Nobody needs another annoying salesman knocking on their door, but everyone could use a new friend." I liked that. Rocky had lots of friends. So would I.

So when I started out, I frequented the various hotels and catering facilities and florists, just trying to meet fellow travelers in the wedding industry. Instead of playing the salesman, I was honest and personal. I figured, make friends first, and the rest will follow.

One day I went to the Los Angeles Airport Marriott and got an appointment with the director of catering. At this time I had zero experience. Not a single Storybook Wedding under my belt. One thing I did have—which was cool and very new at the time—was a photographic business card. I knew this would make me stand out after the meeting, but first I just wanted to say hi to these people.

So I walked into this huge hotel and followed the signs to the Department of Sales and Catering. I told the receptionist I was there to meet with Lynne Ramey. I felt like a kid on his first day of high school, with my little sweater and tie and display book. I was itching to give Ms. Ramey a big sales pitch about my Storybook concept and my low shooting fees, but when she let me into her office, all I said was, "Hi, I just graduated UC Santa Barbara. I know this sounds strange but I have a degree in pharmacology. I was supposed to go to medical school but my passion lies with wedding photography. I think I can do really well."

She said, "So, you haven't shot many weddings?"

I said, "No. I've worked with one of the most famous photographers in the world. I've shot receptions with him, as a second shooter. I am confident that I know what I'm doing, but I have not shot any weddings on my own."

There was a very long pause. She said, "Goodness. Well, thank you for your honesty."

She picked up the phone. I thought she was calling Moose in Security to have me tossed out, but she buzzed her secretary and said, "Could you send in all the catering managers, please?" The catering managers poured into the office, looking mildly confused. She addressed them as a group. "I would like to introduce you to Gary. He just graduated from college. He has decided to go into wedding photography because he really believes he can do some great things with it. Would you all take one of his business cards? Perhaps we won't start him with weddings right away. We'll start him with some of our smaller corporate photo jobs, the ones that pop up at the last minute."

So I started doing little "grip and grin" assignments for Campbell's Soup, General Electric, whomever. Executives would attend these hotel meetings with their regional managers. Afterward, each of the underlings would have their picture taken shaking hands with the Big Cheese. Grip. Grin. Snap. It was my job to deliver prints to the executives directly. The hotel didn't want any kickback. They just wanted to make sure their customers were getting the service they wanted.

Eventually they started sending me weddings.

Marketing Without Advertising teaches that people are usually passionate about at least one product or service that they have told multiple friends about. "Oh my gosh, I have the best accountant," or, "You've got to go to this place for bagels." If you can create client/ allies who become the trumpeters of your product, the book says, you will never have to worry about business again.

How could I charge lower prices yet still have the financial results to convince my parents that I was not destined for a life in a white lab coat?

I hoped that I had come up with a solution, in Storybook Weddings, that would miraculously achieve both simultaneously. I hoped that I had found a way to be both cheaper and more profitable. All I could do was cross my fingers.

Sometimes, when I come up with a strategy, I play the game out in my head, from all angles. I stroke my chin a lot, staring into space, thinking of all the pros and cons. Not all of my decisions are coin tosses. I honestly do a lot of thinking before I launch a project, and the Storybook concept was one of them.

Bill and Julie, My First Wedding

Bill and Julie's wedding was the first Storybook Wedding. I don't know what brain surgeons say to their first patient, but I sure didn't tell Bill and Julie they were my first clients. When I say *first*, I mean I had shot many weddings before but had always been the second shooter, with somebody else directing. This was my first time flying solo, and my first time trying out the Storybook concept.

It was nerve-wracking. I got there two hours beforehand and just paced around, trying to find places for my lighting and posed shots.

Back then we shot film, of course. That meant people had to put a lot more faith in the photographer. Today, with digital, you know right away if the photo didn't come out. Not so with film. Film was locked away in this dark chamber whose contents would only be revealed when magic elixirs were introduced.

In those days, the most common question people would ask me was, "Aren't you afraid the pictures won't come out?" The answer: Yes, terrified. There was an agonizing ten days in which you didn't know if the photos would be acceptable, or if some lab technician with a hangover was going to completely botch them. And if those pictures didn't come out, oh boy, were you screwed. You couldn't exactly do a re-take.

I remember, after Bill and Julie's wedding, calling the lab over and over. "Hey, did the film come out yet? How does it look?" Once they finally processed it they said, "The negatives look okay." Then the prints came out and they told me, "They look good." They didn't say "great," but they did say "good."

I was so excited when I left for the lab that I put my shirt on inside out. I got all the proofs, almost a thousand of them. I laid them out on my table and thought, "Okay, how am I going to do this story-book presentation? How am I going to arrange them?" I could lay all the photos out on a table, but that would be too messy. So I got a notepad, about 3 x 4 inches, and tore all the sheets out. I folded this stack of paper in half and stapled it in the middle. Which basically, once folded, became a little three-dimensional mockup of a book with turning pages.

I quickly developed a system. I would sit down with the proofs and put them in storyline order. Then I would draw a map of the design, of how the photographs should sequence. The first page might be the picture of the invitation, taken with a close-up lens. Then you would turn the page and there would be two 5 x 7s of the mom and the dad. Then across from it, maybe one 8 x 10, both parents together with the bride. Every page had a theme and followed a storyline.

When photos were to face each other on a page, I had the people in the photos face each other. Say the best man was giving the toast. Most photographers would have the best man, bride, and groom in the same picture. I would have them face each other in separate photos. I might take one of the bride and groom facing sideways. Then I'd get one of the best men making a gesture like he was giving a really passionate speech. Then I might wait until the bride and groom doubled over in laughter or something, and get another shot of that from a different angle. When I would present this album to people, it would be action and reaction rather than static shots. The photographs related to each other. Telling a story.

5.5
The Storybook Concept © 1987
relative placement-first toast

in my Storybook concept, I would stand at angles that would create "action and reaction" sequences. Here the best man toasts the couple. While it looks like one image, it is actually two, taken at different times

People got very excited about their book having a beat and a storyline.

I laid out Bill and Julie's proofs, being as imaginative as I could with my storyboarding.

Rather than have them come over and just pick up the proofs, I told them, "Let me show you my proposed pre-design." They sat down and were enthralled. They said, "Wow, this is amazing. Can we look this over tonight?" I said, "Why don't you take a week? If you want to make any changes or additions, just pencil them in." Having them participate in the album design process was a huge hit with customers.

The Pay-Off

Bill and Julie went home for two weeks and then came back with their selections. From my $150 initial shooting fee, they gave me an order of $1,378! I was blown away. This was my first wedding ever. And this was a middle-aged couple without a lot of money. Their reception had been at a mid-range hotel function room. And yet these folks were ready to fork over this much money for their photos!

What Clint Weisman had shown me was the beauty of a low shoot fee. This guaranteed that my calendar would be filled—couples wouldn't have to spend much on me up front, when their money is already spread paper-thin. I would make all my money later—after the bride and groom had cashed all those lovely gift checks!

That first year I booked forty-nine weddings and earned $64,190. This was unheard of in the days of the $450 wedding photography budget. It wasn't quite my six-figure goal, but I now had evidence in hard dollars that I had stumbled upon a system that could bring in a lot of revenue. The fog was starting to lift on the problem of how to create abundance, and maybe even wealth. For the first time ever, I thought I had a fighting chance of getting that BMW 630 CSI without putting on a stethoscope.

I was still working out of the bedroom of my mom and dad's apartment, though. Still living with a mom who might shuffle in with milk and cookies for my guests. At any time. In her pajamas.

As I started to shoot more, I had more page design ideas. For example, the bouquet toss. Instead of having one photo, like most photographers did, I turned it into four different shots. First I would have the bride holding the bouquet up in the air and looking back over her shoulder. Then, for the second shot, I would ask the girls to hold their hands up like they were getting ready. I know this is super cheesy, but no matter. Those would be the top two photos on the page. The bottom left photo would be the girls catching the bouquet, and the bottom right would be a posed photo of the bride with the winner.

I also invented "Greatest Hits." There are several different parts of a cake-cutting ceremony, for example. I memorized a series of five-shot sequences that I knew would create a left/right page setup in my pre-designs. Basically what happened was, although the *events* weren't cookie-cutter, the way that I shot them kind of became that way. I was making triple what the typical wedding photographer made, just based on that innovation alone.

By my second year I shot sixty-three weddings and earned $121,900. This was when gas was 60 cents a gallon.

The Storybook concept was a formula that worked over and over again. It didn't matter if the couple was having the wedding in their backyard or at the Pebble Beach clubhouse. I often joke that my wedding career started and ended shooting in backyards. It's just that in the beginning it was all fruit punch and vinyl tablecloths. Toward the end it was tennis courts and riding stables. But backyards are backyards.

Here's the really cool part. It didn't matter where the wedding was or how much they spent. All that mattered was that the bride and groom were entranced by their photographs. Once I delivered a beautiful book, the happy couple would show it to everyone they knew. Their friends would then say, "I want the name of your photographer." That's when my business really took off. All on word-of-mouth referrals, just like it said in *Marketing Without Advertising*. And all I had to do was make people happy.

Not too shabby.

chapter four

Seeking Closure

As a wedding photographer with a $150 starting fee, you really get the "salt of the earth" couples. ("Salt of the earth" is one of those euphemisms you use when saying anything else will get you in trouble.) Those weddings were a lot more exciting and unpredictable than the ones I did later in my career, where people were spending $100,000 just on the flowers. When you're spending $100,000 on flowers, you pay a lot of people a lot of money to make sure everything else goes smoothly.

When you're getting married in a gym, well, anything goes.

There was one early wedding where the groom's ex-girlfriend showed up at the church uninvited. In fact, she did more than just show up. I remember hearing someone yell, "Oh my God. His ex-girlfriend's here and she's wearing a wedding gown!" Being the curious, yet professional architect of memories that I was, I ran outside like Seabiscuit with his tail on fire.

This girl was hot. I'm talking *stunning*. Indisputably hotter than the bride-to-maybe-be. And she was indeed wearing a wedding gown and holding a bridal bouquet. I guess she figured she'd better be dressed for business, just in case the scales tipped wildly in her favor.

She was sobbing and saying, "I need to see him, just for five minutes. He needs to see me like this. I know he's making a mistake and we have to talk. Just have him come out here and see me."

I felt terrible for the bride, because, first of all, what an awful situation. Second of all, this gal was so damned beautiful. I was fantasizing about asking her to marry *me*, even knowing what kind of psychiatrist bills that would obviously entail.

A steady stream of live reports began flying back and forth to the bride's and groom's rooms. I wanted to be in two places at once. I decided to stay with the ex-girlfriend for a while. That's where the action was. Eventually the entire church congregation filtered out on to the front entrance to get a peek. They were all gawking at this beautiful, nutty girl on the church lawn, begging to see the groom.

As for the groom, he would not come out. Absolutely refused. Smart man.

Finally the best man informed the sobbing ex, "He wants us to call a cab and get you out of here." She said, "No, no. He doesn't know what he's doing. Just tell him, just five minutes. Let me go inside."

The ushers basically made a human wall between her and the church. Walter Payton couldn't have broken through this defensive line. Mascara was now running down the girl's face and she didn't look quite so hot anymore. Finally a taxicab pulled up and the ushers forced her into it, crying and screaming. The ushers started throwing money into the cab. Twenties, tens, fives, ones, change. Everybody was throwing money in the window and holding the door shut.

The best man told the cabbie, "Keep going until you run out of money. Just keep driving and don't stop for anything. Don't even stop for red lights. Do not let this girl out of the car." And off she went, sobbing and pounding on the rear window.

The poor bride was upset for the rest of the day because nobody would talk about anything else. I mean, how do you make small talk about the Cobb salad after something like that? All day long, people would be whispering to each other, "I wonder where she is now," and taking bets on whether she'd make it back before the wedding singer got drunk.

I still wonder sometimes where that crazy, beautiful gal ended up and what she's doing now and whether they've found the right combination of meds.

The Nightgown

One wedding I shot was scheduled for 8:30 on a Saturday morning. That's especially early for those of us who don't have a nine-to-five job! But it was the only time the church had available, so the bride had snagged it. Which meant I had to start at 7:00 in the morning, since I typically started photographing the bride and groom and their families an hour and a half before the ceremony.

I arrived at the bride's apartment and she opened the door. She had this glassy-eyed look and began bouncing from room to room like a pinball. I asked her, "Wow, what time did you get up this morning?"

She said, "I didn't."

"What do you mean, you didn't?"

"I stayed up all night long, drinking coffee." I'd heard of wedding jitters, but typically these are not caused by an all-night caffeine jag.

I inquired reluctantly as to why she had stayed up drinking coffee on the night before her wedding rather than attempting to get some rest. She said, "Because the hair and makeup people wouldn't come this early in the morning. I had them do my hair and makeup last night and I sat in this chair all night long. I kept drinking coffee to make sure I wouldn't fall asleep."

My mind tried to wrap itself around the image of this poor girl sitting in a chair for an entire night, trying to keep her head still, because she was so determined to look good for her wedding. "What did you do to keep yourself busy?" I asked. "Watch TV?"

"No, it was kind of boring so I started sewing some lace onto my veil."

A little red flare went off in my mind, but only for a moment. "Oh, what kind of lace did you use?"

She said, "Actually, sitting here on this rocking chair, I noticed that we had all these little doilies." (These were those little lacy, stringy coasters that you put on a table to help prevent water stains.) She continued: "I sewed them on my veil, one after another, to stay awake."

Odd choice, I thought, but then, caffeine and exhaustion do strange things to the mind. I didn't give it another thought. Until the processional.

The church doors opened and in she walked with brothers on her arms. She looked perfectly lovely until she pulled the veil over her head, at which point a terrible tragicomedy unfurled: Two of the lace dollies ended up directly in front of her eyes. I didn't know what to do. I thought, "Should I really be taking pictures of this? Will she kill me if I do? Will she kill me if I don't?"

I dutifully snapped away, though, as she and her brothers walked up the aisle. She was wobbly and shaky, a state I attributed to the mass quantities of caffeine she'd ingested all night. But then I heard her say quietly, "Guys, I can't see." Evidently the eye-patches were too thick.

I just couldn't figure out why she *had* to have the hair and makeup artists come the night before. I guess that, in her mind, having a hair and makeup person onsite was non-negotiable, and given the scheduling problems, sitting up in a chair all night was the only solution. Having a hair and makeup person was perceived by her as a "must." But was it really a "must"?

the bride sewed doilies from the top of her china cabinet onto her veil. It blinded her, so she had to have her brothers guide her down the aisle

If she'd talked to me, I would have suggested that she take her veil to a hair and makeup specialist a few days before the wedding and do a trial run to find out exactly what would work for her best look. Then, when she was happy with the look, she could have purchased the same makeup products and practiced the hairstyle and application of the veil so she could do it herself on the big day.

But this girl was a strict conformist who had a rigid Greek Ortho-
dox wedding, replete with massive doses of dogmatic ritual. Ritual
must have called for a hair and makeup artist on her wedding day.
Yet such a thing is by no means a necessity. I've seen many, many
brides do their own hair and makeup, or have a friend do it, and
look great.

This was clearly a duel between sticking to conformity and letting
common sense rule. And conformity won, with an absurd price tag.

I've always bristled against conformity. This girl's incomprehen-
sible wedding behavior helped me to see that in the absence of rigid
rules, common sense becomes one's guide. The rules lock you into
an immovable position, whereas the absence of rules permits you to
respond fluidly and come up with creative solutions—the best solution for the here and now.

The Original Bridezilla

I used to do this arrangement that was my own private artistic expression of whether I thought a couple would survive or not: I would
take a photograph of the cake when I got to the reception, and if I
thought the couple was going to make it, I would make their champagne glasses touch in front of it. If I thought they had no chance, I'd
keep their champagne glasses apart. (Of course, I didn't tell anyone
that—it was my own thing.)

A thousand couples are now riffling through their wedding albums
to see if their glasses are touching. To them I would say, "I didn't always do this ritual!" And I won't say when I started. But I will say *how*
I started. It was during the wedding of the world's least compatible
couple. Not only were these two not in love, they didn't even belong
in the same zip code. They should have exchanged their wedding
vows with howitzers.

The ceremony was a disaster from the start. During the processional music, everybody in the synagogue stood and looked toward
the door. No bride. The parents just stood waiting at the end of the
aisle. The entire song played, and still no bride. So they played the
song again. Still nothing.

I ran back to see what the heck was going on because, in case you hadn't guessed, it's odd for the bride not to appear for her own processional. I found her standing in front of a mirror, fixing her hair and making microscopic adjustments to her makeup. I said, "Umm, your processional is . . . proceeding."

She had a kind of French Moroccan accent and said in an off-handed tone, "I know, I know. But I'm not ready to go yet." I gave the organist a "cut" sign to the neck that she wasn't ready to walk down the aisle just yet.

Now the groom was thinking that maybe he had himself a runaway bride. I assured him that no, he wasn't that lucky (I didn't use those exact words), and that she was actually kind of stuck in front of the mirror. A dark expression—not one of surprise—overcame the groom's face. His jaw clenched and his shoulders tensed. I had the strong sense that this was not the first time he and his blushing bride had had such "issues."

Finally I was able to coax the bride away from the mirror. She was fascinated by her own reflection. It was as if she'd never seen herself in the mirror before. She kept taking one last look as I pried her away with my invisible crowbar. She finally headed down the aisle and made it to the altar, or, as it's called in a Jewish ceremony, the *chuppah*.

Bride and groom stood at the bottom of this stage, not looking at one another, emitting waves of hostility so thick you could feel them in the back row. After the rabbi said a few words, the two of them were supposed to go up the stairs together and stand under the covered *chuppah* for the remainder of the ceremony. As they ascended the six steps, the groom accidentally stepped on the bride's veil. Her head jerked backward.

She started screaming at him. "You fucking idiot! Why are you always so stupid? Do you take pills for it?"

To which he replied, "I only stepped on your veil. Sor-*ry*!"

She wouldn't let it go. "You're going to wreck my hair! You're going to wreck my hair! Is that what you want?"

What was Mr. Right's response? He reached over and yanked her veil off, uncoiling her carefully coiffed hair. The hair she had agonized over in the magical mirror. He pulled the veil off and threw it on the ground. Her hair stuck out in thirty-seven directions. She looked like a cactus.

"*That's* what I think of your veil," he said.

We all waited for the mushroom cloud to erupt, but remarkably, she didn't do a thing. I've heard that flies have memories of about five seconds; hers appeared shorter. So we went on with the rest of the ceremony.

The rabbi kept the good times rolling by saying one of the most inappropriate things I'd ever heard. He was talking about the rings, how they are circles, how they have no beginning and no end, and then he added, "I may not be an expert on jewelry, but I need to know for myself, are these rings real?" Everybody in the temple murmured in disbelief.

Suddenly one of the ushers started to wobble left and right. Now, it's not that unusual for wedding party members to take a dive. I knew it was coming. The two ushers on either side of him knew it was coming too.

Before he did a face-plant, the two groomsmen caught him. His mother screamed and ran up to the stage. He was lying there with his mouth open while they patted his wrists. Then they dragged him down the steps, with his shoes clattering like a corpse's. All the time this was happening the ceremony continued.

Bridezilla carried on uninterrupted, as if nothing at all was wrong. Oblivious, smiling and nodding.

I knew right then that I needed to do something to immortalize my feelings about this blessed event—to find a way to speak now or forever hold my peace.

So when we got to the reception, I set up those champagne glasses just the way I wanted and took the photo. It was a way to release my anger and frustration.

Shortly after the honeymoon—big surprise here—the couple broke up. I don't know if they liked their wedding album or not. I think they were signing their divorce papers before they even had a chance to look at it.

So I never had to answer any questions about why the champagne glasses were teetering off opposite ends of the table.

About twenty years later, I actually ran into the groom. Happily married (to someone else, of course), with a wonderful family, he had finally found what he was looking for. He shared with me that the only reason he got married to his first wife was that everyone in his family had told him that this girl was a nightmare and that the wedding was a mistake. This angered him so much, he decided to go through with it and prove everybody wrong.

That is not the type of energy that the universe looks kindly upon when people are taking solemn vows of marriage. And when you are doing things for the wrong reasons, clues start to pop up in your face (like toppling groomsmen or a "misplaced" foot that tears the veil off the bride's head).

I am convinced that when you are on the right or wrong track, the universe gives you either affirmations or danger signs. Affirmations often take the form of remarkable coincidences, like the Rocky Gunn story in *Life* magazine appearing on cue, as if to tell me loudly and clearly, "This is your next guru." That one was a giant billboard painted in safety-orange letters, but once I became open to the idea that these clues were at work in the world, I began to notice clues of a subtler variety. Both good signs . . . and warning signs.

Great Expectations

The expectations for a wedding day are tremendous. This is especially true when you're dealing with average working people, as opposed to members of high society.

My friend Denis Reggie (a top-dollar, high-society wedding photographer) explained it this way: "For the working-class bride, the wedding is a fantasy where she gets to be queen for a day. For the society bride, it's just another day for the queen."

Putting so much expectation on a single day is a recipe for disaster. A wedding should just be a confirmation of a couple's love and commitment. But it turns into something else.

I remember one gal who took "expectation" to a whole new level.

She marched into my studio one day and told me about her wedding plans in encyclopedic detail. How she had booked this perfect venue for the ceremony and the reception. How she had chosen this really great florist, pastry chef, and band. How she was s-o-o-o-o excited about me shooting the wedding. She even described the monogrammed matchbook covers and how she'd gone with the wide format, even though that cost a little more.

This was an attractive, professional-looking woman wearing a crisp Chanel suit and sporting an alligator-skin briefcase. I was excited to photograph her because I knew she would be an exceptionally photogenic bride. I said, "Well, this is going to be neat. I just have a few questions for the groom. When do I get to meet him?"

She said, "Oh, well, ha, ha, ha. There's actually a funny story behind that."

I thought to myself, is he away at war or working internationally and won't be able to show up until just before the wedding? I'd heard stories like that before.

She looked at me and said, without flinching, "I haven't met him yet." Um, a mail-order groom? That was new.

I said, "I'm sorry, did I miss something here?"

"No, you didn't. There *is* going to be a beautiful wedding. I *am* going to have a wonderful groom. I just haven't met him yet."

The expression on my face told her that more explanation was needed.

"I went to a goal-setting seminar," she told me. "In this seminar they explained that in order to make your goals a reality, you need, number one, to put them in writing. Number two, you need to have a specific deadline. And number three, if your goal doesn't happen, there must be a cost to you. My goal is to be married before I'm thirty. So I set a date and I am leveraging against myself financially and socially to make sure this will happen." Shades of Zig Ziglar.

I guess I shouldn't have been shocked. She looked like the type of person who wouldn't be caught dead without a to-do list in her purse. Everything completely organized and on track. I could not imagine this girl not in a suit.

I said to her, "I'm sorry, but you're asking me to set aside June twentieth. That's a very high-demand date. I know you're willing to pay a deposit, but I make my real revenue on the albums I produce. I can't afford to risk such an important business day."

She looked at me with steely eyes. "Do you doubt that I'll achieve my goal?" she challenged.

"Well, it is an odd arrangement, I must say."

"I have a lot of people who want to take me out on dates," she said. I had the sudden impression that she was about to pull out a pie chart or a PowerPoint presentation to back herself up. "Men are *always* hitting on me. Attractive, successful men. I *can* find a husband. That's not an issue. I just want to make sure that I get serious with myself and make it happen."

I didn't want to get in an argument with her. But I did begin thinking how strange it would be to date this woman. On the first date she'd have to find a way to work in the question, "What's your schedule like for June twentieth?" I tried to imagine how the groom-to-be would feel when he learned she had already picked out his tuxedo because she already had the wedding planned down to the minutest detail. How would it feel to be a walk-on role in someone else's fantasy movie?

I handed the check back and said, "I'm sorry. I know we've signed the contract, but I can't honor this. I'm very, very sorry." She glared at me like a rival Mergers and Acquisitions executive at a hostile takeover. She gathered her things and stormed to the door. Before leaving, she shot me a piercing look and said, "I *will* get married."

Interestingly, this bride had come into my life with her goal-planning fever the same day I got rid of mine.

I had tried setting goals, and I'd realized that all it had done was make me miserable. Heading straight for a destination with blinders on prevented me from looking at the scenery along the way. And it was within the scenery that I usually spotted the detours that led to the next glorious destination. These new opportunities were then affirmed by mysterious "clues" that told me I was on the right track.

This bride-to-maybe-be probably did get married on the day she targeted, and she probably now has the white picket fence and manicured lawn that was on her goal list, and she probably got it all accomplished before her self-imposed "old spinster" deadline.

Good for her, I guess. But had she been more open to the infinite possibilities that the world offers on a daily basis, maybe she would have made a fortune inventing something amazing out of the blue or met her true love on a ship to Singapore.

chapter five

Storybook Takes Off

I was a very determined young photographer. I wanted to ensure that my income and demand kept increasing. So I bent over backward—I mean, my hair was mopping the floor—to make sure that I not only had excellent photographs, but excellent designs too. As time went on, the album books became fatter and fatter, because each new referral would know that I had done their friends' wedding and how much it cost. And they were always prepared to spend just a little more.

Even though I started out with kind of a *Jerry Springer* crowd, as time went on, they would tell their friends, who would tell *their* friends, who would tell *their* friends. The universal chorus from all of these potential brides was: "All the other photographers' work looks exactly the same. Your albums are so different. They're what we were hoping for!" I never bought any advertising in magazines, never did any of the big bridal shows or anything else to try to get the bookings. The booking calendar filled by itself.

The business and the wedding books kept growing larger and larger, and by my sixth month, Art Leather Manufacturing, the album maker I was dealing with, ran out of their model with the widest spine. I had bought them all. They had never seen so many large books go to one client, much less a client who'd only been in business for six months.

Art Leather wanted to talk to me. They wanted to know my secret for selling large books (the larger the book, of course, the more photos you're selling). They sent over their regional representatives, Dan Sprague and Tom Miller.

Art Leather, it turned out, was not only the most esteemed album supplier to wedding photographers, but was also highly involved in sponsoring educational seminars for their clients.

As I mentioned earlier, their number one spokesman for years had been my mentor, Rocky Gunn. Rocky had had a close relationship with the owner of Art Leather—that friendship thing again—but both he and Rocky had recently died. Now the owner's son was in charge. A new generation.

Art Leather had an unexpected proposal: They wanted to put me on a lecture tour. A small tour in the beginning, because no one knew who I was. But they thought that because of my rapid success, people would want to listen to me.

Flying Solo

The first mini-tour was three cities: San Diego, then San Francisco, then Seattle. It was the first time I had ever done any public speaking. I had played in bands, but that's nothing like having to write a seminar and deliver it.

The first stop was a three-hour program in San Diego on my Storybook concept of wedding photography. We had thirteen people sign up. I had about six weeks' notice before the speaking date. So I sat down and tried to write out my speech. It was important to me that my talk ended on time, so that I could have a few minutes at the end for questions. I always thought it unprofessional when a speaker ran out of time and didn't field questions, or finished the program with time to spare and left early.

It was important to me that I deliver what I promised. People were paying good money to see me; I wanted to give them value.

So I not only wrote the speech, but also recited it in my apartment. I timed the whole thing to see how it played. The rhythm, the transitions, the pauses, the whole thing.

Orating to my fridge didn't help build my confidence, though. I was terrified.

As I packed up and started the two-hour drive from Marina del Rey to San Diego, my girlfriend Annette, who worked part-time in my studio, accompanied me. She would later become my first wife, though after reading this story you might rightly question why.

Annette kept asking me to give my speech in the car. I said, "No. It's fresh in my head. I don't want to be fatigued by the time I present it."

She said, "Okay, then, tell me what's on your outline."

I took it from the top: "Okay, thanks for coming. The reason I'm here is blah, blah. In the last few weeks I've sold thirteen large albums—"

She immediately interrupted, "That's not exactly right. You didn't sell thirteen albums. Eleven have been sold, but two haven't been delivered yet. You should say that."

I said, "But what's the difference? They bought the albums, which are being custom made. It's just a technicality whether they've actually received them or not."

She said, "You should be accurate."

I said, "Okay, I'll consider that." I moved on to my next point, "I learned wedding photography from Rocky Gunn, who was an amazing mentor—"

She cut me off again. "That's not right. You learned photography from the John Hedgcoe book. Rocky did not teach you photography."

"But . . . " I sighed. This was going to be a long ride. With resignation in my voice, I moved on to the next part of my outline. "The reason I've sold so many large albums is because of the storyboarding technique that I use."

She said, "It's not called storyboarding, it's called a Storybook."

"No, the pre-design is called storyboarding. Like in the movies."

"Whatever," she said. "If you give the program like this, you're going to flop."

Boom. The magic words had been uttered. I was upset now. You don't tell a nervous person about to give his first-ever public address that he's going to flop! You just don't do that. No matter what your opinion is, you keep it to yourself and you offer the person encouragement.

I snapped, "Look, you're really starting to freak me out! I would appreciate if you would stay in the hotel room while I give my presentation!"

She graciously responded something to the tune of, Screw you, no way am I gonna do that.

I thought, Okay, fine. I have dealt with formidable obstacles before in my life. I am going to give the program, with her in the room, even though we have just had this fight. And I'm going to do it *my* way. I'm going to do the best job I can, regardless of her petty, stupid, pointless, and totally unhelpful input.

Annette was now really, really mad about my giving this program. I had no idea why. What was I supposed to do? Cancel it? Rewrite a three-hour speech in twenty minutes? I couldn't imagine what she wanted me to do or why she was trying to sabotage me at the last minute.

We drove on. The good news was, we didn't have to waste any of the car's A/C. The air was chilly enough without it.

My First Presentation

We finally got to San Diego. The space they had reserved for us was a tiny classroom. Pretty sad. Though I guess it would have been even sadder if they'd given us a giant assembly hall and only thirteen seats were filled.

I waited until the lucky thirteen had arrived, then launched into my presentation as if I was addressing the UN General Assembly. I had not yet learned that the size of the room should dictate the style of the delivery. It was among the many things I had not yet learned about public speaking.

But I calmed down as the talk progressed and I found my rhythm.

As part of the program, I wanted to share a technique that Rocky had taught me: The Name Memorization Technique. When I first starting shooting weddings with him, I was struck that he could walk into a room where there was a wedding party of twenty and within a few minutes, he'd be posing the whole group by name: "Lucy, come in just a little bit. Hey, Ralph, can you go behind Vanessa over there?" How in the world did he memorize the names so fast?

He taught me the secret.

He said the key is to address each person at least twice. Look them in the eyes and feel their name being formed by your mouth as you say it. A lot of memory techniques say you should use mnemonic devices, like when you're putting a boutonniere on Chip, check to see if he has a chipped tooth. But those methods take a ridiculous amount of time and mental effort. Thanks to Rocky, I learned to just clear my mind and say, "Hey Chip, my name is Gary." I would feel the word Chip come out while looking at him in the eyes. Then when I'd put the boutonniere on, I'd say, "Okay, Chip. Thank you very much."

When you do this, what happens is the minute you look at Chip again, your lips kind of form the name automatically.

Anyway, it worked really well for me, so I wanted to teach it to the group. I only had thirteen people to work with, but I told them about Rocky's technique and then I addressed all thirteen people by name. They were impressed. I did get stuck on one of them. He said, "Oh, my name is Jim too." There were two Jims, that's what had tripped me up. No biggie. I explained that the method wasn't perfect, but pretty darned good.

Clearly they were persuaded; they were all taking notes. They wanted to be better wedding photographers, and it was a huge advantage to be able to pose groups by name. Rather than, "Hey, you in the red," or "Oversized blond in the back row," they could establish instant rapport. They ate it up.

My program ended on time and I actually got a standing ovation—thirteen people standing in this tiny room. Annette shocked me by rushing up to the front and saying, "But Gary, aren't you going to thank Bill, Terri, Jennifer, Chip, Sam, Jim, and the other Jim?" For some strange reason, she decided to upstage me at the last minute by recalling everybody's names perfectly—including the one name I'd missed. (Of course, she'd had all evening to take notes from the back of the room.)

The little crowd became quiet as she reprimanded me like schoolteacher: You forgot to thank this person and that person. It was really embarrassing and it pretty much negated all of the warm feelings that had been generated by the successful speech and standing ovation.

Later she sat down with me and said, "You know, I think I could be a speaker."

I said, "Oh really?"

"Yes, I think I have what it takes. Plus, I'm really tired of you taking credit for everything. I do a lot around here." Which was true. She did help me with lab production and tasks like that. Cutting negatives and putting them in an envelope. But she didn't participate in the booking process. She didn't devise marketing or presentation strategies. She simply took whatever lab work was lying around and cleaned it up.

The problem was, a part of Annette resented my success. I should have noticed this—it would have saved me a lot of grief. Career success was a sore point between her and her parents. They would say snippy little things like, "Well, it must be nice to be with someone who is so smart and successful." There were deep issues with her family. All her life, Annette had been made to feel she wasn't worth much.

So she decided she was going to find that sense of worth by forcing herself on my seminars.

After we got married.

Fly With Me Instead

When Annette and I met in college, it seemed like we shared so much. But looking back, all we really had in common was college. Everything we did revolved around the University of California Santa Barbara. Riding our bikes, shopping in the health food store, studying for exams. College life was our glue.

Once we got into the world, I discovered that we were completely different people. I was driven to attain success. I was terrified of poverty. For me, success wasn't about being rich; it was about getting as far away from selling wigs and delivering newspapers as I possibly could. As a result, I was very serious. I was on time for everything and always prepared. Even my to-do lists had to-do lists.

Annette, on the other hand, was constantly late for things, including client meetings and wedding shoots. One time we were so late for a shoot I barked at her, "Goddammit, we've got to leave *now*!" I guess my urgency got through to her. She put such a hustle in her step that she fell down the stairs!

I felt so terrible, I decided to make it better by doing what any idiot would do. I asked her to marry me. I was twenty-four years old.

We set the date for February 14th, Valentine's Day. We hired Rembrandt, my favorite nine-piece band, booked the church, and planned the reception. Friends bought airplane tickets.

Then, just a few weeks before the event, I broke down in tears. I knew I didn't love her. I cancelled the caterer and the band, and told everybody the wedding was off.

Annette was devastated.

When I tried to explain things to our friends, one of the brides-maids said, "Gary, you are an idiot. She is the most awesome girl! You two are incredible together. You will never find anybody else as good as her, as long as you live."

That scared the hell out of me. When you do something as dramatic as calling off a wedding, you are overwhelmed with guilt anyway.

I talked to Annette about it, and she just sobbed. At the tender age of twenty-four, I was incapable of rational behavior in the presence of female sobs. I said, "Well, I guess we could go ahead. I just had the jitters." She took me back.

Now, if any of my female friends went back to a guy who called off a wedding, I would smack her on the head with a flyswatter and say, "Wake up!"

No one smacked Annette. Or me. We reset the wedding for July and went through with it. The turnout wasn't as big as it would have been the first time around. Everybody was feeling kind of awkward.

One glance at our wedding photos tells the story. The look on both of our faces can only be described as abject animal panic. There's one picture where she looks as if she's on her way to the guillotine. There's another one of me waiting for her at the end of the aisle, and my eyes have that look you see on a frog the moment it realizes it's staring at a snake's tonsils, not a fly.

If digital photography had been invented, someone might have had pity and shown us those pictures before we said "I do," and a lot of unhappiness would have been avoided.

But alas, technology did not save the day. We had a Catholic wedding ceremony in a Catholic church. Then we hopped on a plane and flew to Hawaii. It was my first trip to Hawaii, and I remember sitting on the plane thinking, "What have I done? What have I done?" I had married someone I knew I really didn't love. I had committed emotional suicide of my own free will. Why?

As if to rub cosmic salt in my wound, every flight attendant on this plane was drop-dead gorgeous. They kept coming up to us and saying, "Oh my gosh, are you two on your honeymoon? Let me see the ring. Wow, you are such a lucky girl! I would trade places with you in an instant."

I remember thinking, "Okay, let's do it. Let's trade." Not a good thing to be thinking on your honeymoon. Every time they would walk up and down they would wink or smile, and my heart would plunge into my stomach.

Even on that flight, I knew I had two very large issues. One, I wasn't ready to be tied to one person forever. Annette had been my first real girlfriend. I hadn't been independent for long enough. Two, I was devoted to making my business work, not to being a good relationship partner. I should never have gone ahead with this.

When we got to Hawaii, I recall having such a strange mixture of emotions. The beauty of the place—the air itself smelled fragrant with flowers—intoxicated me, and yet I felt black doom inside.

I couldn't live with myself. I knew I had to make a choice. So I made the decision, right then, that I was not going to be a quitter. Period. My parents had gone through plenty of hard times and had managed to hold their marriage together. I was never going to get a divorce.

On a beautiful beach in Hawaii I committed myself to the marriage and swore I was going to make it work, come hell or high water.

Then I had to crawl into bed with her.

Flying Tethered

After the wedding, Annette essentially gave me an ultimatum: Make me part of your seminars or else. I guess this was part of that "hell or high water" deal I'd made with myself, so here was my chance to prove it.

"Fine," I said.

I took my outline and divided it up. "Okay, you take this part of the program and then it will come back to me and then you can take this part."

So that's how we began our joint seminars. I would give the first part of the presentation, and then there would be this awkward moment where, after building some momentum, I'd have to say, "Okay, now Annette is going to explain the next section to you." It was artificial and stilted.

Annette would step up and say "Ahhh" into the microphone, instantly canceling out all of the tingly energy in the room. Then she would say, "Hello, my name is Annette and this is how we do things." With a grandiose and condescending manner, she would lecture the audience on what we (I!) did in the studio. I would always cringe at her needlessly authoritative style.

After delivering her portion, she would toss it back to me and I would say, "Thank you Annette. That was nice. Now back to how to ensure reorders . . ." The audience would perk up again. We would do the switch-off a few times during the seminar. It was received politely at best.

But somehow the dual presentations became popular. The crowds began to grow. They went from thirteen to sixty to ninety to a couple hundred people. Whenever we would break there would be a crowd around each of us, asking us questions. One night we were in Chicago and I was selling a book I'd written called *The Storybook Concept*. Back then, how-to books could be extremely expensive. This one came with a videotape and sold for $495. We did well that evening. Annette, for the first time, gave an exciting, up-tempo speech. She was in more of a rhythm than usual and was making a connection with the audience. There was less of her typical condescension.

I complimented her later. "You're really getting the hang of the speaking thing."

With doubt in her voice she said, "Do you think so? I'm not sure. Thanks for saying that." I hoped we were now going to reach a new level of quality with our seminars.

My hopes were dashed at our next engagement. This was a large and prominent event. She stepped to the microphone and lost her train of thought. She just mumbled, "Um, um. *Hi*. Um . . ." She started shuffling through her notes and then reading directly from the page as if she were reciting a list of names. It was a major setback. We weren't back to square one, we were back to square negative forty-three.

We got into our hotel room afterward. She said, "Can you believe how freakin' great I did? I mean, I *had* them. I completely kicked ass."

It was one of those moments in life where I had no idea what to say. How could two people experience the same event in such different ways? No words were formulating in my brain. What could I tell her? "You sucked out loud"? "You made Ben Stein look like Martin Luther King"? If I'd said that, I'd have been paying for it for the next six months. So I did the brave thing: changed the subject and asked her what she felt like for dinner.

On another night she did fairly well again. But during the breaks there was no crowd around her. Everyone was around me. She just stood there looking uncomfortable.

Annette loved it when people approached her. She would lapse into her Harvard professor routine: "You know, the thing that's really important is . . ." or "Here's. What. You. Need. To. Do . . ." It always made my butt clench when she would talk like that. I'm sorry, but she didn't originate any of these ideas. She had no authority to speak that way. As for me, I always preferred to give commonsense answers—why this works and why that doesn't—rather than telling people they "need" to do anything.

Anyway, this one evening she was standing all by herself. Not a single person came up to her to ask her a question. I couldn't explain why, but neither was it a big deal to me.

We finished the program and I said, "That went well. We sold a lot of books."

At which point she announced, "You know, I never really wanted to be in business. I'm not a businessperson. This is dumb and I don't want to do seminars anymore."

Part of me was thinking, "Thank God." But the more survival-oriented part of me said, "You know, if that's what you really want to do . . ." It's not as if I argued with her. The fact was, I didn't think she was good at it. It kind of broke up the show to have two of us talking, especially when one of us was being a pompous ass. So I said, "Okay, you're out."

There was only one little hitch. We had already committed to a twelve-city tour.

Stuck With Each Other

I called Art Leather to tell them that from now on it was going to be just me. I got a very angry return phone call from the tour promoter. "What the hell is going on?!"

I calmly explained that my wife no longer wanted to do the tour, but that it wouldn't be a problem because I could easily carry the entire presentation. I explained that I had written the whole program myself anyway and that the portions she did were just taken from my notes.

He said, "That's not the point. The point is, a lot of customers are eager to see how a husband and wife operate a photography studio together."

Oh.

I hadn't really thought about that angle. "Can't we say she dropped out for health reasons?" I asked.

"I am not going to start lying to my customers! You guys made the commitment! The brochures have already been sent out!" He was way more upset than I thought he would be. It didn't seem like a big deal to me, because I knew the value my program offered, and it had nothing to do with the number of presenters. In truth, I believed the program would improve considerably by letting me do it alone.

I went back to my wife and said, "Okay, I notified them."

About a week later I got a fax from a friend of mine who was a sales rep with the company. He said, "Gary, you have to read this and call me back." It was a memo to all of the representatives, nationwide, from Art Leather. It said, "Regarding Gary and Annette Fong, do not enter into business deals with these two people. They are people who do not honor their commitments and cannot be trusted. Therefore, do not, ever again, enter into ventures with these people."

Annette was numbering negatives on a table in our bedroom. I dropped the fax on the table. She read it, looked at me and said,

"Okay, I'll go."

That was that. I contacted the organization and the tour was back on. We didn't discuss the contretemps; we just did the program as if nothing had happened. It was a giant success. The crowds were larger than I ever would have dreamed.

Then I found out why. There was, at that time, another very famous photographer named Hanson Fong. People thought I was him.

The Wrong Fong

Not only did Hanson Fong and I share the same last name, but, to add to the confusion, Hanson had also been one of Rocky Gunn's students. We were Rocky's two protégés. I was one he had encouraged *not* to follow him; Hanson was one who'd become his disciple, the living, breathing reincarnation of Rocky. Hanson's wife even bore a striking resemblance to Rocky. Hanson was very devoted.

In a true passing of the keys, Rocky had died while playing basketball with Hanson. Rocky had a heart attack and dropped dead right in front of him.

With Rocky gone, Hanson became as popular as all the Bruce Lee look-alike stars after Bruce died.

You may not know this, but there are not many surnames in the world more popular than Fong. Lee and Fong. Why? Because there are so many Chinese people on this planet. Sometimes the name's spelled differently, like Phuong or Feng or Fung, but it still comes down to a whole lot of Fongs.

In the photography world it caused quite a bit of confusion.

I would come to cities such as Birmingham, Alabama, or Cleveland, Ohio, and the room would be packed. People would rush up to me and say, "Are you going to do that Fred Astaire and Ginger Rogers thing? With the fog machines?" That was the way that Hanson taught a technique called Classical Flow Posing. He would use dance models and ice machines. Hanson was very, very . . . different.

He adored elaborate poses. One shot he would do involved a photographer standing behind the bride, holding a remote-control unit, which would light up her veil like a Jesus halo. He often had the bride pose with the wind blowing and seagulls flying in the background.

He was known to spend fifteen minutes on a single photograph of the bride—posing and positioning her fingers with her wrists cocked backward and her fingers fanning out like a peacock's tail. My friend Denis Reggie, another lecturer on wedding photography, used to ridicule his style. "A bunch of brides doing kung fu poses," he would say.

Hanson Fong was also a Master Photographer, meaning that he had excelled at numerous print competitions.

One time, when I was lecturing in Hawaii, there was a large state convention of photographers. I was scheduled to speak about my Storybook concept. They asked me if I could come one day early to be a judge in a photo print competition. I was flattered. I said yes.

I came to the print competition, never having witnessed one before and obviously never having judged one. I was on a stage with two "highly esteemed" photographers as my co-judges. After introducing them, the announcer said, "And the third judge is Gary Fong, a photographer from San Francisco, California. A highly regarded Master Photographer."

None of those things were true about me, though they were true for Hanson Fong. I was not from San Francisco, nor was I a Master Photographer. I had absolutely no idea what was considered an award-winning print.

Turns out, these contests have a lot of formal rules. Who knew?

I motioned for the announcer to come over and whispered, "Hey, I'm not a Master Photographer."

The guy said, "What are you talking about? You are a very famous Master Photographer."

I said, "No, that's Hanson Fong. I'm Gary Fong."

He looked like he had just swallowed a lump of hot charcoal and said, "Oh. Well, just do the best you can."

They put this electronic keypad in my lap. It had ten keys, zero through nine, just like a telephone. I was supposed to punch in the score of every print that was presented.

The first print came up. It was turning on this carousel, lit by two lights, and set at a very specific distance and angle. It was a black-and-white shot of a smiling Hawaiian girl wearing a lei. It had a mauve felt mat. I thought was a nice print. The announcer gave the name of the print and said, "Judges, enter your score."

I thought, "That sure is a lovely print. I bet my mother would like it." I gave it a score of 100.

All of a sudden an incredibly loud siren went off. The announcer said, "We have an automatic challenge. The average score among the judges was sixty-eight points. Mr. Fong scored it a one hundred." Five hundred people behind me groaned and started mumbling to each other. I started to get nervous. I didn't know what an automatic challenge was.

The first judge was given the microphone, and in a deep, booming, authoritative voice (I've always hated authoritative voices), he started rattling off everything that was wrong with the print. "First of all, the mat around a black-and-white print shouldn't be mauve. That distracts from the print, makes it look bland and ugly. The print quality is bad," he noted as well, adding, "While it is a pleasant expression, it is nowhere near the standard of professional photography." He ranted on and on. His final comment was, "Any idiot would know better than to score this print any higher than seventy."

"Well, thank you very much for those comments," the announcer said. "Now, for a follow-up comment, we have Mr. Fong." They put the microphone in my hand. I couldn't have been more embarrassed if I were naked and peddling around the stage on a miniature clown bicycle. Here I was judging a contest, and not only was I ignorant of the rules, I hadn't even known there *were* rules. They asked me, "Why did you score it so high?"

I said, "Well, I think it's a nice picture. I mean, she's smiling and she's a cute girl. I am sure her mom would love it." The laughter behind me was uproarious. I wanted to pour acid on my head and melt into my shoes.

Then they went to the third judge, who said, "Yes, I would like to echo what the first judge said. This print really cannot score anything over a seventy. Anyone can see that."

I found out that an automatic challenge occurs when the score of one judge is twenty points above or below the score of another judge. I did the math and concluded that if I scored everything at 75, then I would probably never again trigger that horrible fire-alarm buzzer. It seemed unlikely that both the other judges would score any prints at 95 or higher, or at 55 or lower.

So for the rest of the competition, I just sat back in my chair and pressed 75 for every single print that went by. The automatic challenge was never heard again. I made it through the print-judging competition without making a further spectacle of myself. But I have never judged another competition—and I never will.

Nor have I ever entered one.

As for those two other "highly esteemed" judges who sat with me on the Hawaii stage, I have never heard of either of them again. They're probably sitting on a stage right now, in the Kalamazoo Knights of Columbus Hall, trashing some poor photographer's hard work.

Never to Be Forgiven

After the contest-judging debacle, I went back to speaking and doing my program. A lot of people appreciated my take on the business aspect of things, even though I obviously wasn't equipped to judge a photo competition.

One thing I did know how to do was sell a big, fat wedding book. And that's what people really wanted to learn.

That seminar tour included nineteen cities across the country. All my life, I had never been off the West Coast. I had been south to Tijuana, east to Arizona, and as far north as Canada. But never east.

Seeing the whole country was a blast. I got to see Graceland. I got to see Niagara Falls. I got to see New York City. I had a wonderful time. My book and videotape were selling like hotcakes. (Actually, in my experience, hotcakes are not particularly high-volume sellers. My books were selling more like porn in a prison library.) At the end of that tour, the book and video sales had brought me $88,000 in cash. Pretty remarkable for only nineteen cities. It gave Annette and I enough money to put the down payment on our first house, a five-bedroom place in a nice section of west L.A. It was such a great benefit to have that down payment, and it wouldn't have happened without that tour.

After our final engagement, my friend Wayne Byrne threw an end-of-tour party. He gave us big tearful hugs at the end of the evening.

We flew back from Florida with almost $90,000 cash in our pockets, along with lots of memories of making really great friends and energizing a lot of people about their careers. Wedding photographers are usually on the bottom tier of the totem poll in terms of society status, right alongside car salesmen and telemarketers. You don't see them at the local country club unless they've got a Nikon in their hands. But we'd left them feeling really proud and inspired about their work. Not bad.

With all of that great energy flowing in my system, I was positively glowing on the return flight. I looked over at Annette and said, "Aren't you glad you went?"

I'll never forget her reaction. She paused for a moment, looked at me, and said, "For as long as I live, I will never ever forgive you for making me go on that God-awful tour."

I think it was that moment that our relationship became unsalvageable.

We lapsed into a holding pattern, while I concentrated on the business, which was taking off with the power of a Saturn V rocket.

Years later, when I began marriage counseling, my psychologist was baffled as to why I was so confused about how to handle my personal life. She saw me as a capable, bright, in-control person who knew exactly what he wanted, adopted creative strategies for getting to the destination, and had the persistence to keep trying different approaches until the result was achieved. She could not understand why my personal life was hobbling along like a Ford Escort with a blown cylinder.

Only years later did I realize that there was a complete disconnect between how I handled my personal life and how I handled my business life. You see, *I* dictated my business life. My personal life, on the other hand, was subject to the veto power of others.

My career decisions had always been considered ludicrous by others. "Why are you going into wedding photography when you have a pharmacology degree from a prestigious university? What the hell is wrong with you? Everybody knows wedding photographers can't make a decent living!"

Those words fell on deaf ears, because I understood my business. But when it came to my personal life, the advice of my friends suddenly had the power to cancel out all of my intuition.

I knew that getting married to Annette was the wrong thing to do. First of all, there was the trifling matter of not being in love. But I allowed others to have the deciding vote in my personal life. Only later in life did I learn to heed that inner voice telling me to follow both my heart and my mind.

I've learned that when you do something for someone else, you are not the only one who gets hurt. In fact, it's usually the person you're trying to help who ends up getting hurt the worst. If I had held fast to my decision not to marry Annette, she would have been stung for a few weeks, then she would have gotten over it. Instead, I forced us both to live through the pain of a long, unhappy dissolution.

chapter six

The Nights Under the Desk

In its second year, Storybook Weddings earned over $120,000 on sixty-three weddings. The third year I made over $170,000 on sixty-nine weddings.

And I was still living in my parents' apartment.

At first I would meet people at their homes, to avoid having them see that I still lived with mom and dad. But soon that arrangement became impossible. The wedding photo business requires numerous meetings—from first inquiry, to paperwork, to pre-event meeting, to presentation of proofs and album pre-design. I just didn't have enough hours in the day to keep driving all over town.

So I bought a sofa and loveseat with throw pillows. And since I took credit cards, I slapped a sticker on my bedroom door: Visa/MasterCard Accepted Here. I was ready to see clients in my home office.

Sort of.

Clients would come to the apartment building parking lot, where they would be instructed to dial 122 on the keypad. This would ring my phone, and I would say, "Okay, I'll open the gate, you wait there and I'll come down and show you where to park."

I would then lead them upstairs through a dark hallway to my parents' apartment. Upon opening the front door, they would be met by a cloud of kimchee-and-fried-fish odor. Though my mom was no longer combing wigs at this point, she had begun making her own kimchee in jars. I'm not sure which was worse—the hairspray or the kimchee. Probably the kimchee. Kimchee jars lined the kitchen counters, reeking a pungent garlic odor that got past the plastic-seal lids with no difficulty.

I would try to hurry clients past the kitchen to a quick left turn down the hallway to the first room on the right, the one with the MC/Visa sticker over the knob.

Sometimes I wouldn't whisk them fast enough, though, and they would glance to the right and see our kitchen. It had lime green linoleum floors and a Formica dinette set with four chairs. One of these chairs only had a center pole sticking up out of a starfish-shaped base on wheels, because I'd broken the seat part off by leaning on it. The top part of the chair lay on the floor next to the erect base, and we all intended to fix it one of these days.

One evening I had a potentially lucrative inquiry appointment. This couple both worked in one of L.A.'s top law firms. They were both dressed in suits and were very professional in appearance and demeanor. Their wedding was to be at the Bel Air Bay Club, an exclusive venue. The date was open on my calendar and I really wanted this gig. So I tried to play everything right. I whisked them past the smelly kitchen. I sat them down in my office and started in. My pitch was going really well.

My mom used to take some type of medication before bed that, for the fifteen minutes before it knocked her out for the night, would make her wander about and mumble incoherently. It was commonplace in the Fong home to see Mom stumbling about in the evening, issuing random statements from the dream world. But this could be a shock to the uninitiated.

I was about to close the deal with Mr. & Mrs. Bel Air Bay Club, when, right on cue, my mom made a zombie-like appearance in the hallway, with her messy hair, droopy eyelids, and bare feet, clad in bright yellow pajamas. Thankfully, she passed the door and continued on, straight to bed.

Then I heard the shuffling sounds coming back toward us.

My mom walked right into my room and, in a barely intelligible, heavily Korean-accented mumble, introduced herself to my guests and asked them if they wanted some milk and cookies.

The guests were very polite and gracious, showing no unusual reaction. They declined the offer for refreshments and didn't even flinch as my mom took the next ten seconds to turn awkwardly around and shuffle out the door to her bedroom, closing the door with a rousing and unintended slam.

I lost the gig. And that's when I knew I had to get out.

A Real Studio

I had heard of a photographer named Jeff Bryan. He was this interior designer/decorator/architect dude who also consulted on giving photographers game plans. Jeff would work with photographers to help them get financing, and then he would go nuts spending their money.

I sat down with him. I wanted to at least explore the option of creating a professionally decorated and designed photography studio. Of course, anything was going to seem professional compared to Kimchee Alley!

Jeff pitched me on the idea of not limiting myself to wedding photography, but expanding into portraiture. He said that I had a legion of loyal clients who loved my wedding photography, so why miss out on the other photo business I could be doing? Family portraits, baby photos, graduation shots—that sort of stuff.

Well, the reason I was missing out on those other business avenues was because I had absolutely no interest in pursuing them.

It would have been handy if I'd thought to mention that to Jeff, but I didn't.

Jeff convinced me to expand my wedding photography studio into a portrait *and* wedding studio. He asked me how much money I had in savings. I said, "Fifty thousand dollars."

"You've got to be joking. You have fifty thousand dollars in savings?"

I thought he was making fun of me. But he was actually impressed that I had socked away that much. Turns out he thought it was *too* much. "Oh, that's silly," he said. "Saving money is for old ladies. You need to grow your business."

I couldn't think of a rebuttal.

I signed a contract with him and within minutes, literally, we were driving around L.A., looking for a suitable place to house my photography studio. We ended up going to this building in Culver City. Culver City, in case you're not familiar with it, has some spiffy parts and some not-so-spiffy parts. Among the not-so-spiffy parts is the Target where I would later get arrested.

I wasn't too thrilled with the idea of opening a studio in Culver City. Plus, Jeff picked a building I didn't like much. It had that same trapezoid shape the Palace Court apartments had. I get depressed whenever I see a trapezoid.

Had I been fully engaged in the process, there are many things I would have done differently. But I let Jeff drive the bus. We took that studio in Culver City and I signed a lease: three years, $1,800 a month.

I'd never before had that kind of expense. Up until then my business and living expenses were pretty much the same because I had a "home office." Now I would have the additional overhead of a professional location. Which meant new phone lines, new furniture, and the works.

We burned through my $50,000 in a hurry. I even let Jeff talk me into a grand opening party with a budget of $5,000. We hired my favorite nine-piece band and had a disappointing turnout of about sixty people. I wore a tuxedo and the whole thing was pretty pathetic. It would have been more productive to spend the $5,000 on Chia Pets.

My new business was no longer Storybook Weddings; it was Storybook Studio of Photography. I had samples of baby portraits, portfolio photography, and nice frames. This was all under Jeff's direction. But I didn't have the passion for portrait photography. My niche was weddings. I knew how to merchandise them, sell them, and make them into a thriving business, one that was streamlined and focused.

Now it was becoming diffuse. I had a photography studio set up in the back, complete with squeaky toys to make children laugh, a big plastic football we could put kids inside of (so they could pop out for a "peek-a-boo!" shot), giant crayons, colored gels, and a flash system.

I didn't get very much business from portraiture because, as I said, my heart wasn't in it.

Eventually that back studio area became my office. On the rare occasions when we'd have portrait sessions, we'd have to cover the desk area and shove all the accumulated crap into a corner. It was pretty clear to all involved that I just wasn't into it.

So even though it was called Storybook Studio, I pretty much stuck to weddings. The portrait idea was a flop while the wedding photography was running nicely on its own.

But it was no longer a challenge to me. I started getting antsy.

The Money Machine

One day I was walking around a photography convention and I saw someone demonstrating an amazing thing called a Bryce Automated Letter Printer. It was this $12,000 Hasbro Mousetrap contraption where you'd stick a pile of envelopes in one end and it would individually address eight thousand envelopes per hour.

I sat and I watched this machine churn and churn. I was fascinated with it, and for some stupid reason I decided that I had to have one.

A lot of my businesses have begun by me being the first one to buy some new toy, and then figuring out how to make money with it. So, for reasons I couldn't possibly explain, I signed a lease for this $12,000 automated dot matrix addressing machine. I had it delivered to the studio with absolutely no idea what I was going to do with it.

For a month or two, this beast just sat there in my office, quietly mocking me. "Nice move, Mr. Rockefeller," it would say. "Way to spend twelve grand on a paperweight." I got very testy whenever anyone asked me about the Bryce Automated Letter Printer, because I could offer no explanation as to why it was occupying space in my studio. All I knew was that I was shelling out expensive lease payments every month. I kept wondering, what the heck am I going to do with this? How am I going to make money with it?

One day I was looking at a brochure from the print shop that had made my first photographic business cards. They were always sending me stuff, saying not only do we do business cards but we also do photographic postcards, posters, and 8 x 10 brochures! They also did full four-color printings on 8½ x 11 stock that they called "catalog cards." They were really cool looking, but you had to order thousands of them to keep the unit cost down. I was fascinated with the idea of printing thousands of copies of my photos, but the price was too high.

Meanwhile, every day, in my mailbox, there'd be some type of announcement from a real estate agent. It would list a local address and say something like, "Just sold in your neighborhood, please call for a market analysis of your home. Now is the time to sell!" These cheesy photocopied flyers went directly from the mailbox to the trash. Every day.

That method of marketing is called "farming." The way it works is that a real estate office will give an agent a certain number of addresses in a certain neighborhood. That agent is supposed to go to that pre-assigned neighborhood and "farm" it, sending out notices, knocking on doors, and trying to get new listings.

A friend of mine who was a realtor told me about the huge amount of work and dedication required to send out mailings to farm an area with discipline.

I started thinking (always a dangerous thing). What if instead of sending out those crappy Xeroxed paper flyers, a realtor could send out photographic postcards of high quality? A nice, full-color postcard with his or her picture on it, the first of its kind. On the other side would be a printed message, plus the mailing label spat out by my brand new $12,000 paperweight.

If I was able to print four different color postcards onto an 8½ x 11 sheet, then I could participate in what is called in the printing industry a "gang run." A gang run saves money because you group the four jobs together on one sheet and then cut the sheet into separate orders.

I got excited. I started to do some research and learned that the postage for postcards was much less than for letters. At the time it was, like, 11 cents, versus 25 cents for a regular envelope printing. Then, if you registered with the post office, you also got a discount for automated bulk printing and bulk mailing, and so saved a few cents more.

By using gang-run methods, I could produce photographic postcards for pennies each. Realtors were already spending a fortune sending out direct mail, and most of it was dumpster fodder.

I did the math. I realized that, with the savings on the printing and the postage, I could offer realtors these beautiful, four-color postcards *for the cost of a normal postage stamp*. Not only could I offer them a much better product for the same money, but also, because my system was completely automated, I could save them a ton of labor. It was a no-brainer.

I started meeting with real estate agents. It was the easiest sell in the world. We'd take a picture of the guy with his foot on the bumper of a Mercedes-Benz holding a SOLD sign. Corny stuff, but it gave the realtor instant face recognition and, because it was in full color, it had high impact.

I began to collect orders for five thousand postcards at a time. As soon as I got four customers, I would bunch them up onto one large 8½ x 11 catalog card and send off the order ganged together. Then the printing company would cut it into fours and send me back separate orders of five thousand 4 x 6 postcards.

The first month, Marketing Concepts Group, as I decided to call it, grossed $72,000. That meant almost a million a year in revenue. The company started to grow fast. Pretty soon realtors were asking me for tailored deals. "Okay, if I sign up with you and give you my addresses, can I have those addresses exclusively?" In other words, no one else could use my service for mailing cards to the same address. I thought, "Okay, fair enough."

I researched the software and found ways that I could run through a new customer's farm list, compare it to the existing lists, and reject the ones that were already reserved.

I was able to guarantee my customers exclusivity, which was a huge competitive advantage for them. The results for my direct-mail farming program were instantaneous.

I decided to sell subscription plans. The way that worked was, I would sell the realtor a year of exclusivity for my postcard business. They had to sign up for a minimum of two thousand pieces, mailed twice a month. That meant that I could guarantee the regular scheduling of gang runs to keep my printer busy and my costs low.

This exclusivity option was a great marketing tool. I learned that, as in any profession, the top 5 percent of realtors outperformed the bottom 50 percent by far. Usually there were two or three people fighting for the top position in any given area. So I would ask around to learn who was the top dog in a particular area. Then I would also find out the names of the number two and three people.

I would send Top Realtor #1 a nice sample postcard, then follow up with a "Hey, I sent you a postcard, did you notice it?"

The postcards looked great, so the agent would almost always want to meet with me. I would give my presentation and tell them about the four thousand minimum purchase and the exclusivity plan.

Well, four thousand postcards a month was a big commitment, so they'd often say, "I'm going to have to think about it."

At which point I would thank them, get up to leave, and say, "Okay, that's fine. I've got another appointment in the area anyway."

They would perk up and say, "With whom?"

Already knowing who his or her key competitor was, I'd say, "I've got a meeting with Sally Smith at two o'clock."

The agent would instantly develop a nervous tic and become extremely . . . energized. Frantic, one might say. "Well, what if I signed up right now?"

"Are you saying you want the exclusive?"

By this point, the guy would practically be climbing over his desk to grab hold of my lapels. "If I give you a check right now, will you cancel that two o'clock meeting?"

This worked almost 100 percent of the time. I would go from office to office and walk away with a $7,000 to $12,000 check. It was phenomenal. I had an assistant who worked late into the night because we had mailings of fifty or one hundred thousand pieces that would have to go out twice a week. He just stayed in the back, running the Bryce machine, that beautiful $12,000 ex-paperweight that had entered my life for no discernible reason.

One time these two high-end female realtors came to my office for a pitch presentation and I said, "I'd like to introduce you to Dan, my assistant." Dan came out of the back room completely covered in white powder from the postcards, looking like a psychotic baker.

He just stood there kind of awkwardly, and then blurted out, "The best part about what Gary does is he sends out junk mail but it's good junk mail." The two ladies looked at each other. I gave Dan the wide-eyed "these are potential customers!" look.

He tried to smooth things over, "I mean, this really isn't junk mail. What I mean is—"

I cut him off with a, "Hey Danno, ol' buddy, why don't you go out to my car and see if you can find that left-handed hammer I've been looking for?" As soon as the door closed the ladies looked at me and said, "Oh my goodness, that poor boy."

From then on, Dan stayed in the back running the Bryce machine. But the business started to appear as if it had unlimited growth potential. It seemed like it could be repeated citywide, statewide, nationwide, and worldwide. I started to think, Holy crap, this thing could be a platinum mine.

My First Mercedes

Back in the 1980s, the minute you got successful—especially if you lived in Los Angeles—the first thing that you had to do was buy a Mercedes Benz. It was the car that symbolized success and affluence in the '80s. A Mercedes was not just a status symbol, it was a badge of credibility, just like a professional photographer having a Hasselblad camera.

When I buy cars, I always pay cash for them—it's been ground into my head since birth that I should never take out loans. So after a particularly flush period at Storybook, I bought myself a Mercedes Benz 500 SEC, their top-of-the-line two-door coupe. It was an $88,000 car, but I bought it slightly used, so I paid a mere $42,000.

It was cherry, though. Hand-built, with a gorgeous burgundy interior. It had one of the first anti-lock brake systems, and I would take friends out for a spin, slamming the brakes until we would nearly pass out from the G-force.

The Mercedes even impressed my mom. She considered it a rite of passage to the big time.

When her cousin visited from Korea, my mom asked me to come to their apartment and show him the Mercedes. I think that moment was the validation I had been awaiting since the day she'd "disowned" me for deciding to be a wedding photographer instead of going to medical school.

I absolutely could not believe that I was a wedding photographer in my twenties and I had this pimpin' car. Turned out, I wasn't the only one who had trouble believing it.

From the moment I signed the bill of sale, I got pulled over by the cops more often than a Krispy Kreme delivery truck. For example, one time I left my friend's house quite late and drove the two blocks to my house. I was so tired I forgot to turn my headlights on.

All of a sudden, this giant searchlight with the wattage of a supernova ignited in my face and I heard a bullhorn shout, "Mercedes Benz driver, stop your car immediately and get out of the vehicle!" Well, continuing to drive wasn't really an option, not with the Light of God shining directly in my eyes.

As I stumbled blindly out of the car, the unseen beings behind the alien light ordered me to lie face down on the concrete, lace my fingers behind my neck, and cross my ankles. What was I going to be asked to do next—get up and Riverdance?

I couldn't really see the cops because my retinas had been melted, but I did hear them order me to hold still while they searched my car. They asked a bunch of questions and then demanded to see my ID, which was in the car, as was my registration.

After they radioed everything in, it was established that I was indeed the legal owner of the car. They explained to me, after they'd helped me to my feet, that they had pulled me over because my lights were off and I didn't have a front license plate.

Fair enough, but why the Jeffrey Dahmer treatment?

The cops said that my behavior fit the profile of stolen vehicles—lights off and plates removed. That didn't make sense, though. That kind of behavior would only make one look *more* conspicuous. I was about to point this out, but I decided I'd had enough fun for the evening.

They let me go with a warning: Driving that car, in that neighborhood, made me look like a drug dealer.

They had a point. Once I bought that car, everybody *did* seem to think I was a drug dealer. They'd take one look at my car and ask what I did for a living. When I'd tell them that I was a wedding photographer, they'd give me this look like I was Tony Soprano claiming to be in waste management.

Then they'd say, "Dude. No, really, what do you do?"

That 500 SEC caused me a lot of trouble.

HE HAS A GUN!

A week or so later, I was driving on a semi-highway through a not-super-great part of town when the cops pulled me over again. Just checking to make sure everything was kosher, I guess. I had my ID and registration at the ready. (I learned to carry them like a traveler's passport.)

Now, it happened that I had purchased this little CO_2 air pistol for my friend's kid. It said on the package, "For ages twelve and up." It came in a colorful box that looked like one of those things you buy fireworks in. I think it had a picture of a cowboy on it. It was a gray gun made of "genuine metal" that looked 100 percent toy-like and had a sticker on it that said FOR USE ONLY WITH ADULT SUPERVISION.

I pulled over on the shoulder and two officers exited their cruiser and approached my car. I was becoming so familiar with this procedure, I was wondering if I would know the officers by name. One of them came up to my window and asked me for my license and registration, which I started to hand him.

Then I heard the other one scream, "Partner! Gun!"

I actually laughed for half a second because I thought he was joking.

The next thing I knew, the officer at my window had drawn his *real* gun and was pointing it at my head. His hands were shaking like a junkie's on his first day of detox.

I knew I had to take charge or bad things were going to happen.

I lay my hands on the wheel very deliberately and said, "Officer, please remain calm. I will do whatever you say." He was shaking so badly, it was like watching Barney Fife try to apprehend a terrorist. I was petrified, thinking he was going to squeeze the trigger by mistake. "Officer," I repeated, "I need you to remain calm."

He tried to tell me to do something, but his voice was all shaky and garbled and I couldn't understand him. I again instructed him to remain calm and told him that everything was going to be okay and that I would walk him though this. I already knew the drill. I said, "I am going to step out of the vehicle and lie face down on the concrete. Then I am going to lace my fingers behind my neck and cross my ankles."

I slowly did everything I'd promised, and he cuffed my hands behind my back.

Finally, the second officer pulled the toy air gun out of the car, laid it on the hood, and said, "We have the weapon under control."

Meanwhile I'm lying there on the concrete, wondering who was going to drive by and see me.

The cop with his gun drawn backed cautiously away from me and approached the hood of the cruiser. I heard this strange high-pitched sound that might have been a laugh or a sob. It was not a sound one typically associates with mental health.

Then he said, "*That's* the gun? Made by Whammo, adult supervision required? That's the weapon in question?"

His partner cleared his throat and replied, "I observed a weapon and followed protocol."

"Geez, let's help this poor guy up." They helped me to my feet, uncuffed me, and profusely apologized.

They explained to me that ever since the L.A. Riots, everyone on the force had hair-trigger nerves. When they saw me in my Mercedes, they thought I might have been a gang member up to no good.

I guess being young, successful, and Asian American was a more serious crime than I'd imagined. I would learn to be more careful in the future.

Targeted at Target

I forget what I had to buy, but they only had it at Target. Being in Westchester, California, I was exactly between two Target locations. One was in Culver City; the other was in Manhattan Beach.

I went to the one in Culver City. Big mistake.

While walking down one of the aisles, a large African American woman barreled into me with the full weight of her body. A deliberate body bump. I thought it was pretty strange, but I didn't want to make a big deal out of it. Then she shouted out loudly, for the whole store to hear, "Excuse me!"

I mumbled something lame and hurried on my way.

When I got through the checkout, a woman in a red Target vest was standing with two beefy Target security officers behind her. The large black woman, also waiting at the front of the store, said, "That's him, officer! Arrest him!"

I looked around to see whom she was referring to. It took me a few seconds to realize that they were all staring at me. Just to make certain there was no doubt in anyone's mind, the large black woman shook an angry finger at me and said, and "That's him! That's the man who tried to kill my baby!"

Uh-oh.

A five-year-old boy was clinging to the woman's trunk-like thigh, and I noticed for the first time that she was pregnant. *Really* pregnant. Either that or she was Budweiser's number one customer. Shock and puzzlement were swirling around in my head.

The Target security guys calmly informed me that I was accused of attacking this woman in the store. They said they had no authority to detain me, but that they had contacted the Culver City police, who were on their way. They "suggested" that I stick around for questioning. They said I was free to leave, but if I did so, they would have to report my license plate number to the P.D.

The strange thing was, they were apologetic and courteous, even as this woman was screaming in rage that I was her assailant. They even offered to help me with my three bags of purchases as I followed them to the security office.

In the Target security office we stood in front of a bank of security monitors. On one of the monitors, my accuser sat on the floor, spread-eagled, propped up on her doughy arms, visibly panting as her young son stared at her in worry. She was clearly trying to dramatize some kind of injury. Her name, I learned, was Glenda Violet Washington.

About three minutes later, two officers from the Culver City Police Department arrived. At that point I got a little nervous. I mean, here I was being accused of a violent act, and even though I was innocent, I knew it would be my word against hers. Ms. Washington had made sure to body-check me when nobody else was looking. I recalled that clearly. And she had cried out quite convincingly after our bodies had made contact. I recalled that too.

But the officers were really nice. A lot like the Target security guys—courteous, almost apologetic. They certainly didn't make me feel like an accused assailant.

The senior officer began asking me odd questions, like what kind of car I drove. As soon as I said it was a Mercedes 500 SEC, the two cops gave each other a knowing look. "She must've seen him drive in," one of them remarked. They were acting as if Glenda Violet Washington was the suspect, not me.

During the questioning, a Target employee came in, saying that Ms. Washington was asking what was taking so long, and could she get an ambulance because she was afraid that she was going to "lose the baby."

The senior officer told the employee to go back to Ms. Washington with the following message: "She can get an ambulance, but it's eighty-five dollars a mile and she has to pay in advance. The reason it's taking so long is that the police are watching a replay of the surveillance video."

In reality, we were not watching the surveillance video, because you cannot stop the recording in process until after the store closes. But Glenda Violet Washington didn't know that. We all watched on the security monitor as the Target employee relayed the message to her. Immediately, the "injured" Glenda Violet Washington jumped up and started waving her hands animatedly.

"Interesting," said the officer.

The Target employee came back in and said, "She told us you can't review the videotape playback without her attorney present, and she wants to know the badge numbers of the officers and the name of the watch commander." Whoa, this gal had experience!

It finally became clear that I was the would-be victim of an extortion plot. Apparently, from the moment I'd arrived in my Mercedes, I'd been walking around with a giant red Target bull's-eye on my chest.

Since it was her word against mine, the officers said that they were not going to charge me, but that if she chose to make a "citizen's arrest," they would be legally compelled to fill out a citation. So the officers accompanied me out there to face my accuser, where she was told to declare that she was placing me under citizen's arrest.

She said, "I hereby place you under citizen's arrest," in an almost incoherent mumble. I think she was trying to sound injured. Her poor son kept saying, "Momma? You gonna be okay, Momma?"

As they filled out the citation, the junior officer told me that the targeting of Mercedes drivers was not uncommon. He shared a story in which he'd had to arrest a man in the middle of eating dinner with his family on charges of assault, battery, and attempted rape.

It seems the guy had been at a bar having a non-alcoholic drink with a friend. A stunning blonde woman came up to him, saying that she was late for an appointment and needed a ride. She asked this man for a lift and he said sure.

Off they went to his car, a new Mercedes. They hadn't gone two blocks when the woman hopped out of the car and bolted off on foot. Odd, he thought. But he shrugged it off and went home to his family.

A half hour later, unbeknownst to the man, the blonde showed up at the police station, physically beaten, giving the police not only a description of the man, but also an exact car description and a license plate number. She alleged that they had met at a local bar, where he offered her a ride home. He then made a detour to a hotel parking lot where he assaulted her physically and sexually. She managed to get away.

This officer had several reasons not to believe her story and theorized that her intent was to extort the man for a cash payment in exchange for dropping the charges. The case hadn't been resolved yet, though—the guy was still awaiting trial.

Gee, officer, I feel better already.

The next day the Culver City district attorney called me and said that Glenda Violet Washington was dropping the charges. Turns out she was a twenty-one-year-old mother of three (with another bun in the oven) who lived on welfare in Venice. She had tried this scam before and had been warned not to do it again. The D.A. said that I could sue her for fraud, but that she "didn't have a pot to piss in."

He offered his apologies, and that was the end of that.

Glenda Violet Washington most likely went on to deliver a healthy baby, sans an ill-gotten windfall from me.

Antoine

An exceptional thing happened one Saturday evening after work. I guess what with the whole Glenda Violet Washington affair freshly behind me, karma was giving me a chance to improve my attitude about race relations.

I had arranged to meet a friend of mine at a movie theater. I'd just shot a wedding, so all of my expensive camera equipment and all of my exposed film from the wedding was in the trunk of my car.

I was late getting to the theater, so I parked the car and walked away from it in a hurry.

We saw the movie, and it was a long one. At the end of it I was tired, so I told my friend, "Ah well, I guess I'll head home." I stood up and instinctively felt my pants pocket for my keys. Nothing. I felt my back pockets and jacket pockets. Still nothing.

Oh shit, had I left the keys in the car?

I ran down the street like the Six Million Dollar Man. I was relieved to see my car still there. When I got to it, there was a note on the windshield. It read, "Dear Mercedes Benz Owner, you left your keys in the ignition. I have them, so please page me when you get this. Take care, Antoine." What a kind Samaritan act, I thought.

This was before cell phones, so at the nearest pay phone I called the number Antoine had provided. His voicemail message started with a loud, thumping rap song. Then his recorded voice came on and said, "Shit man, this is Antoine. I say leave a message and I'll call you back if I feel like it."

My hopes for a speedy and painless resolution evaporated.

I said, "Um, excuse me, hi, Antoine, this is Gary Fong and I'm the guy who owns the Mercedes Benz." I was thinking to myself, "What's the deal? If he's going to screw with me, why didn't he just take the car? Is he going to ransom the keys back to me? Is he going to lure me to an alley, take my wallet, *then* drive off in my car?" Glenda Violet Washington had put all sorts of unkind thoughts in my head.

I left the pay phone number and waited. After a while the pay phone rang and a voice said, "This is Antoine."

I said "Hi, I'm the guy with the car."

"Yeah, shit, man," he said. "That wasn't so smart, leaving your keys in the door like that. Someone could have stole your car."

I said, "Yeah, I know. I can't even tell you how grateful I am."

He said, "So I'm at the movie theater pay phone now. When the movie's over I'll give you a call, around 10:30. We'll meet by the car and I'll give you the keys."

My friend and I went and had an appetizer at a nearby restaurant. I was feeling very nervous because my life was no longer in my control. It was in the control of "shit, man" Antoine. Not only did he have lordship over my Mercedes, he had lordship over every single piece of camera equipment I owned, plus some shot wedding film that was irreplaceable.

I tried to enjoy my friend's company, but every second I kept thinking, *Please God, I hope Antoine's not psychotic. I hope, I hope, I hope.*

Around 10:15 we went to the car and waited nervously. I looked across the parking lot saw this black man the size of a linebacker approaching. Big baseball hat, baggy clothes, gold chains. I silently prayed that this would not be Antoine, and that Antoine would end up looking a little more like Spike Lee.

But of course, it was Antoine. With his cute little girlfriend. He came sauntering up as if he was listening to a rap video, then just stood there for a moment, moving in place.

"Shit, foo, that wasn't too smart, leaving your keys in the car like that," he said. "Someone could have stolen it."

I said, "Oh my gosh, thanks for the note. You see, I'm a wedding photographer . . ."

"What? Shit, man, do not lie to me," he said. (He probably thought I was a drug dealer.)

"No really, I'm a wedding photographer. In that trunk is not only all of my camera equipment, but all of the film from a wedding I shot today."

He shook his head and said, "That's not too smart man, not too smart. You coulda lost it all. This is not a good town for leaving your keys in the car door."

And with that he handed over the keys.

"Oh my gosh, I can't thank you enough. Can I give you a reward?"

He looked slightly offended and said, "No, man, that ain't right. Just be more careful next time."

With one simple gesture, Antoine had saved my life and shattered any racial stereotypes I had ever held. Mind you, this was right after the L.A. Riots, so racial tensions—especially between Asians and African Americans—were at an all-time high.

This one saint of an individual single-handedly erased all memory of Glenda Violet Washington and gave me back the most valuable gift I could hope for: trust in my fellow man.

While he was saying a few words to my friend, I went to his girlfriend and said, "I'm not going to be okay with him refusing a reward." I asked her for her phone number and she gave it to me. The next day I called her up and said, "You have to give me Antoine's address."

Not knowing what else to do, I called FTD and sent him a big bouquet of flowers. I had no idea what else to send. It also had a bright red coffee cup that said, "You're the Best!"

Thanks, Antoine.

The Stranger in My Bed

The postcard business was thriving, but I couldn't say the same about my marriage. I woke up one morning and realized that ignoring the eight-hundred-pound gorilla in the room was no longer possible. The game was up. I could not spend another night in bed with this person. I just couldn't do it.

Annette and I separated and I filed for divorce. As a lovely follow-up, when I told my mom about the end of our marriage, she sided with Annette. Mom called her and apologized that I'd turned out the way I had, saying she'd tried her best to raise a great son, but had obviously failed.

I didn't speak to my mom for nearly two years following that stunt.

Though my personal life was crumbling, my business was showing a lot of promise, which served as a great distraction. During this time

I met a Filipino realtor who was phenomenally successful. He had something like eight associate realtors under him, and all of his success was due to farming. He contacted me about my postcard-mailing service.

Remember, we were offering a fully automated service. A large part of a realtor's time back then was spent licking stamps and addressing flyers. My service freed them from that burden, at a price that cut their costs.

So this realtor was ready to sign a $1 million-per-year contract before I even made my sales pitch, and he didn't want a discount.

There was only one little problem: my divorce attorney. She must have gotten her law degree from the West Covina School of Cosmetology. She advised me not to take the $1 million account because "Your soon-to-be ex-wife could claim that he is her client, too."

Now, there's a basic fact of family law that post-separation earnings belong to each separate party. This means that once we filed for divorce, there was an official date of separation. Past that deadline, if I were to win the lottery or discover the secret to cold fusion, all that money would belong entirely to me.

But this moronic attorney advised me not to take the $1 million deal, and her moronic client took her advice.

My big realtor client was, shall we say . . . upset. He was ready to sign a one-year contract for a million bucks and I turned him down.

Shortly thereafter, the real estate recession of the late '80s hit California. It was brutal. By July 1989, the market slammed on its brakes and every single realtor client I had, even the most successful ones, said, "Please stop the mailings. I have a warehouse full of postcards and no cash flow."

The Bryce Automated Letter Printer that had paid for itself many times over went silent. Overnight, Marketing Concepts Group ground to a halt.

Though Storybook Weddings was still doing great, my financial circumstances took a sharp turn for the worse. The house we had bought when Storybook started to take off was now worth less than what I owed the bank.

I decided to acquire some roommates to help me feel better about having a mortgage worth more than the house. I traveled a lot, too, so I rented out three of my five bedrooms. This brought my living costs down to less than $500 a month, and with that I was able to reconcile the fact that I wouldn't be able to unload the house for a while. I didn't know when the market was going to turn around again.

I was heartbroken, despondent, and lonely. I felt tremendous guilt for having left my marriage for something as ambiguous as lack of love. Annette hadn't wanted me to leave, and it was very painful for her. So I assumed all of the responsibility for ending the marriage. All my life I had believed that once you get married, you stay with the person through thick and thin, you talk things out, you persevere. But I simply couldn't do it with Annette anymore. I took that failure very hard.

The Stranger in My Bed, Part II

I started going to the gym daily, where I was surrounded by people just like me. Apparently when people break up, they head straight to the gym.

This gym constantly played Taylor Dayne's "Love Will Lead You Back" in its song loop. The lyrics to that song are tough to hear when you've unilaterally ended your marriage. I imagined Annette (who wanted me back) singing the lyrics, "Someday I just know that love will lead you back in my arms . . . where you belong . . ." Once I actually started to sob while doing bench presses.

As fate would have it, the next (and second-ever) girl I slept with was a flight attendant. My in-flight experience en route to my honeymoon must have left a subconscious impression on me, because it turned into a potent fetish for flight attendants. And as I was walking out of the gym (located at an L.A. Airport Hotel) one day, this soon-to-be-bride randomly selected me to help her figure out some unfinished psychosexual business in her life.

She didn't tell me her name. Turned out she was getting married on Saturday, and, this being Thursday, she wanted to have one last fling before committing herself forever to a deeply controlling and stifling guy. As one who had just failed at marriage, I thought I could talk her out of what she was about to do.

"Shhh, don't talk," she said repeatedly, back at my place. I tried to ask her name, but she said she didn't want me to know it, and she didn't want to know mine either. I was lonely and found myself with a total stranger. I don't know how most guys can do this serially, because to me it was a heart-scorching experience. It's like walking into a Thanksgiving dinner with a close family you've never met before and sharing dinner with them, while nobody addresses you or even bothers to find out your name.

That's what sex with a stranger feels like to me.

When she woke up in the early morning to catch a cab for her flight out of town, my newly intimate friend-stranger gave me a most endearing nickname: "Um."

"Um, excuse me, but do you have any orange juice?" "Well, Um, that was great." I caught myself about to say, "Good luck on Saturday," but my head flew into a stupor. With nothing at all meaningful to say, I was silent as she got into her cab.

I felt as alone as if I were on the deck of an unmanned aircraft carrier, adrift in the Indian Ocean, at midnight, with no blanket. It felt a lot like the night I spent under the stairs at the sheriff's station.

I was so sad that I couldn't really do anything that day. The day turned into weeks. When I woke up, I would get sleepy again. And then I would get hungry again, and then sleepy again. I think they call it depression. Of course, it was really about my failed marriage, but the mysterious flight attendant had set it in motion with her strange, sad, nameless goodbye.

Giving Up Hope

I had hired a teenage girl, Terri, who started as a production worker and eventually became a very good photographer. She knew how to run the Storybook business. This afforded me the luxury of not working. Which was good, because I *couldn't* work. I pretty much spent the year in pajamas, feeling sad and miserable all the time.

Since the Storybook company had become successful very early in my marriage, much of its worth was considered community property. So I ended up owing a huge settlement to Annette. I couldn't pay it all at once; it had to be spread out over five years. I lost hundreds of thousands of dollars and suddenly found myself right back where I'd started.

I had no money in the bank, tons of credit card debt, and a large five-year settlement to pay off. I felt gut-shot and weary, as if I'd lost everything. Which I pretty much had.

One day I was driving around, mulling over the failure of Marketing Concepts Group, stewing over the fact that I had been cleaned out by Annette's excellent attorney. I felt so low I barely had the motivation to keep the car between the painted lines.

That's the day I happened to see the bumper sticker I told you about at the beginning. It read: SINCE I GAVE UP HOPE, I FEEL MUCH BETTER.

All of a sudden—no joke—I felt an enormous weight lift off my shoulders. I started to laugh, all alone in my car. My cackling grew louder and louder. That bumper sticker really got to me. It was, in fact, the funniest thing I'd ever seen.

I thought, *I want to feel better, so I'm going to give up hope*. It may seem strange, but it felt like nothing less than a spiritual awakening.

Right there in that moment, I decided I was not going to worry about *anything* anymore. I had worked my ass off in business and had absolutely nothing to show for it. In fact, I had more debt than cash and a future that appeared bleak. But I just said, "You know what? I don't care. I completely and utterly don't care."

I'd never felt better in my entire life.

Next stop? Club Med in Nassau, Bahamas.

chapter seven

The Intruder in the Spider Outfit

I didn't pick Club Med in Nassau out of the blue. I had a friend named Charlotte who was a party planner in Sherman Oaks. Tall, attractive, slender, and in her mid-twenties, she was a director of catering for a nearby hotel. She and her Day Runner, always inseparable. Picture Courtney Cox in *Friends*, only taller.

Charlotte and I reconnected when my marriage ended. She was a generous listener and a phone person. I am also a phone person, so we would stay up late into the night solving the mysteries of life together. She was single, career-driven, and always complaining about never meeting Mr. Right.

At this point in my life, I should confess that I had a problem that my marriage counselor called "Body Dysmorphic Disorder." Without going into detail, I had this firm belief that I was terribly ugly. I only had it for a brief spell, right around the time I was friendly with Charlotte.

Back in those days, I had a problem maintaining eye contact. My eyes would dart around the room, trying to avert any long gaze. I was literally ashamed of my own face.

This is what someone would expect from a burn victim, but my reason was because I believed I was super-ugly. Psychologically, this freed me from having to enter the singles scene again.

Rather than date, I resolved that I would be the cool guy-pal. The guy that girls love and trust, knowing that romantic chemistry is out of the question. Kind of like the gay guy friend. Only not gay. All the girls love their gay guy friends because they're safe. Being hideous (at least in my own mind), I retreated to the position of being the safe, heterosexual guy friend.

I am happy to report that, later on, in counseling, my therapist got me over this hurdle with a simple paradigm-shifting exercise. She suggested that I stand in a line at a public place and take an inventory of how I objectively compared to the other men in the room. When I did the exercise, standing in line at a bank, I discovered to my surprise that I was not wrinkly, fat, bald, knock-kneed, duck-toed, or buck-toothed. Nor did I wear Coke-bottle glasses, lime green polyester pants, or pocket protectors, like other men in the room. In this one bank-teller line, I realized that the entire idea of being super-ugly was an illusion of my own creation.

However, I had not yet had this epiphany when I was hanging out with Charlotte. This made us an absolutely toxic pair. She was on a lonely quest for Mr. Right, baring her soul to me nightly on the phone about how there are "no great guys available in L.A." I, being the non-gay guy-pal that I believed myself to be, was doing everything in my repertoire to convince her that she was beautiful, charming, and an unbelievable catch. I could do this openly because there was no way she would be interested in me!

One of her corporate jobs was an event for Club Med. Club Med had offered her a land package in exchange for her services. I think it was a seven-day package, which meant they didn't pay your airfare, but once you got to Club Med it was all-inclusive. You got seven days and seven nights with all the meals and all the fun of Club Med.

She approached me about it and said, "Hey Gary, I have this package for two. You've got frequent flyer miles. Why don't you take care of the airfare and we can go to Club Med in the Bahamas together?" My mind couldn't come up with a good reason not to spend a week in the Bahamas, so I said, "I've got nothing going on here. Sure, I'll go."

We went to the Nassau Club Med and they gave us a room with two beds—because we weren't a couple, we were just friends. It was my understanding that we were just going to do whatever each of us wanted. No expectations. From the moment I got there, I met so many people that I was up until 4:00 in the morning every night. I had recently given up hope, and that made me a much more fun person! I don't drink, but my new friends and I would hang out in the little bar, dancing and laughing. Playing tennis all day. Lying in the sun and doing beach sports.

I was having a blast until I started to realize that Charlotte was getting more and more . . . frosty. I would come back to the room and she would be sitting there with a little black cloud of anger over her head. And this cloud would be shooting bolts of lightning at me.

"Were you having fun?" she'd say. "'Cause you have certainly been up late."

I'd say, "Yeah, I know. Oh gosh, I'm tired." Then I'd jump into the sack and fall dead asleep.

In the morning I'd say, "Hey, let's go to breakfast." We'd eat together and then, as soon as breakfast was over, I would run off with a new group of friends.

I didn't think of it as being impolite to my date, because she wasn't my date, she was just a travel buddy. Okay, she was more than a travel buddy, she was my good friend. A sincere friend who would laugh riotously at my jokes (always a plus). Once she spit out her drink all over the table when I caught her with a good line mid-gulp! Her eyes would sparkle whenever I told her she had an infectious laugh. Then she would grab my thigh and lean on my shoulder, at which point I would pat her on the hip, straighten her out, and continue with my story.

I explained to her that as a natural-born people-person, she radiated all of the qualities I so wished my ex-wife had possessed. Annette had been a shy wallflower, and oh, how badly I wanted to be with someone who was a people magnet like myself. Shy people, I theorized, practice a form of self-hatred. Whenever they are thrust into a social gathering, they retreat into self-criticism. They measure their shortcomings against the prettiest, liveliest, most glittering people in the room, and then assume that everybody hates them.

Shy people are naturally attracted to the social butterfly, the "life of the party." However, in time, if the shy girl finds herself *attached* to the "LOTP," her self-loathing intensifies, building a mountain of resentment toward the natural sparkler. This causes insurmountable problems in a marriage. Therefore, I vowed that my next significant other was going to be one who was never ill at ease around strangers. I explained my theories in great detail to Charlotte, who was a natural sparkler.

And what a sweet friend she was! Once she came over to my place after my cat had kittens. One of them was stillborn, and I was kind of grossed out by the little pink grub carcass decaying in the box next to the nursing litter. All I had to do was mention something about it, and along came Charlotte, with a new set of dishwashing gloves and a small bottle of vodka. She explained that the vodka was to calm her nerves after helping me discard the dead kitten, because she knew she was going to freak out.

Who was I to deny such an offer of help? Who wouldn't want a gal-pal like this? She was the best! I would always say this as I gave her a playful little punch in the shoulder at the end of a fun evening.

I remember once, under a starlit sky, standing on the harbor after a candle-lit dinner and a long evening of opening our souls to each other, telling her that she was going to make some lucky guy the happiest man in the world.

We ended up staying at Club Med longer than the seven nights because I just didn't want to go back to Los Angeles. She stayed on because she was a party planner and had a block of free space in her calendar. I made an offer with the management at Club Med to do some tennis instructing in exchange for my lodgings.

As the days went by I noticed that Charlotte had started to wear less and less clothing when she climbed into her bed. At first it was sweats, then shorts. Then she was down to lingerie. One night she was wearing this teddy that looked like a spider web. It was black, it was sheer, it had all these streaks, and it was very revealing. It made me uncomfortable, plus I was getting some creepy vibes from her. I remember saying something like, "Wow, that's certainly fancy. All right-y then, I'm going to bed. See you at breakfast tomorrow." I rolled over, turned the light out, and fell asleep.

The next thing I knew, I kind of half woke up, and I could have sworn she was on top of me with her hair hanging in front of her face.

I remember thinking, with dream-like logic, "That's really wild, she's riding a bronco or something." Her head was swiveling back and forth and she was rocking up and down.

Then all of a sudden it occurred to me: I'm awake! This is not a dream!

In shock, I threw her off me.

The room had ceramic tiled floors. I heard this loud crack as she landed on her knee. She was holding her leg and bawling like a wounded animal. I was screaming out at the top of my lungs, "What the hell are you doing? Are you out of your mind?!" It was not a Club Med Moment.

When the wailing and gnashing of teeth had subsided, I said, "You are going home tomorrow or I'm getting another room. I'm not staying with you." She said, "Yes, I understand, I understand." She was weeping incessantly and I felt completely violated—I had never really believed a man could feel that way, but trust me, he can.

The next morning, at first daylight, I was at the desk applying for a different room. They said if I was going to do that I would have to become a full-time instructor. I liked tennis instructing, but I didn't want to do it full time, so Charlotte and I made a deal. We would continue to share a room, but we were not going to talk, we were not going to discuss anything, we were just going to go our separate ways until it was time to fly back to Los Angeles. There was not even a friendship between us anymore; we were just roommates. You can probably imagine how comfortable *that* arrangement was.

But then it got even weirder. She started showing up at the tennis courts with a different guy whenever I'd be instructing. She'd start making out with them furiously, with one eye looking at me. What was she thinking?

We returned to L.A. a month later. She flew back with me. I don't remember how we wound up going back together, but we did.

She had left her car at my house. So we came into the house from the cab and I said, "Well, that was interesting. Goodbye." Normally I'm a hugger, but I just shook her hand.

I don't know what she was expecting after the spider-bronco episode. But she finally understood that I was completely done with her. Over. The end. She said, "Fine, yes. A firm handshake to you too. Okay then, farewell." She always made it a point to speak with perfect diction.

She grabbed her bag and headed for the exit. Now, I have French doors with openings on either side of them. The openings are covered with screens. Rather than go through the center doors, she walked right into one of these screen-covered side openings.

Typically, a person would say something like, "Oops, wrong way," then back up, open the actual doors, and walk through them. But she kept right on going. Not only into the screen, but *through* the screen, ripping it completely out of its frame. Stepping over the crumpled wreckage, she walked robotically toward her car, holding her head up with whatever dignity she could muster.

And that was the last I ever saw of her.

What Inspired Me to Become an Inventor

At one of the photo conventions, I met a designer named Enzo. Enzo had become wealthy by inventing things. He and I had a talk that forever changed the way I saw the world and my place in it.

Just as a passing curiosity, I asked him what his secret to success as an inventor was. He said that most of his success didn't come from pulling new ideas out of a magic hat. Inventing wasn't at all the way it was portrayed in the cartoons—light bulbs over the head and fevered cries of *Eureka!* You don't wait for inspiration to strike you like heaven's ball-peen hammer. You don't even need to be particularly creative or technologically savvy.

The secret, Enzo said, is that if you look at *anything*, you will see that it can be improved. Any object or service, especially the ones you use often, has features that just aren't working for you. You simply have to learn to identify those things and propose solutions. Most of your ideas won't stick, but some of them will.

We happened to be standing next to his suitcase at the time; he had just arrived from the airport. He pointed to it and said, "Just for the heck of it, tell me at least five ways this thing can be improved." Now, at the time, luggage had not changed substantively since the steamer cases of the '30s.

I said, "It's a suitcase—it is what it is. How could anyone improve on it?"

"Give me five ways," he urged. "You can do it."

Okay, I thought, I like a challenge. "Well, it could use wheels," I said. "That would be great."

He said, "Exactly. Now ask yourself why it doesn't have wheels. Is there a reason preventing it?"

I couldn't come up with one. He spurred me on further. "Give me another improvement."

I said, "Well, if it had wheels, it would need a telescoping handle so you wouldn't have to bend down to wheel it around."

He cheered, "EXACTLY! Why *don't* suitcases have handles that telescope?"

Again, I couldn't come up with a reason. I thought for a bit longer and then said, "It should be expandable, with snaps or a zipper, sort of like an accordion." That was improvement number three.

Number four followed quickly: "How about a combination lock?"

Enzo was positively giddy with delight. All I needed was one more improvement. "Ah, how about a hard back, so when you slide it up a ramp, it doesn't scuff the fabric." I'd done it! I'd named five ways to improve the "un-improvable" standard, the suitcase.

Enzo said, "Bravo, my friend—now go and patent those ideas and make yourself a fortune."

I'd like to say that's exactly what I did, but in fact I did absolutely nothing. Zippo. When suitcases hit the retail market featuring my exact list of improvements, I kicked myself up and down until I was psychologically black and blue. I swore that if I came up with an idea like that again, I would never let it go by. And I've tried to live by that promise.

People come up to me fairly often now, saying that they had the ideas for the Puffer or the Origami or the Lightsphere or the Flip-Cage (some of the photo accessories I've invented and marketed) and were kicking themselves because they hadn't done anything about it.

My advice for becoming a successful inventor? Develop a low tolerance for self-inflicted blows from the foot.

So I Invented Montage

Now that I was back at the photography studio, with no Marketing Concepts Group to run and my studio manager having relocated to Northern California, I would spend my days alone in an empty room with piles of negatives, prints, and order envelopes. Little yellow Post-it notes sported cryptic phrases with differing levels of urgency indicated by the color of the ink. For example, "114-Smith/Klein 1620 Canvas" would be written in red Sharpie and stuck on a computer monitor. This was meant to be an expedited request for a 16 x 20 print on canvas (red Sharpies meant "Look!"), but nowhere on the note did it say whether the order had been sent out yet.

So I'd go looking for the Smith/Klein box, wherever it may be. Look for negative 114 out of 1,200. If it wasn't there, I'd call the lab to see if they had that order in-house. On a sticky note, there's no progress grid, no dates, nothing. I was lost so I decided I would devise a production system.

I spent a whole day making forms. That helped with future orders, but not with the ones in process. When a customer would call asking for the status of an order, I had no idea what to tell them. I had no idea where to look, but I did know that I was knee-deep in kimchee.

I spent endless lonely nights in that studio trying to keep up with things. Worst of all, I resented it. I had started the postcard company and then shut it down when all of my clients went tits-up in the real estate recession. Going back to work at Storybook, my established, mature company, felt like going back to high school.

So there I was in the studio, with a massive pile of orders and appointments, and a phone ringing constantly. It was a busy half-million-dollar-a-year wedding photography business and it was the 1980s. Email and the digital era had not yet kicked in. That meant a lot of phone calls and a lot of 8 x 10s. And I was dreadfully alone.

Wedding photographers are woefully underpaid for the amount of labor that goes into producing a wedding album.

Every print required that a negative be cut from a long strip, placed in an individual wax envelope, and numbered on the outside, with the print order checked off in a box. If a person wanted an 8 x 10 print in vertical (as opposed to horizontal) orientation, this would have to be marked on the envelope. The negative would then be put into an order bag. The process was tedious, time-consuming, and prone to error.

Now imagine what happens when two days later another person wants a photo made from that same negative. If the negative has been sent to the lab, you'd put a sticky note on your computer monitor saying that when Smith/Jones #112 comes back, make a 5 x 7. Managing negatives is like trying to lasso crickets.

The waste factor was tremendous, due to error. You could order twenty 8 x 10s of the wrong photo, and it wouldn't be the lab's fault. It wouldn't be the client's fault. It would be your fault. So you'd have to eat the cost. Worse yet, if you hired an employee to do this, and they did it wrong, you'd not only have to eat the cost of the prints, you'd have to pay the person for doing it wrong, and then you'd have to pay them again to do it right. And *you'd* get to be the one to explain to the client why their order was late.

I was clueless and I had no help.

After many weeks of being back in my production room, I began to fantasize about a simple life on red clay courts, running tennis drills.

I wondered, why couldn't we use computers to organize and print this stuff out automatically? It would be like with Quicken financial software, where you just type out your check and the program does everything else. Why not lab automation software?

And since I was designing wedding albums that needed to incorporate these print orders, I thought, why couldn't somebody design an interface that allowed you to arrange photos in an onscreen photo album, then let the software do all of the backend printouts? The program could record descriptive labels for each negative, along with how many prints in each size for each order. It could also automatically fill out the order forms for client invoicing as well as album ordering.

So often I've heard the world's greatest copout phrase: "If it was such a great idea, then somebody would've done it by now." Oh man, that phrase irritates me! If everybody believed that stupid saying, progress would never occur. Yet, like everybody, that nagging doubt always pops into my mind as I am deep in thought about how to merchandise my next great (and thoroughly obvious) invention.

I Become a Software Guy

As I was noodling on the software idea, I happened to attend a trade-show where Art Leather Manufacturing (remember them? The largest manufacturer of albums in the world?) was showing their new integrated album design and productivity solution. I was intrigued. Their software programs, in theory, allowed you to enter print numbers in a graphic template so you could quickly create wedding albums and automatically track all of your photo data. I was stoked and wanted to buy it.

I called the manufacturer and spoke to the president of the company, Mark Roberts, whom I knew from my lecture gig. I asked him if I could buy the product they were showing. He said that the software had never gotten finished. He had sunk a lot of money into it, and not only did it never get done, he couldn't get the programmers to call him back. Basically they took the money and ran.

Sounded like an opportunity to me. If I could create this software, I had the largest album company eager to distribute it.

Only thing was, I didn't know how to program software. I called my super-genius buddy from UCSB, Jeff Gold, but he didn't program for Macs. Instead, he referred me to a very talented programmer named John Keating. John was working for one of the large electronic game companies. We met for dinner at the Red Rose Café in Venice, and, at a gas-lit outdoor picnic table, I explained to him my idea for the software.

Sketching on the proverbial dinner napkin, I drew two open pages of a virtual wedding album. I explained that each page should have matted spaces for photos that were consistent with what the album makers were producing (for example, one 8 x 10 or two 5 x 7 prints per page, etc.). The software should allow you to pick the setup for each page, and, once the setup was selected, allow you to select the prints to insert.

When all the info was entered, the computer should:

1. Collate all the order information and print the labels
2. Print the lab order (number of negatives, total number of prints in sizes, cost for the order)
3. Automatically print the order form for the album company
4. Create a directory of all of the prints so the photographer could check and verify that the prints were returned to him without lab error

If software like this existed, it would be impossible to make mistakes. It would save a professional photographer, by my calculations, at least twenty hours per wedding.

All I needed to do was convince Art Leather that John and I were the team that was going to finish the project, and not desert them as had the other team.

Pitching Montage

Art Leather bought us plane tickets to New York. John and I shared a seedy room at the Pan American Hotel in Brooklyn. It smelled like an old bus and there wasn't enough space to walk past each other on the same side of the bed.

But we felt like traveling executives.

In the morning, after a bracing McBreakfast and sour orange juice, we were picked up and driven to the meeting in a Lincoln Town Car. With tinted glass. The only thing missing was the Sicilian mandolin music.

When we pulled up to the factory there was this huge sign: Art Leather Manufacturing, the World's Largest Manufacturer of Wedding Albums and Folios. This building was about the size of a city block.

We took the elevator to the executive offices. They were on a very busy floor with lots of cubicles, lots of worried faces running around, and lots of ringing phones. We said we were there to meet with the president. We felt really special. We were escorted into the boardroom where the president and a bevy of other people in suits were waiting for us. They looked like . . . honestly, they looked like a jury.

Our presentation was jerry-rigged because we hadn't been able to get the software to work correctly in time. Technically speaking, there *was* no software. I'd cobbled together a demo that *looked* like working software, provided you clicked on certain buttons in sequence. It was like a PowerPoint presentation. It showed what we were going to accomplish but did not provide the benefits of actual functionality. In short, the whole thing was ready to blow up in our faces. But we had our fingers crossed.

Over the course of the meeting I did disclose to them that this was a prototype version, and that not all the pieces were working yet. (I did not disclose that the percentage of pieces that *were* working properly was currently zero.)

We must have done something right because they decided to go with us. We all shook hands and the room was abuzz with the prospect that we would have the first software product for album manufacturers. We said we would be able to get them the working version within one month.

John and I were stoked. We went back to our miserable little hotel room and told ourselves we might have a pretty darn big deal here.

Energized, we flew back to Los Angeles and set to work. John did the programming and I did the graphics and artwork.

Montage Wraps

We finished the wedding album software only forty-five days late (which is actually on time in the software business) and took it to a national photographers' convention in Denver to demo. As part of this trip, we would also be meeting with Art Leather to finalize our deal.

The software surprised us by actually working. Really nicely, in fact. It was powerful and was printing out the reports, just like we promised. We had something here. Knowing that Art Leather had some thirty thousand active clients, we projected that, at a sales price of $495, if we were able to turn 10 percent of their clients into customers, it might be worth about $1.5 million.

We had agreed in principal that we would work with Art Leather, but nobody knew how the deal was going to be structured. The extent of my current thinking was, "They will open a checkbook and give us lots of money." Art Leather, of course, wanted something a little more specific. So we had this "deal-definition meeting" scheduled with the executives of the company. The idea was to decide how to exchange value with each other for this now-very-valuable commodity, which we named Montage.

The night before the meeting, John and I sat down at a restaurant and tried to figure out exactly what we wanted. Did we want to sell the software outright to Art Leather? Or did we want to sell it ourselves and only use Art Leather for marketing? We really didn't know. Art Leather had promised that we could retain all of the revenue for the software in exchange for our dedicating it only to their albums.

We figured we had a product with a couple million dollars of sales potential. The question was: outright sale or strategic marketing alliance?

The next morning, we met with Art Leather in a makeshift boardroom in the presidential suite of a very nice hotel. One thing Art Leather knew how to do was spend money. Everything they did was for appearances. They would fly in a piano player from England for their tradeshows. They'd always have a grand piano, too. Now that I'm in the tradeshow business, I know how costly that was, based on union rates and union rules, plus the expense of all of the rentals. Art Leather just loved to incinerate the old greenbacks. Everything was more expensive than it needed to be. I've never been able to follow that reasoning. "Hey, look at the way our company wastes money—don't you want to do business with us?!"

We sat down in the overly expensive boardroom, with our overly expensive lox and mineral water, and they said, "Okay gentlemen, we all know the software is valuable. What would you like to see?"

John spoke first. "Well, we figure that with the thirty thousand accounts you have, if we can sell to ten percent of those accounts at five hundred dollars each, that's three thousand copies of the software at five hundred dollars, which is one and a half million. Using the multiples typical to company valuations, if we took eight times the revenue, the enterprise value is twelve million. The first way we could do it is a simple buyou—" Before he could get the word "buyout" out of his mouth, he felt the hand of the company president, Mark, grasping his elbow and yanking him toward the door.

"Can you step outside for just a second?" was all Mark said.

John and I were whisked out the door so fast our heads were spinning. We didn't know what was going on. Before we'd even caught our breath, their Information Systems Director, Keith, emerged from the room and said, "Guys, can you step inside?"

We went back in and the boardroom was completely empty. In fifteen seconds. No drinks, no snacks, just one guy and an empty wood table. Talk about "leaving the table"! The only person remaining with us was Keith.

"Guys, it seems you've got your heads jammed up your . . . completely in the clouds. Let's be reasonable."

Evidently Art Leather had money to spend on grand pianos but not on software.

"We didn't say we wanted twelve million dollars," I explained. "We simply wanted to present both scenarios. First a straight buyout and then—"

"I know that," he interrupted. "But you guys must be nuts to think there would be that much money in it. We want to be in the album business, not the software business. The only deal we'll take is a co-marketing agreement where we do all of the merchandising and marketing and you boys sell us the software at unit prices and keep all the revenue."

We thought about the tinted glass on the company Town Car and decided we were okay with a co-marketing deal.

The idea was that this $30-million-a-year company would market our automated album software—tied to its products—to all of its photographers. We would get all of the software revenue. They would generate more album sales, because the software only worked with their products.

With that understanding, we went to our first tradeshow to introduce Montage. We set up a very elaborate booth with these little Mac Color Classic computers, right near the grand piano, which was being played by the Earl of Worcestershire Sauce or whatever the hell his name was.

All day long, John and I, along with about twenty Art Leather representatives, pitched the hell out of this amazing new software product. Mark, the president, even held a contest: The rep who sold the most copies of Montage that first day would get a $100 bonus. We were literally dragging people into the booth to demo our software.

At the end of the first day, with twenty reps working the floor and thousands of photographers walking around, we had sold a grand total of three units. Not three hundred. Three. For $1,500. It wasn't catastrophic, considering that it was just us two splitting the money, but it certainly wasn't anything close to our projections.

The problem was—and this is always a problem with new software—nobody understood it, even though we were clearly demonstrating its wondrous capabilities. It was so frustrating! These people needed our product badly, and $495 was a very reasonable price. It would save them twenty hours per wedding! We posted a list of all the tasks you would no longer need to do manually if you used Montage.

And everyone looked at us like we were selling trout-breeding equipment.

My Lecture Career Resuscitated

Art Leather was not as disappointed as John and I were, and they continued to mount an ambitious marketing effort for the software.

I was part of that effort. The plan was for me to embark on a cross-country speaking tour, sponsored by Art Leather, to pitch Montage to as many photographers as possible. I reasoned—correctly, I think—that nobody would come to a seminar if it was marketed only as a presentation on the computerization of wedding photography. If the software product wasn't flying off the shelves, I didn't think a two-hour pitchfest about the product would fill the seats either.

I believed that photographers would attend a seminar about the overall business of photography, given by a well-known photographer. They would then be receptive to whatever tools this well-known photographer was using to make his business grow.

The only problem was the "well known" part. I'd dropped out of the seminar circuit five years before, and my name had sunk back into relative obscurity. It became the mission of Art Leather's marketing department to make me a renowned photographer again so that I would have the credibility to recommend the software I was using to made my studio as successful as it was.

Mine was, in fact, a very successful studio, and we were still doing the Storybook concept for weddings. The cool thing was, I could now show how it was being automated through the use of this software.

The seminar then became about the computerized Storybook concept. I visited thirty-two cities and saw over ten thousand photographers. I showed them not only the Storybook concept of shooting, design, and layout, but also how the software convinced couples how great their designs were going to look.

It went exceedingly well. Except for one thing: Nobody bought the software.

I then made an astonishing discovery: In order to use computer software, one must have a computer. This was back in the early '90s, and it turned out that most photographers didn't. Of those who were computerized, very few of them had Macs because the Mac cost a lot more than an IBM clone.

Our software was for a Mac, because, well, I used a Mac.

We scrambled to create a Windows version. Once that was ready, sales picked up. This took over a year, but we eventually wound up selling five thousand copies of Montage software, which made it a very lucrative venture for us.

At the end of the run, Art Leather expressed an interest in buying the copyright and the future rights to sell the software for $550,000. That was fine by us, because John and I had made a lot of money already, and to end our relationship with a $275,000 paycheck each was perfect. We signed a deal transferring the copyright to Art Leather.

Art Leather didn't give us the $550,000 up front, of course. They spread it out in payments over three years. I was careful not to include that money in my lifestyle budget because I knew that if I did, at the end of three years I would have a giant financial hole to fill. Plus, with all of the preaching my dad had done about saving, I made the decision to save all of it.

I opened a separate savings account, and every check that came in for the Montage buyout, I deposited it there. The idea was that I was going to invest in real estate and prepare for my retirement. It was fun to watch my savings account growing and growing with compound interest because I wasn't spending a penny. Everything was going according to plan.

The world was not only embracing the concept of the personal computer, they were starting to connect computers together. The World Wide Web was weaving people into a faceless international community.

The Virtual Masquerade Party

In between the hours when I was helping produce our multimillion-dollar software project, I had begun communicating online with complete strangers all around the country.

Once computers got connected, they became a safe, anonymous cloak for representing yourself to the opposite sex in any way you damn well pleased. If you were looking for strictly fantasy conversation, you could instantly don a pseudo-identity and start chatting.

Dating had certainly changed since the last time I'd been "on the market."

Before America Online, there was an evolutionary product called Apple Talk Remote Access, Personal Edition. As soon as you signed in, there were two graphic interface buttons—one said The Lobby, and the other one said You've got mail. I know this sounds really primitive, but if you hit Lobby, you hooked into this hub that was like a party line on a telephone, where everybody could talk at the same time.

Inside each numbered lobby was a maximum of maybe thirteen people. People who had different handles (screen names, as they are now called) would aimlessly cluster inside the room. There was a list of names, and anyone could just randomly type and all thirteen people would see what was written. There was no way of defining the discussion, no way of saying, for instance, "We are all here to talk about the sexual habits of mudpuppies." It was just thirteen anonymous people from anywhere on the globe inside a numbered lobby, "chatting" about whatever they fancied. Yay.

For the privilege of communicating in this manner, I shelled out about $800 a month in connection charges.

Eventually, this online service would become AOL.

AOL eventually figured out that a more productive way to organize lobbies was by allowing them to select the topic for their rooms. So now you could choose to join a room dedicated to politics, religion, dwarf-bowling, or singles. This narrowed the focus considerably.

Needless to say, the singles rooms were a trip because you had no idea if someone was lying about who they were. A person would type, "Hey CheerleaderHotXXX, what are your measurements?" And "she" would answer something ridiculous just to get things moving. There were no photos, no way to validate anything that was represented there. Your mind would fill in the blanks in a wildly optimistic sort of way that rarely corresponded with reality.

Everyone had hilarious stories about meet-ups.

My first live hook-up was with a woman I will call Shauna. I was single and doing a lot of traveling at the time, so if I would be going to San Antonio, for example, I might go into a chat room marked SAN ANTONIO and say, "Hi, what's there to do in town?" I'd strike up a conversation and often it would be, "Well, when you get here I'll give you a list of really cool places to go and maybe we could meet for a drink." This was the beginning of online dating.

Shauna was this really sweet girl in Texas I met online and became very friendly with. We finally exchanged numbers and started talking on the phone. She was terrific. I liked her voice. She was going through a breakup and had kids, but she seemed like a person I wanted to know better.

Eventually the idea of exchanging photos came up, so I sent one of mine and she sent one of hers. (You had to send photos by snail mail in those days, because there were no scanners and no digital photography.) About four days later I got a photo from her, and she was a really cute girl who looked just like her voice. That was always the mystery, of course—you'd be talking on the phone with someone and then you'd see the photograph and go, "Wow. *That's* the person I have been sharing my deepest secrets with?" But Shauna looked like I'd thought (and hoped) she would.

She and I talked on the phone for hours, losing track of time.

She owned her own little store, which I found charming. After our snail-mailed photo exchange, we deemed each other interesting enough to meet in person.

We cooked up a crazy plan involving airplanes. The idea of jumping on a plane to meet her was thrilling, daring, intoxicating. I felt like a character in a Woody Allen movie.

We planned on meeting in Los Angeles, so she bought her tickets. Yes, I did say tickets. With an *s*. Just before hopping on the plane, she phoned me. "Gary, there's something I need to come clean about—those photographs I sent you were not of me."

"What do you mean? Who are they pictures of?"

"My cousin," she said. "She looks a lot *like* me, though."

"Okay, what's going on?" I asked. "Are you still coming?"

"Well, that's the thing," she replied. "I'm not sure if I should cancel my seats or not."

Seats? What the hell was going on here? "Who is the other person you're planning to bring?" I queried, growing testier by the moment.

"Well, actually, that's the funny part. I needed to buy an extra seat because I've . . . put on a few pounds."

I blinked. "What are you talking about?"

"That photo of my cousin, that's what I *usually* look like. I've just been going through a rough patch lately, so I've gained a little weight."

"Well, okay. What are we talking here?"

"I'm five-three, three hundred pounds."

I hadn't prepared myself for that. Suddenly my mind started rewinding the tapes of our talks together. I remembered there were a few times when she'd actually snored on the phone. I found that a little odd. I also remember her mentioning once that her daughter was jumping on her like a trampoline. I didn't realize she'd meant it literally. All of a sudden it all made sense.

I said, "Okay, why would you lie to me? Why would you send me a photo that isn't you?"

"Because I thought if you really got to know me as a person, you would like me and then you wouldn't have a problem with my weight."

I said, "Well, the problem I have is that you were lying to me." (Of course, I had the other problem too, but why bring that up?)

"I guess you don't want me to come now, do you?"

"No, I'm sorry. I don't." I hung up, and that's the last I ever heard from her.

I decided maybe it was time for a new screen name.

Alex Really Is a Girl

I continued chatting with women online, but thanks to my two-seated friend, I had become pretty skeptical about anyone I met.

Online dating is usually a wipeout, but the pitfalls weren't widely known back then. When someone sent you a photo through the mail, you only got one shot, and it was usually ten years and twenty pounds ago, and taken from the most flattering angle. And yet, you would build an entire 3D visual library around this one mirage.

When you met in person, the shock was usually visceral. So you learned to savor the fantasy for as long as you could. Still, I did get caught up chatting with this one individual who went by the name of Alex. In those early days, there weren't a lot of normal people hanging around online; they were typically software engineers, mostly guys, many of whom had a nasty habit of pretending to be women in order to make juicy conversation. A lot of latent homosexuality went back and forth, embedded in code packets.

This Alex person was an Information Systems Director at a small company and ran the AS400 mainframe or something like that. All indications were that she had about as much estrogen running through her as a diesel engine.

So I ran a test on her, a set of questions I'd devised for separating the real women from the pseudo. For example, I would ask, "What is a speculum?" I still don't know, but I knew if *she* had the answer, she was definitely female. I would ask her dress size or shoe size, and if she answered, "Medium," that was an instant red flag. Things like pantyhose come in sizes A, B, and C, but guys don't know that, so I'd ask questions to uncover such ignorance.

Alex passed the test. I was now pretty sure that she was female, even though she went by a man's name and was a computer nerd. She thought my instant lie detector test was hilarious. So I scored a few points with her that way.

I'm a fool for girls who think I'm funny. We started talking in earnest. Why is your name Alex? Short for Alexis. Where do you live? Cincinnati, though constantly traveling. Tell me more about yourself. She had a Russian boyfriend named Boris and they were having problems. She was great to talk to, and so talk we did. And talk and talk and talk.

Well, *type and type and type* on the keyboard anyway.

I wouldn't talk to her on the phone because, after Shauna, I didn't want to give my number out. I thought everybody on the 'net was a wacko. But I finally caved in to her pressure and said, "Okay, we can talk on the phone, but why don't you send me your photo first?" So she snail-mailed me a series of photos.

When I got them I was totally bummed. They were really nice photos. Unfortunately, they were really nice photos of supermodel Niki Taylor. How stupid did Alex think I was? Did she think just because I could use a computer that I lived under a rock? Niki Taylor was one of the most famous faces in the world. Alex (if that was even her real name) had even tried to give the photos a realistic touch by making them a little fuzzy. Photos of photos, I guessed. (This was pre-Photoshop.)

"Did you get my photographs?" she asked the next time we were chatting online. I said that I had.

"Well . . . what did you think?"

I replied, "I think you are a liar and I am just really tired of people trying to be what they're not. I don't care what you look like. I was just trying to see if you are honest or not. To send photos of Niki Taylor, that's ridiculous."

She said, "I get that all the time."

"Yeah, I'm sure you do."

"No, really. People always ask if I'm Niki Taylor."

This line of conversation wasn't moving her any higher up the credibility scale. I was about to log off when she said, "Gary, look at that couch behind me in the picture."

I looked. It was a tweed, multicolored monstrosity, just like the one we'd had at the Compton wig store. There were cigarette holes in it, and some tragic knitted thing on one of the armrests.

"Why would Niki Taylor be in a photo with a couch like that?" she asked.

I had to think about that one. "Wow, you're right. That would be weird. How the hell did you get that couch in the photo of Niki Taylor?"

She sighed (not easy to do in text chat). "Will you just freakin' call me?"

A Real Conversation

I called her and she really was a young woman. She wasn't gruff or transvestite-y sounding at all. The more we talked, the more we laughed, and the more we laughed, the more comfortable I felt with her. I finally said, "I guess I'll never know if you were telling the truth or not with those photos."

She said, "Why not?" Meaning: What's to stop us from meeting in person?

I told her my little story about Miss Two-Seater and said that meeting in person was out of the question. She kept nagging me and daring me and making playful little slights on my masculinity. I hate playful little slights on my masculinity.

As it happened, I had to fly to Cincinnati for business soon, so I gave her my flight information and said, "If you want to show up, show up."

She said, "Okay, I'll be the blonde in the tan business suit holding a copy of *Allure* magazine and looking suspiciously like Niki Taylor."

I landed in Cincinnati.

How do you meet a person in an airport with just a photo to go on? I should have planned this better, I thought. I hadn't sent her my picture, so she had no idea who to look for.

But I figured I could look for somebody with an *Allure* magazine, and if I didn't like what I saw, I could walk out to Ground Transportation and jump in a cab.

I got off the plane and slunk over to the far side of the gate area. (This was back when people could actually greet one another at the gates.) Without giving away that I'd just come off the plane, I wanted to see if anyone was looking for me.

And there she was. She was the girl in the photo. She hadn't been lying. She was sitting there with an *Allure* magazine. She got up to look around, then sat down again. I let her wait a few minutes as I absorbed the fact that this person actually existed. This hilariously funny, warm person that I had so much in common with, she existed and looked exactly as she'd described herself.

Then came a wave of doubt: She thinks I'm a hoot online, but as soon as she meets me, she's going to be disappointed. I'm not going to be what she expected.

Oh hell, Gary, I told myself. Go for it! I took a deep breath and started toward her.

As I approached, she looked up. I said, "Alex? Hi, I'm Gary." She jumped up and gave me a really big hug. It was the oddest thing. It was like meeting an old friend, yet someone brand new. A stranger that you know really well. There we were, laughing and talking. Not *really* nervous, but sort of nervous. The more we talked, the more we got used to the whole idea. We seemed mismatched because I travel really, really casual. I had on a baseball hat, t-shirt, and jeans, and she was dressed to the nines in a business suit and heels. We made a really odd couple.

Of course, the next step for us was to move in together.

Cohabitation

A few months later, Alex sold everything in her apartment, quit her job, and moved to Los Angeles.

I've always admired people who can make instant life-changing decisions. But being on the receiving end of a spontaneous whim is terrifying. At the time, I was tremendously commitment-phobic, newly recovering from a bout of Body Dysmorphic Disorder, and so nonconfrontational that I couldn't even summon the nerve to say, "Maybe we should discuss this over coffee."

When she trumpeted the words, "I'm moving in with you," I reflexively spat out this totally meaning-free, single-word response: "Awesome."

What does "awesome" mean in a situation like this? It doesn't say that I agree, it doesn't say I want this; it just says that this is something that inspires awe. Such a detached reply would alert any girl with an ounce of self-preservation that a red flag was flying high.

What would happen if we didn't click? Where would she live? With what furniture?

The answer to that, of course, was, "We'll find out soon enough."

When Alex moved in, the range of our activities outside of the house was wonderful. We went on bike rides. We explored L.A. We went shopping, or drove up through Malibu or down to Laguna Beach in the convertible.

It was when we got home that things got testy.

Everything from not having an extra dresser for her clothes (she'd sold all her furniture, even the nasty, matted couch in the Polaroid) to the fact that I still had three female roommates (this was back in the days when I'd rented out the extra bedrooms of my five-bedroom house) became an issue. All things in our domestic life, big or small, were issues.

For example, she brought her massively shedding Maine Coon cat with her. Cat fur was everywhere. And so was cat pee—everywhere, that is, except the litter box. And I had that foam rubber padding under my wool rugs, which I discovered to be a permanent record of all cat odors for all time.

She also brought along a truly gargantuan Irish setter, who was a howling, needy, emotional mess.

Maine Coon cat dander was everywhere. My eye swelled shut one morning due to a hair that had gotten in there while I was asleep and caused an allergic reaction. I woke up, horrified and itchy, to an extreme close-up view of this miniature lion purring at me with the most contented look. Next to me was Alex, wearing her pink blindfold with the sequin-studded word BABY embroidered across her eyes.

How had I ended up here?

One day, when the friction was building but was still at the point where we were both ignoring it amicably, we were riding our bikes in Venice Beach looking for the next amusing thing to do.

Street performers along Venice Beach are legendary for their randomness. Chainsaw jugglers perform alongside artists who can write your name on a grain of rice, in city-issued sidewalk grids reminiscent of my days at the swap meets. Fortunetellers wearing turbans and burning incense vie for the attention of passersby.

Except for one completely aloof, older white guy in a sailor's cap. He sat with dark sunglasses and arms crossed at a card table with a chalkboard in front of it that read PSYCHIC BOB TELLS PAST, PRESENT, AND FUTURE. He stood in stark contrast to all of the wannabe swamis, and this to me was worth exploring.

I had never been to a tarot card reader before, and so it was all new to me and Alex. He asked for twenty bucks and proceeded to tell me the most ridiculous forecast I had ever heard in my life. He said that within six months I would be married to somebody I had not yet met.

Dude, have you no manners? I thought, mortified. This is my girl-friend here! She sold everything she had to come to L.A. to live with me! And we met on the internet! Are you crazy? We will be together forever!

I laughed off the idiotic reading, and Alex rolled her eyes behind her imitation Chanel sunglasses.

Six months later, of course, I was married to somebody I had not yet met.

Things between me and Alex disintegrated immediately after the silly (I thought) card reading. We got in the stupidest fights about absolutely nothing. Once we were on our way to Universal Studios and she decided to wear super-high, strappy heels. Not only did she tower annoyingly over me when she wore heels, but going to an amusement park in heels designed for evening-wear was ridiculous. Mistakenly, I shared my opinion with her.

Alex was fuming all day. Late that night, I woke up and heard her talking in her sleep.

"Oh really? You think I'm beautiful? Well, not only am I beautiful, but I can be a lot of fun (chuckle). Oh really, you want to find out? Maybe you should take me home . . ."

I had a sneaking suspicion that I was not the person being ad-dressed in her dream. I made a mental note to chat with her in the morning about the fissures in our relationship, and dozed off.

At 7:00 A.M., she was gone. Clothes still here, Maine Coon cat and crazy Irish setter still howling in the dog run.

Oh God, she'd left. But with what car? Mine was still in the garage.

The next three days were tense. She never called. The first twenty-four hours went by and she was officially missing, but here's the most terrifying part: We had met on the internet. This would be bound to raise a lot of suspicion from the police if I reported her missing. But if I didn't, would I be a suspect if she wound up *really* missing . . . or worse?

So I called Alex's stepmother to explain the situation, and from that point forward made it a point to be with people (translation: with an established alibi) at all hours of the day, so that I could always cite my whereabouts. No renting of little fishing boats, no purchasing of duct tape or quickset concrete until I knew for sure where Alex was.

I made random long-distance phone calls to prove that I was at home.

With each passing hour, the weight of the unknown settled on me more and more heavily. I paced the floor.

She had simply disappeared. No note, and all of her things still at my house.

Panic made a home in my chest.

There was so much unexplained about her disappearing in the middle of the night. Where did she go with no car? Did she *walk* somewhere in the middle of the night? We lived in a suburban bedroom community in Los Angeles. It was a safe neighborhood, but I wouldn't walk down Manchester Avenue at 3:00 A.M.—especially not without a dog. Manchester Avenue is the main thoroughfare to Inglewood, a scary, gang-ridden part of town. And a few miles further down the gray brick road was my old nemesis, Compton. Anybody wanting to go from South-Central L.A. to the beach would typically pass within two blocks of my house.

So while I didn't live in a bad neighborhood, let's just say that I lived right on the *way* to one. So why hadn't she taken her dog?

By the third day, to keep myself calm, I went back to that old comfortable community of invisible strangers (chat rooms) to seek answers. What would motivate somebody, I queried, to disappear in the middle of the night without saying goodbye or leaving a note? The responses ranged from "What a bitch" to "Are you sure you didn't do something to her and don't remember?"

Alex called me on the fourth day, asking if she could come by and pick up her things. I was speechless. There was so much to say, and there was absolutely nothing to say. I chose the former, and after a long flurry of unprintable words told her that I would put all of her belongings in the garage next to my car. I placed her cat in an airport-approved cat carrier and left him in the garage. I put her dog in the dog run. When I came home that day, all of her belongings and creatures were gone.

Okay, done.

About three weeks later, an Israeli chiropractor from Venice, California, called my cell phone in a panic. He said that he had found my number on Alex's phone bill and wanted to know if I had any idea where she might be. I told him that the same thing had happened to me less than a month earlier. He was shocked because Alex had concocted some tale about my being a "family friend" she had come to stay with while she got her bearings in California.

Apparently what had happened was Alex had gone rollerblading on Venice Beach. This Israeli chiropractor approached her while she was sitting on the seawall and declared her "the most beautiful girl in the entire world," at which point Alex decided to move in with him. Sound familiar?

Part of me wanted to tell this chiropractor, "She's your problem now." But I felt bad because he'd been had by this very confused young lady. He said we should get together, and I thought that would be interesting, but it never happened.

Mom Dies

When I'm on tour I live in this oddly insulated little bubble, even though I'm bouncing from city to city and jumping on and off planes. All other aspects of my life get put on hold and fade into the background.

I was in Orlando, in the middle of a nineteen-city tour, when I got a phone call from my dad that mom was in the ICU at the local hospital.

Now, my mom spent a lot of time in the hospital, mostly to register weird constellations of symptoms that would typically result in batteries of costly tests that then led to diagnoses of "clean slate, nothing wrong." Doctors opined that she had a "low pain threshold." *Hypochondria* was probably a more accurate term for it. She would normally be in the hospital about once every month and a half.

But this time it was different. My dad called and asked me to come home. Unlike my mom, there was never the hint of "crying wolf" about my father. Mom was in the ICU, he said, and unresponsive to treatment.

My tour promoter immediately got me a plane ticket back to L.A. As soon as I got to the hospital, I was told that Mom had massive internal bleeding and that her body was grotesquely bloated.

She was in a coma.

We'd had a testy relationship for years. For most of my life, I guess. I'm a very sensitive person, and my mom had a habit of saying awful things that I couldn't easily forget. And, having inherited the gentle personality characteristics from my father's side, I wasn't the type to fight fire with fire. I simply made myself scarce. Often weeks turned into months and months turned into years, with only the obligatory visits on holidays.

We never had that gut-wrenching, cathartic blowout that unseated deeply buried issues, followed by apologies, hugs, declarations of love, and Hallmark-card walks on the beach at sunset. Neither of us got the chance to say sorry.

And now it was too late. The doctors said that nothing could be done, that she was suffering from total organ failure. They ushered us into a conference room to meet with the doctors and sign a non-resuscitate order. This basically meant that if her heart stopped, we authorized them to not attempt to revive her. It's a weird paper to sign; it feels like signing a death warrant.

But she was in a coma and her kidneys and liver were gone. If her life were artificially prolonged, she would have to spend the rest of her days strapped to a dialysis machine. Even if she were ever able to regain consciousness, the quality of her life would be zilch. So we signed the form, and Dad and I drove around doing nothing but waiting for the call that she had passed.

At one point I turned off my cell phone, because every time it rang it shattered my nerves and I couldn't get any sleep. When I turned it back on after just a few hours, there were twelve voicemail messages. That's when I knew.

I played the messages and got the news that my mother had died. A friend of mine had lost both of her parents at a fairly young age, and for some reason, only a few months earlier, we had spoken about what it was like to face the loss of your parents.

"It's like you walk the earth alone," she'd said.

I really got that now. It was one thing to write a Declaration of Independence, recognizing that my parents might not be the best guardians for me, but facing the fact that they really would not be here *at all* was a different matter. After all those years of *feeling* like I walked the earth alone (with the exception of my dad), now I really *did* walk the earth alone. Mom was no more.

Mother's Day and Easter were the hardest for my dad and me. I felt an aching loneliness, a deep chasm in my soul that needed to be filled sooner rather than later. With anyone.

I wanted someone to hold me and keep me from shuddering at night, someone who would sit next to me on the couch as I watched *The Tonight Show*. Somebody I could go to the movies with. Someone with whom I could forget for a while.

I yearned desperately for a safe place to park my heart.

Again, when one focuses on the goal rather than the process, one can be easily led astray. I wanted to instantly find a place to give my heart a soft landing, but I didn't allow myself enough time to heal. I knew better, but in my pain, I eagerly cast that knowledge aside.

Well, whenever we neglect the hard-earned lessons of life, life has a tendency to deliver a monkey wrench between our eyes. Just to get our attention. I was about to find myself in big trouble again.

The Stranger at the Altar

It's hard for me to remember the exact sequence of events that plopped me down on a little creekside gazebo in Pigeon Forge, Tennessee, on a snowy Christmas day. All I know is that my wedding day had arrived, and I was about to say "I do" to a recent acquaintance, almost exactly six months after Psychic Bob's prediction that I would marry someone I had not yet met within half a year.

When I was frantic with worry over Alex, I became close to another girl online—we'll call her Mary—who was planning to assist me on an upcoming wedding. I noticed that she frequented a chat room called MILLIONAIRE'S LOUNGE, but since I wasn't one, I figured I wasn't her type, romantically speaking, and proceeded to have long, platonic, non-threatening (I thought) conversations with her.

Mary was from Tennessee, and she was superb at playing the part of intimate stranger on Instant Messenger. Eventually we started talking on the phone, too. Lengthy long-distance calls were not only an emotional balm, but also a handy alibi in a potential investigation about the disappearance of internet Alex.

Of course, it never did occur to me that this could be perceived as serial behavior.

Eventually Mary came out to Los Angeles to stay with her friend Ben, and we all met for dinner. I remember thinking, "She sure is a great girl." She was kind of tomboyish, wearing a baseball cap all the time and hardly any makeup. She was nowhere near as good-looking as Alex, which made her "safe" as far as possible relationships went.

Insanity, we are often told, is defined as repeating the same behavior over and over, hoping for different results. Having welcomed a complete stranger into my home once, with somewhat disastrous results, I decided to go ahead and marry this tomboyish stranger only months after we'd met, just like ol' Psychic Bob had predicted. Of course I didn't remember his prediction at the time, but had I yielded subconsciously to his power of suggestion? I sometimes wonder.

It was a lonely ceremony for me. Her parents came, but nobody from my side did, not even my dad, who later told me he'd predicted this marriage would not work.

As it was Christmas day, it had been nearly impossible to find someone to officiate. The only guy available arrived at the gazebo wearing a University of Tennessee Volunteers ball cap and a matching orange windbreaker. It was just the two of us, her parents, and the football fan.

A flock of geese followed us to the gazebo, but as soon as we took our positions, they flew away. You can learn a lot from nature.

Mary's parents acted as the witnesses, snapped some photos, and recorded a handheld video of the ceremony. All of which were mercifully misplaced forever.

That evening the four of us had dinner in a colonial-style restaurant. Her dad ordered liver and onions, and I had the rib eye. I don't remember what the ladies ordered. Liver and onions for a wedding day dinner, though, that was a real Lifetime Television moment.

During dinner, I remember staring out the window, past the flickering candle on the windowsill, toward the partially thawed snow on the grass, feeling for a moment like I was actually sitting outside. On our wedding night, we checked into the honeymoon suite of a Dollywood motor hotel and did the best we could with the loud, grinding, linoleum-lined Jacuzzi and the odd-smelling bed with its flowery comforter. I would snap in and out of Zen consciousness throughout the evening. Detachment seemed the only logical strategy.

chapter eight

Two Wedding Photographers in a Federal Jury Trial

As I mentioned earlier, I had hired this nineteen-year-old girl, Terri, to work at my photography studio, and I was impressed by how hardworking she was and how well she understood the trade. I taught her everything I knew. Before long I had practically cloned myself. She mastered the business side and became an excellent shooter, and eventually I made her my general manager.

At a young age, Terri was earning serious bucks. I was happy, she was happy. But all good stories come to an end. After five years she got married and decided to relocate to the San Francisco Bay area. She loved the "storybook wedding photography" concept and wanted very badly to start her own business. I felt that, armed with the training and experience I'd given her, she would become a big success and I would take great pride in her.

So we made an agreement that she could use the name "Storybook Weddings" as long as she didn't confuse her studio with mine and her marketing reach did not extend outside the San Francisco Bay area. We wrote a contract and signed it.

Some months later, when I saw Storybook.com on the web, my jaw hit the table.

I learned that this domain name, as well as StorybookStudio.com, was registered to Terri. I was flabbergasted because that meant

I would now be excluded from using my own company name on the internet. I called her and said, "Terri, you can't do this. We have an agreement that says that you can only use that name in the San Francisco area. The internet is the whole world."

We calmly discussed the problem, like friends, for a few minutes, and then she said, "Well, what are you going to do about it?" This was shocking to me because I had allowed her to use the name as a gift. For no money. All I asked was that she restrict her use to San Francisco. The friendly part of the conversation was over.

I called a law firm. They said, "Yes, you do have previous ownership of the trademark because you originated it and you used it in what's called *interstate commerce*." Previous ownership via interstate commerce means that if I ship a print, for example, across state lines, it automatically becomes a trademark and demonstrates common law ownership. That meant that I didn't need to register the trademark, because I had already asserted my rights prior to Terri's.

I had copies of the agreements and the invoices I had sent across state lines, so I went to this law firm with my little box of papers. They said, "All we need to do is write a letter and assert your rights." We wrote a letter to Terri saying, "You have an agreement stating that this name is to be used in San Francisco only. Mr. Fong owns the common law rights to the Storybook trademark, and you are in infringement of it." In essence, the letter told Terri that she had been put on notice, and if she continued to use my trademark, she might end up owing me a bundle.

This letter generated a speedy reply from Terri's newly hired attorney to my own. He said something like, "You are mistaken as to the business relationship that occurred between Mrs. Houghton and Mr. Fong. In fact, your client used to work for her. *She* was the one who employed *him*."

I laughed at first. I mean, this had to be a joke! No, my attorney assured me, this did not appear to be an attempt at comedy writing. I went from laughing to seething in 0.3 seconds. I said, "We're going to take this to court."

"Okay, that'll be a ten-thousand dollar retainer," I was told. (Apparently, to file a lawsuit in federal court is, well, to make a federal case out of it.)

I dipped into my real estate savings and my Montage royalties. I felt I had to do it.

I filed suit asserting a breach of what is called *fiduciary duty*. Fiduciary duty basically means trust between an employer and an employee and vice versa. I also filed claims for breach of contract, trademark infringement, and copyright infringement. We were off and running.

I served the complaint through a law firm I'd found in Culver City. It was a tiny firm with only a couple of attorneys, one senior partner who was pushing ninety (soon to be pushing daisies, too, by the looks of him), and a couple of associates. I retained one of the associates because his hourly fee was so low. This, it turned out, was much like hiring a discount brain surgeon.

One thing I have learned after years of working with attorneys is that passing the bar exam does not automatically give a person wisdom, talent, or even basic competence. It's not like that diploma thingy in *The Wizard of Oz*. It is, in fact, quite possible to escape law school knowing almost nothing about the law. This attorney proved it. He charged only a hundred an hour, yes, but when I got the bills, they would come to five to ten grand a month. Why? Well, apparently our little night school dropout had to consult with his senior partners on pretty much everything—how to use the coffee machine, how to save a file. I wound up getting double-billed, paying not only for the entry-level clown, but also for the $350-an-hour senior partner. Just so these two guys could talk to each other about stuff the younger guy should have already known.

So there were these massive charges and we were getting nowhere. I decided to seek alternative counsel. But first I made myself an expert on copyright law.

Now, one thing I have noticed is that if you take a guy with a second-grade education, living in a trailer in the wilds of Alabama, and tell him he has cancer, within days he'll be spouting medical terms that only an oncologist can understand. Why? Because the cancer *belongs* to him. He owns it.

The same thing happened with me. I studied all the possible

ways we could seek damages. I interviewed attorney after attorney. I immediately knew something was wrong with this one guy in Century City when he made it a point to show me the size of his copier. He also slapped a legal brief the size of a Manhattan phone book on the table as if to say, "Beat that!" I pointed out to him, though, that they call them "briefs" for a reason. They're supposed to digest information in the simplest way possible so that a judge can actually *read* them. Calling this thing a brief was like calling the Chicago fire a flare-up.

I met with eight different attorneys before finding the right one. This much I have learned out about working with attorneys: Experience matters. People will say, "Oh, you don't need a big fancy lawyer because all they do is overcharge." Not necessarily. I have found that the more experienced, more expensive attorney will dispatch his work much more efficiently than a green attorney who's still trying to figure out that a negligence tort does not come from a pastry shop.

Enter Ed Schwartz. He worked for one of the largest intellectual property law firms in California. The whole firm reeked of prestige— maple-paneled walls, brass fixtures, oil paintings of hunting dogs, the works. We sat down and he said simply, "Can you show me everything that's been filed in this case so far?" I gave him a thick wad of papers and he fanned them out on his shiny, $3,000 table as if they were tarot cards, moving them around and plucking out the ones he didn't need. After about five minutes he gave me his "reading": "Okay, this is basically what's going on. You have a case of blah, blah, blah . . ." and he started rattling off legalese that would make your head explode. Clearly his grasp of this situation was already light years beyond what it had taken Counselor Night School months of his time and thousands of my dollars to figure out.

Ed asked me how much I had paid my previous attorney, and when I told him he said, "That's ridiculous." Without blinking he told me his fee was $550 an hour, and he promised that he could get me through this. I couldn't hand over the retainer fast enough.

He got tons of work done in the first month: scheduling, discovery, subpoenas. When I got his first bill, it was surprisingly low. When I examined his billing, I'd see that he would take ten minutes to draft a letter that it would have taken Counselor Night School six hours to do. I was actually *saving* money by paying $550 an hour!

One of the first things that happens in a lawsuit is what's called a *venue motion*. In my case, even though Terri lived in the San Francisco Bay area, we wanted to move the trial to Los Angeles. First of all, that's where my attorney resided, so it would keep the cost lower than if he had to fly to San Francisco for every court appearance and deposition. Secondly, it's more expensive for the other side if they lose the venue battle.

The court found that because the agreement was reached in Los Angeles before the defendant moved to San Francisco, the venue should be Los Angeles. Terri's attorney—the one who wrote the letter saying, "You're somehow mistaken, Mr. Fong actually worked for my client"—revealed further dimensions of his staggering incompetence when he sent us a letter stating something like, "Yes, you have won. While the venue has been defined as Los Angeles, it is far more convenient for me if you come to San Francisco to do the 'meet and greet.'"

Needless to say, we scheduled the meet and greet—the initial meeting in which both parties assert their trial positions and exchange documents—in Culver City.

The guy pulled a no-show. So we filed what is a called a *default motion*.

His response? A letter stating that our attempt to have the meeting in Culver City was unconstitutional and could be considered kidnapping. Kidnapping? Yep, kidnapping.

He went on to define the criminal code for kidnapping, meaning a person held against his will, etc. (At the end of the trial this guy was sanctioned $16,000 for his ridiculous tactics. He had to write me a check from his personal account, as it wasn't covered by malpractice insurance. That was freaking sweet!)

Now that I had my really great attorney, I figured it would be smooth sailing because our case was actually a simple one. It shouldn't take two years and a federal jury trial to understand that we had a signed contract and she had broken it. Kind of a slam-dunk, really.

Well, except for the fact that one party can be deliberately unresponsive and burden the other with endless costs and paper-work.

"But come on, this isn't Enron," you might say. "This is two wedding photographers suing each other. Why would they need a lengthy trial in a federal court?"

Answer: The defendant was insured. You see, under many commercial insurance policies, there is a little-read clause called "Advertising Injury." Advertising injury exists because you might accidentally put a full-page ad in the *New York Times* saying that Macintosh apples are ten cents each when they should been thirty-nine cents. Your store then gets overrun with customers and, in order to make good on the advertising, you have to sell the apples at a loss.

The defendant in this case went to her insurance company and claimed Advertising Injury, saying that she had registered these websites for advertising purposes, was being sued, and, therefore, needed to be covered. Under Advertising Injury, the insurance company will provide a legal defense for you and will pay the claim as long as the act was not willful. When the insurance company took over, they brought in a new attorney.

This was not good news for us. It meant she now had a free attorney. Bottomless pockets. *They* were now the ones who began running up the tab—and forcing me to run up my tab as well. My savings were disappearing faster than dignity at a Star Trek convention. But I had to see it through because the alternative was even worse—losing all the money I'd spent on two different law firms, plus losing the ability to advertise my own photography services on the internet. I really had no choice but to chase this thing as far down the rabbit hole as they wanted to go.

Neither side had any incentive to settle. Me, because I had the money from the Montage sale and I knew I was in the right. Her, because the case was costing her nothing. And so, Terri and her attorney made the tactical decision to try and outspend me. Not a good strategy if you're in the wrong. It was a mistake they would regret.

Caught Red-Handed

A deposition's a pretty scary thing. Your attorney is present. The opposing attorney is present, plus the opposing party. And then there's this court reporter who stoically records everything you say. Verbatim. No wiggle room.

Both of the attorneys give you careful instructions on how to say "yes" and "no" clearly. Don't say "uh-huh" or "uh-uh," or nod or make faces. And only answer in yes/no responses. Because anytime you start to ramble, it can become very problematic for you.

Witness examination is a skill that is finely honed by attorneys, who are specialists in litigating. For example, let's say they ask you a question like, "How tall was the man?" and you say you don't know. They'll say, "What do you mean, you don't know? You must have *some* idea." You'll say, "Okay, well I have some idea, but . . ." Then they'll say, "All right, was he two inches tall? Less than two inches tall? Sixteen feet tall? Was he taller than sixteen feet?"

On and on, back and forth, they go until they get you closer to an answer.

We flew up to San Francisco for the deposition.

I remember Terri sitting on the sofa looking at me with this expression of "Hey, it's me, can't we just be friends?" But by then the case had gone so far, it was ridiculous to think I would suddenly make it go away. Our side was planning on going all the way to trial. The statements she had already made in her response to the lawsuit guaranteed that we would have a very favorable trial situation.

My attorney conducted the deposition. No sooner had he asked three or four questions than Terri began to sing like a canary—a canary auditioning for *American Idol*. Every single charge that she had denied in our lawsuit, every single allegation that we had accused her of in our lawsuit, she copped to. I guess it's much easier to say whatever you want in a written response than it is when the other party and a court reporter are staring at you in a small room. She reversed all of the statements that were in her formal response, and we felt that we now had her for perjury as well.

We were completely incredulous. We waited for the settlement proposal to arrive.

Days turned to weeks and weeks turned into months, but no settlement proposal came. So we proceeded, knowing that we were going to win this case for sure.

At the deposition, the attorney for the insurance company obviously knew she had a dog of a case. She was also young, and inexperienced, and let a lot of testimony get into the record that she should have objected to.

When you're suing somebody, it's easy to get mad at the other attorney. But if the other attorney is incompetent, they become your best friend. I was still kind of mad because they were doing so many things to drive up my legal fees, but I knew enough to keep my mouth shut and be polite. When you're in a legal proceeding you pretty much have to act like that wolf and sheep dog in the old cartoons: All very friendly and civil until the gavel falls and you start trying to kill each other. That's how it is with lawyers.

Anyway, nearly two years later, we were finally assigned to Judge Collins in the Los Angeles Federal Court. Judge Collins had been appointed to her bench by President Clinton himself.

When you go to a federal court, it's nothing at all like Judge Judy. You enter this very imposing building with armed guards and metal detectors. For me, it was a long-awaited day of justice. I felt more relaxed than I've ever felt in a mud bath. I remember running my fingers along the granite tabletops of the richly appointed courtroom. Seeing the American flag and the gigantic seal of the United States of America behind the judge. Taking in this massive, massive, courtroom, built at enormous taxpayer expense. It was all very sobering, but I felt good.

On television, they make courtrooms look beautiful. There's this dramatic lighting and there's always this really long walk from the attorneys' tables to the witness stand. All for dramatic effect.

In real life, even in federal court, there's only a small distance between the plaintiff's and defendant's desks and the witness stand. You're right on top of each other. So it can be intimidating. But it wasn't to me, because my law firm had prepared me well.

They actually had an exact duplicate of a federal courtroom where they would practice with their clients for long sessions. There was a witness stand. A judge's bench. A jury box. Attorneys used this mock courtroom to teach clients what it's like to walk up and to be sworn in. They would fill the jury stand with interns to simulate the experience of having nine people listening to your every word. Ed trained me not to look at the jury directly.

We practiced answering questions like, "Did you know this person?" I would say, "Yeah," and he'd say, "It's not *yeah*, it's *yes*." They taught me to only say "I don't know" if I really didn't know, or else I would open myself up to another line of questioning. They told me I should never say, "I guess this could be the case." Rather, I was taught to say, "To the best of my knowledge, this is the answer." Things like that.

There's a lot of skill to being an effective witness. For example, every time a question is asked, you wait about a second and a half before answering, which gives your attorney a chance to object on your behalf if needed. Because once you start to answer, whatever you say is admitted into testimony.

By the time I got to the court, I was well rehearsed and comfortable in that environment. The defendant didn't have that advantage.

The first thing we did was jury selection.

If you're the defendant, you have the option of saying, "Hey, I want a jury to hear this." Terri opted for a jury trial, which was the biggest mistake she made. I think her intent was to try to intimidate me, but actually it wound up being far more scary for her.

When you do jury selection, there is an interview process where both sides are able to accept or exclude a juror. You only get, I think, three exclusions. When the jury pool walked in for consideration, it was about thirty people.

Each side would ask the potential jurors questions, like what do you do, do you have any knowledge of this person or this case, are you involved in photography, have you ever hired a wedding photographer, and stuff like that. And so we slogged through the selection process.

I remember watching Terri when the selection process started. She looked as if she was going to faint. I think that's when the magnitude of the whole thing hit. She was petrified.

The Jury Is Staring

As we went through the jury elimination process, it seemed as if all the jurors we wanted—i.e., people with measurable IQs—were getting excluded by opposing counsel.

Soon we were out of elimination options and we ended up with a crew that looked as if it had been plucked from the Department of Motor Vehicles on a random Tuesday afternoon. I was worried. I had been waiting two years for my day in court, and now the decisions were going to be made by nine people who (1) obviously didn't want to be there, and (2) didn't seem to know a thing about intellectual property law.

My attorney wasn't worried. He looked at me and said, "We've got a great jury."

I wasn't so sure. Ed told me to relax.

I didn't feel relaxed. I said, "But nobody here knows a thing about intellectual property, trademark laws, or anything of the sort!"

Ed said that if they did, they would have been disqualified. The real skill in litigation is to tell a story that makes sense to anyone off the street. He explained to me that while individually none of these people seemed particularly bright (or even sentient, as I pointed out), nine people together are brilliant. They miss nothing.

I supposed that made sense. Although I would've preferred to be judged by nine Ph.D.s, I guess that only happens when you get to the Supreme Court. In federal court, you get the Maury Povich studio audience.

My attorney's opening statements were brilliant. He talked about how the defendant had perjured herself and violated federal laws with an attitude of impunity, how we would present clear and convincing evidence that would lead the jury to come to no other conclusion than "guilty."

Terri's attorney's opening arguments were, well, sad. She went on about how this was a young mother, and that the jury would find her to be a really nice person who does really nice photography, and the really nice evidence would show that she had done nothing wrong.

I thought we won the case at the opening bell. But it was due to be a long trial. My attorney was prepared with a slide show, a whiteboard with pre-drawn diagrams, and boxes and boxes of evidence.

The defendant's attorney had only brought a couple of dog-eared manila folders. But, then again, what *could* she have brought? This was such a simple case. The defendant had already admitted wrongdoing at the deposition. I wondered for the hundredth time why we were even here.

As the case unfolded, testimony was heard on both sides. We called Terri's husband, who did everything I'd been instructed not to do on the witness stand. He answered yes or no questions with "maybe." He rolled his eyes while answering. He sighed petulantly—always a big winner with juries. Day after day it was victory after victory for us. But the coup de grâce was our "rebuttal witness."

Prior to trial, each side has to show the other side all of the evidence they intend to present, along with a witness list. This eliminates the element of surprise. It's not like in the movies when the courtroom gasps as the fiery young attorney reveals some surprise witness. That doesn't happen in court—unless someone lies.

If someone lies, or makes a statement that can be rebutted, opposing counsel can call a "rebuttal witness." A rebuttal witness does not have to appear on the pre-trial witness list, and therefore rebuttal witnesses often *do* pack the element of surprise.

The smart litigator knows when to call in a rebuttal witness. The *genius* litigator knows to make sure that the rebuttal witness is *already there* at the courtroom, waiting outside in the hall, to completely blow the doors off a false statement.

In a scene straight out of *Perry Mason*, our defendant made a statement that my attorney knew in advance she was going to, and which was false. A big part of the case depended on whether she had been my employee or not. If she'd been my employee, then two major things would be proven: (1) that she had never been my boss, as she had said in her lawsuit response, and (2) that she owed me a duty of loyalty by not using my intellectual property to her own unfair gain.

When asked if her tax return showed that she had been my employee, she responded no.

Bam.

Waiting right outside the courtroom doors was her accountant. He was sworn in, identified himself as her tax preparer, and promptly identified her tax return.

Then the defendant was brought up to the stand. Ed asked her if this was her tax return (yes), if this was her signature (yes). "Can you please turn to page fourteen of your return and read to me what it says under 'Employer' at the bottom of the page?"

Her body language was a more stunning admission of guilt than Jack Nicholson shouting, "You can't handle the truth!" She literally turned her back to the jury, hunched over the return, turned bright red, and mumbled the answer we wanted to hear: her employer had been Storybook Weddings Photography (my company). Just for effect, Ed asked her to repeat her answer again, loud and clear.

It was the big moment I had been waiting for. For two years.

One of the jury members appeared to be nodding off, and another one seemed to be mentally communicating with the mothership, but at least we had seven jurors paying attention.

Then, after two days of trial, Terri's attorney suddenly announced, "Defense rests." What? Did I hear right? They were rolling over with barely a fight? Why had they even let this thing go to trial?

The case was handed to the jury.

Busted

Waiting for a jury verdict is agonizing. You're crammed into a tiny waiting room with the opposing side. You cannot leave, because at any moment the jury could reach a decision. So you all act moronically cordial.

You read magazines, you write letters, you kill time. Game Boys hadn't been invented yet. The book I chose to read was called *Stupid Criminals*. It was a humor book about idiots who make horrible mistakes while committing crimes, such as bank robbers who leave their wallets at the teller window. I made it a point to prominently display the book cover to the other side. I thought it was hilarious.

Nobody else shared my opinion.

Hours went by. I couldn't understand what could be taking so long. Even though I'd been confident all the way through the trial, I began to get more and more nervous. I asked my attorney and he said not to worry, it's all about lunch.

What?

If the jury finishes before noon, he explained, they don't get a free lunch. So they typically drag it out until 12:00 so they can get their federally provided meal. He predicted a verdict would be handed down about five minutes after the jury ate.

He was right. After lunch a federal marshal burst in and said, "Parties and counsel are asked to come to the courtroom. The jury has reached its decision."

Talk about intense! I could feel my heart pounding in my throat, in my temples, even in the soles of my feet. I was actually woozy. I couldn't even imagine how Terri must have been feeling. As hard as it was on me, it had to be much worse for her.

We had asked the jury for "special questions." Rather than a blanket "guilty or not guilty" decision, we asked them to split the decision into twelve separate questions of guilt or non-guilt. For each guilty verdict, we asked the jury to assess a damage figure.

The defendant was found guilty on all twelve counts. The total of the damages was $245,000. I was dreaming it would be a lot more, but come on, this was a lawsuit between two wedding photographers. It was a very good award.

The most important thing my attorney did was *not* to ask whether the jury found the defendant's actions to be willful. Of course they *had* been willful, but by not asking that question specifically, the insurance company was on the hook to pay the bill. If we had asked the jury if the acts were willful, we might have been able to collect triple damages, or nearly $750,000, but—and this is a humongous but—the insurance company wouldn't have covered it. We would've had to go after Terri's personal assets and future wages.

We knew she was a mother of young children. It would not have been fun to force her to sell her house, impound her business earnings, etc. Though I was mad at her, I wasn't going to be a monster about it. So we skipped the question of willfulness. And with that question out of the way, we got a check from her insurance company within a week.

I did the most fun thing I could think of to do with a sudden windfall. After I paid back my savings account, I bought a beautiful ski chalet at Big White Ski Resort. That was my third property on the mountain, and by far the finest.

Oh, and as I mentioned before, I also got awarded that money from her original attorney's incompetence. I bought a sailboat with that and mailed him a photo with me waving from the deck.

After two years, the case was closed. And I had a new sailboat and a new chalet to show for it!

A $240,000 Paperweight?

I came back from a trip to Egypt with a bunch of vacation film, which I took to a local one-hour photo. When I got the prints back they were the nicest I had ever seen. I was impressed. I looked over the counter and noticed that the operator was looking at a computer monitor that had six different images on it.

Having worked in many a one-hour-photo lab, I knew it was impossible to view six images at a time. I asked, "Is this digital?"

He said, "Yes. What it does is it takes the negative and digitizes it. Then it shows you six on a screen so you can color-correct them faster."

I said, "Well, if it's digital, is there any way that you can take the negative and turn it into a digital file?"

He said, "Absolutely. I can give you your negatives on a CD if you want."

It was a eureka moment. This was the bridge between traditional photography and digital. Without further ado, I called up Fuji, who made that one-hour-photo machine. Just as I'd done with the Bryce Automated Letter Printer, I leased the machine right there on the spot.

I was one of the first people to have one. It was called a Fuji Frontier, and it cost about $240,000. I figured I could use this machine for my photography studio, save the money I was spending on retail labs, and use the savings to pay for the machine.

I soon made the unwelcome discovery that if you don't run a lot of prints through the machine, the chemistry goes bad. That meant I had to process at least three hundred 8 x 10s every single day or else put in $120 worth of new starter solution.

On top of that, I discovered that the machine required 220-volt power, which my studio didn't have. I asked the management how much it would cost to have it put in. They said it would be about a $13,000 onetime fee.

I felt the familiar flutter of panic I have known before in my life when I've made a hasty decision with my gut rather than my brain. I had committed to this quarter-million-dollar, moving-van-sized machine, even though I couldn't use it myself, had absolutely nowhere to put it, and didn't have the correct power supply.

Yay!

The next thing I did was to call my friend Jason, the CEO of Pictage. Pictage was a "brokering" business that displayed wedding images online and made its revenue by charging a 10 percent commission on top of any print orders that were ordered on the Pictage. com website.

Problem was, Pictage was still hand-scanning its paper proofs on a flatbed scanner. Each image took time. Employees would put color prints facedown on the scanner bed, hit the Scan button, and rest their heads in their hands until the glowing light extinguished. Repeat same, hundreds of times. No way this company could be thriving with that model.

I said to Jason, "Dude, you really need to be in the lab business." I told him how all the people I knew who owned labs had their own private jets, things like that. I said, "All the money is being made in the lab business."

Pictage had attracted financing by telling investors that by simply taking 10 percent on the resale of images, they would have a profitable business.

I knew better. I also knew that hand-scanning each of these proofs, one at a time, would not only create a massive bottleneck in the work flow, it was also unproductive. But back in the late 1990s, the internet was *full* of unprofitable business models that people were throwing money at. Like Webvan, where you could put in an order online for a single Snickers bar and someone would deliver it to your house for just a little more than you would pay at the store. No one bothered to ask, "On what planet could this idea possibly make money?"

I told Jason that if they were going to be putting images online, why not produce the images themselves?

He was skeptical for a few reasons. One, because he didn't want to go back to his investors and say, "Hey, I was wrong about the model. We need to have a lab." Two, because he had grave doubts about printing images on the same equipment they used at one-hour-photo labs. Three, where would they get the money to take on a $240,000 machine?

the Fuji Frontier. I leased this $240,000 printer without a plan, and it wound up making me a small fortune

Boy, I said, did I have a deal for them. I offered to bring my machine into the Pictage offices and create a lab. I would run said lab, and, in return, get a piece of the company. Jason finally ran out of objections and said okay.

I brought the machine over and parked it in what used to be Pictage's kitchen.

Pictage

Word got out that I, a well-known wedding photographer, was now in the lab business. I didn't know how that was going to go over. It was like the Terminator becoming governor of your state—the idea took some getting used to. Were people going to be hesitant to send their film in, knowing that I would be looking at their work? Would they think, "Gary's a photographer not a lab owner; how can we feel comfortable sending our film in?"

I was nervous. So I bought myself a white lab coat. There, that felt better. And all of a sudden I found myself sitting in front of a one-hour-photo machine. The exact same job I'd left as a student many years before. Only now I owned it. Weird.

I announced that I had started a photo lab and waited for the orders to come in.

The first shipment we got from UPS was almost a full truckload of wedding film. There was so much of it, we couldn't fit it into our small offices, and a lot of it had to sit in the hallway. We only had six employees, but one had to stand out in the hallway and guard the film. We stationed another person on the inside, opening the boxes. Now what? Someone suggested we make a form to record what was inside the boxes. Yay, great idea! So we did that. Then we moved this big mountain of film from the hallway into our offices. We didn't know what to do with the film once it got inside. We were literally buried in film.

We went over to the nearest Target and bought a whole bunch of stacking Tupperware bins that could accommodate the contents of a full box of film. We put the film into these Tupperware boxes and labeled them with a dry-erase markers.

We spent almost an entire day doing nothing but checking in film. Once the film was checked in, we started to move the boxes around, organize

we had so much film coming in our first days at Pictage that we had nowhere to put them except in these Tupperware bins. The problem was, the dry-erase markers that we used to identify the client name on the front rubbed off the minute you touched it. So we wound up with many lost orders

them, and put them in different places. (Put that one here. No, over there!) The problem was, the moment you touched the plastic boxes, the dry-erase letters would rub off on your hands. So you'd wind up with a box that had no identifying information.

It ended up that we didn't know who some of the boxes belonged to. So we had to print out sample images and put them on a big stick-up board. We would keep them there until a customer called and said, "Hey, where's my order?"

"Oh, is that the groom with the black tux and pink carnation? The bride had red roses?"

They'd say, "No, yellow roses." Then we'd find it under mystery box 212. It was an incredibly productive system—if, for some reason, you wanted to torture customers and drive yourself insane.

We got so busy, it took eight weeks for us to get a single 8 x 10 out of our lab. You can imagine the big smile that put on our customers' faces. "But if a high-speed machine takes ninety seconds to make a print, why would it take you guys eight weeks?" you might ask. Well, because we had a massive bottleneck. Hundreds of orders going in and only one machine to pop prints out.

For a while we had to stop taking all new orders. It was awful. We were losing hundreds of thousands of dollars a month. We had the orders but not enough staff. We started running ads on Monster.com and got hundreds of resumes. For a while, all I did all day long was interview people.

We were losing money like crazy, yet we had no choice but to keep hiring people. I would interview someone, and say, "Okay, you're hired. When can you start?" They would say, "Right away," and I would say, "How about right this second?"

Of course, we didn't have anyone available to train or supervise these new hires, so there would be people sitting at desks with nothing to do. They would ask me for direction and I would say, "I don't know, just do something. Please."

It got so busy I was working twenty hours a day. I slept under my desk. I would be so tired that I would have meetings and interviews with my head still under the desk. It was commonplace to see four people in my office, talking to my feet.

Some major new disaster struck about once every two hours. Equipment breakdowns, running out of paper, running out of chemicals. Then everything would shut down. We kept getting further and further behind. The harder I worked, the more behind we got. This was absolutely, undoubtedly the most miserable period of my entire life. It made going through a divorce and losing my shirt seem like a sex party on the Hilton yacht.

The CEO Jason and his wife Jennifer had sunk every dollar they had into this business. About once every three days I would walk into his office and say, "Jason, we're completely hosed. We are absolutely not going to make it this time."

He would say, very calmly (with only a tiny tic jittering in the corner of his eye), "I know how you feel and I understand that this is very bad. What can be done to reduce the damage?"

I would say something helpful like, "Nothing. Nothing can be done. We are completely screwed."

And he would say, "Well, if something *could* be done, what would that be?"

"Well, I guess we could stay open a few additional hours. Add a swing shift."

So that's what I would do. I kept adding more hours to the lab until we were running twenty-four hours a day, seven days a week.

Finally, after months of losing money as if we were eating it for breakfast, we stopped taking all new customers and all new orders. We had a payroll of $80,000 coming up and only $60,000 in the bank.

We had an emergency board meeting and one of our directors said, "Let's go ahead and start shutting it down."

Christmas was coming and we were heartbroken. We didn't have payroll and nobody had any more money to invest in the company. Besides, why would anyone invest in a company that was losing money faster than virginity in Orlando during Spring Break?

After the board meeting, Jason and I just looked at each other. Even though I'd had my histrionics and insisted many times that we were never going to make it, deep down I'd always felt this was eventually going to be a tremendously successful company.

Even though we were thoroughly depressed, I said, "You know, I've never failed at anything. In business, that is."

He said, "I know. Me either."

We looked each other in the eye. He slammed his hand down on the table. I slammed my hand down on the table. We said, "We're not going to start failing now!" Our battle cry had gone up.

Okay, done that. We just sat there looking at each other again.

Then Jason's aunt sauntered in and lent the company $100,000. Enough to cover payroll through the middle of January.

The World Explodes

On the morning of September 11, 2001, I signed on to AOL and stared, blinked, and stared some more at the smoldering ruins that would become the icon of our new millennium. Along with millions of others, I could feel my worldview shifting in real time. I now knew exactly what it had been like for my parents. I now lived in a country under attack.

Once the dust settled and the FAA cleared planes to fly again, I kicked into survival mode. Rather than slip into passivity and wait for tons of burning metal to be hurled me at 600 mph, I got intensely motivated. I felt like I had to *do* something.

My first step was to purchase several boxes of survival water packs. Then I bought a huge supply of MREs. MREs, in case you have no Navy SEAL training, are little packages of foil-sealed calories that can be best described as three thousand Rice Krispies hydraulically pile-driven into a tiny "edible" brick. This brick of concentrated sustenance theoretically contained enough calories for one day for an average 180-pound male.

Why did this ritual seem familiar? I didn't realize it at the time, but here I was, once again preparing my Desert Survival Kit. But this time I didn't just have a crunchy, crispy, incredibly loud Mylar blanket, I had a full-body radiation suit.

Yes, I really bought one.

I would tell my personal assistants, only half-joking, that part of their job was to know how to duct-tape the seam between my clothes and my radiation suit and to secure my gas mask before they succumbed to nuclear radiation or anthrax. I would always comfort them by promising they would be "on the clock" for the event, and that I would feel really sad for them as I stepped over their boiling, twitching bodies.

Sometimes my sense of humor plays better in person than on the printed page.

I wasn't joking when it came to the survival thing, though. I had my rations and radiation suit stored on my sailboat in the harbor. My self-preservation plan was carefully laid out. I calculated, for instance, that should Los Angeles be attacked, there would be inevitable looting, martial law, and general mayhem for about a week. (I knew this because I had lived through the Los Angeles riots.) So I figured that if I took my sailboat out into the open sea until everybody got their freak-demons exorcised, I could then return, fully nourished by pile-driven Rice Krispies, sporting a scruffy beard and a dandy sailor's tan to boot—unless, of course, the ozone layer were ruptured in the attack, in which case I would return as a smiling stick of Fong jerky.

My doomsday plan didn't stop at the harbor. I bought a Honda Gold Wing motorcycle. I actually found one painted in camouflage colors (the desert- and jungle-themed gas tank would surely help me disappear into the post-apocalyptic, *Mad Max* landscape). I stored a week's worth of rations in the saddlebags. The idea was that if I couldn't make it to the sailboat for whatever reason, I would probably want to leave town. My Honda Gold Wing had the tank capacity to get me about three hundred miles. That was not going to get me to, say, Oregon, of course, so inside one of my saddlebags was a handy-dandy siphon pump. Once my gas gauge needle started straying toward "E," I would need to stop the bike, step respectfully over some smoldering bodies, unscrew the nearest gas cap, and help myself to enough fuel to power me to pine tree–laden Oregon, where I would live off the land until civilization was restored.

All of the above was my honest-to-God first reaction to this brave new world of living in a war zone. I started to wonder why this drill felt so familiar to me. Was it genetic? Had the shock of explosions from my parents' wartime childhoods somehow become embedded in my DNA? What had caused me to turn into the human that survives with the cockroaches? Why was it so important to me to tough my way through disasters? What forces had turned the twelve-year-old boy sleeping under the staircase in a crispy Mylar blanket into this forty-year-old with a motorcycle, a radiation suit, and a doomsday plan?

The odd thing was, my own father, once again, made no plans whatsoever for his own survival. I would have thought he'd be the expert in navigating life in a war zone, but all he did was sit impassively and listen to the radio. It was just like when we got burglarized at the wig store. He glazed over. Clearly my survival drive was not a result of genetics. The more I thought about it, the more absurd it all became. What weird instinct had fired up in me? Was I really planning to have assistants tape me up in a radiation suit moments before they gasped their last breaths?

All of a sudden, just as my priorities had undergone a sea change on the morning of 9/11, they shifted again. All of my attention went to the survivors of the 9/11 tragedy. I felt a sudden urgency to do something for them. Making rain, rather than waiting for rainfall, had always been my forte. So how could I do that now? Was there some way I could simultaneously help Pictage and help the survivors of 9/11?

It finally occurred to me that it was time to travel again. If there was one thing I could do to help ensure Pictage's success in the coming months, it was to go out there on the national lecture circuit and stir up some excitement and positive vibes for our lab.

And I could donate all the tour proceeds to the 9/11 survivors!

I called my best friend, celebrity photographer Denis Reggie, to ask him if he'd consider joining me. He said yes before I could finish my pitch.

This was exciting. I knew we had something here that would create a buzz. At the time we were the two biggest names in the wedding photography business. By going on tour together, we were sure to raise some dollars—along with some eyebrows.

The 9/11 Town Hall Tours

Denis and I had a blast on the tour. A good chunk of the enjoyment for me was in making fun of Denis. For one thing, he had an uncanny knack of drawing airport security agents to him like piranhas to a wounded guppy. The instant we would lay our laptops on the X-ray scanning belt and step through the metal detector, a squad of uniforms would descend on Denis with beeping wands and frowning faces. He would always be asked to take off his shoes, grab his ankles, cough, walk in circles. All the while, I would stand waiting for him in the "safe" area with laughter mounting on my face.

You see, Denis is of Lebanese descent. But he looks nothing like it. I didn't even know he was Lebanese until about twenty years into our friendship. He looks more Greek to me. But, on the 9/11 Town Hall Tour, he became the butt of my endless teasing, because "his people" were terrorists. We Chinese, I would explain, were way too smart to blow ourselves up for some cause. We would rather invent the technology for *you* to blow *yourself* up. It was completely ridiculous, of course, but that didn't discourage me a bit.

We lugged our bags across the United States, city after city, putting on our dog-and-pony show to packed houses.

When I was young, I think the reason I wanted to be a musician was because I liked the idea of traveling from city to city, playing to huge crowds. In my dreams I would do one city per evening. Atlanta on Monday, New Orleans on Tuesday. Life on the road. Being on tour. Who ever imagined I would do that as a wedding photographer?

I'd heard that Rocky used to play his guitar on his tours. Maybe that's how he fulfilled *his* rock star dreams.

I no longer go on the road, because it's a lot of work, but I've done at least a dozen national tours, sometimes hitting over thirty cities. With each city completed, your program gets smoother, more polished, and funnier.

One thing I've learned about having a fan base is to always be nice. One moment of impatience toward a fan gets repeated thousands of times over the years. Like this time a friend of mine was at the Baseball Hall of Fame. Reggie Jackson happened to be there, and my friend approached him with gushing admiration. "Mr. Jackson, sir, I am such a huge fan . . ." RJ's response to this man, who is a very well-respected industrialist, was a quick and hearty "Go fuck yourself." This happened some twenty years ago. My friend told me the story and now I'm telling you. Now we all probably think Reggie Jackson is a gigantic asshole, but he might have just been having a bad day.

I've learned that the only day that matters is the day you are nice to an admirer. Like the time I was at a convention when a young man came up to me and began asking me a question. I say "began," because the asking of the question turned out to be a procedure that took longer than oral surgery. With the most unnerving case of stuttering I have ever witnessed, he asked me (over the course of the next minute and a half), the following question: "Mr. Fong, could you please look at my portfolio?"

With my habit of laughing at the most inopportune times, I immediately resorted to my tried-and-true mind game: Name all of the states that begin with the letter "A." I had to dig deep, but my expression didn't change, and I made it through. One second longer, though, and I would have gone down in folklore as Gary Fong, the Guy Who Laughs at the Verbally Handicapped.

What I loved most about touring was making new friends. I always abided by Rocky's motto: "Everybody could use a new friend." And I made a lot of friends around the country. One of them, on a later tour, would become my third wife. But we'll get to that in a bit.

Burned Out

Almost by accident, our team at Pictage came up with a way of creating what was called an *image catalogue*. It had nine to twelve photo images on a single 8 x 10 sheet. They were numbered in sequence, say from 1 to 2,000, and coil-bound together. An image catalog allowed the bride and groom to quickly and easily find whatever images they wanted to order. No one had ever offered anything like this before.

We found a way to streamline the production so the catalogues took little time to make. By doing so, we were able to pull about six of our employees off manual assembly. That was the turning point. We took the image catalogue to the large Wedding and Portrait Photographers International convention, and it was a huge hit.

I told our sales people that we offered so many products it had become confusing. Even to us. So we decided to just focus on one hot thing, like Oscar Meyer does with hot dogs. We decided to become the image catalogue people.

From that moment on, we started to generate a positive cash flow and the company began to prosper. In fact, it kept growing and growing. By the time I left, we had seventy-two people. Now there are over two hundred worldwide.

Once we were in the clear, work was no longer an option for me. I was too burned out. I retired. And so did my second marriage.

chapter nine

Remembering and Forgetting

I inherently have a much harder time forgiving than forgetting. When it comes to pain, I rinse clean with very little residue. In fact, if it weren't for my journal, I would have a hard time recalling some of the most hurtful experiences of my life.

Strangely, I would have a hard time forgetting them, too.

My journal, which I've been keeping since I wrote my Declaration of Independence at age ten, is a marvelous tool that helps me both remember and forget. How?

Well, when I have periods of anguish, I write down in my "drama queen" style every last sensation of self-doubt and fear that I harbor. This is very therapeutic. By dumping my feelings onto the pages of a journal, I no longer have to keep them inside, but I don't have to force them on an unsuspecting friend, either. The very act of dumping on paper allows me to forget, to move on.

But recording my pain in black and white helps me remember, too. Whenever I'm going through a difficult period, I can always look back on the worst moments of my life and see that I survived them. It's right there on paper. My journal helps me remember, not so much the suffering, but the healing. If I got through it then, I realize, I can get through it now. This, too, shall pass.

Remembering and forgetting, the twin gifts of keeping a journal.

Now, as I sit down to write about my second marriage, something startling occurs to me: I barely remember it.

If I don't refer to my journal, I realize, I can hardly recall anything at all about the five years and three months that I spent in marriage number two. For the life of me, I cannot remember what Mary was like as my wife.

I don't remember our nicknames. I don't remember what she was like in the mornings, whether she was a cranky slow starter or the type that would pop up in bed at the break of day. I don't remember what kind of sandwich she would order at Subway. I don't remember if she drove a stick shift well, or how good she was at parallel parking. I don't remember if we ever flew a kite together. I don't remember if she curled her hair to look pretty on special occasions. Without the benefit of my journal, I would recall very little at all, and even with it the words are sparse.

I'm either a shining beacon of hope for those who have ended painful relationships or a textbook entry in a psychology book under the heading "Denial." I like to think it's the former.

As I flip through my journal from that period, I see pages and pages and pages about the suffering and shock I experienced when she unexpectedly announced she wanted to end our marriage. I find words such as "unbearable" and "excruciating." I see statements like, "I dread to experience what's coming next." I see descriptions of waking up in the middle of the night, terrifyingly alone, in a concrete, industrial-style apartment building, to the sound of an elevator ascending and descending in its shaft. The loneliest sound in the universe at 3:00 A.M.

I see accounts of early surprises in the marriage that should have alerted me to trouble, such as the day she glibly informed me, right after we got married, "I'm sorry if I gave you the idea that I wanted to have children, because I really don't." Having children had been a bedrock reason for my wanting to get married in the first place.

But here's what's funny: When I close the journal and just try to remember those days unaided, what comes to mind is her dog. I can honestly say with the gift of retrospect that I loved her dog more than I loved her.

Maybe that was our problem?

His name was Dragon and he was the most awesome German Shepherd ever. He looked at me with these sweet amber eyes that glowed in the sun, and his ears perked straight up as he followed my every move. Whenever I went into a restaurant or grocery store, his gaze would stay riveted to the door. One day he couldn't take it anymore. I'd gone into a supermarket and was browsing in the cereal section. I turned left and nearly tripped over him, sitting alertly in the aisle and staring up at me. He had jumped out of the Jeep and come inside to find me, just because he missed me. Another time I went into a bowling alley and he pulled the same thing. The temptation of that big black ball rolling at thirty miles an hour down an alley was too much for his canine instincts to resist. This ninety-pound German Shepherd went barreling after the ball, snapping his jaws and crashing into the bowling pins. I fell over laughing.

These memories, and many more, I can call up on my own. I remember him as if he were still here with me. I can close my eyes and feel his body leaning up against mine. I remember his dank dog smell. I used to say that if you took an X-ray of my heart, you would see the face of my smiling canine friend. That's how much I loved him.

But if I don't look at my journal, the only memories I have of the marriage is that it felt stifling. They say the opposite of love is hate, but that's not true. The opposite of love is indifference. To say that my second wife left a yearning in my heart, or that I have stabbing memories of our bygone passions, would, alas, be untrue.

I sometimes wonder why I got married after having known her for only five months, especially since she cheated on me while we were dating. What I do know is that Alex had just left me in the middle of the night with no forwarding address. My mother had just died. I was trying to adapt to a world that was rocking on its axis.

The only stumbling block to romance was that she was nowhere near as attractive as Alex. It sounds shallow to say it, but it was really hard for me to be excited about an average-looking person after having been with someone who looked like Alex. But as time went on, Mary seemed able to understand things that I didn't or couldn't. And I felt so lost at the time. I remember that when we first recognized that something was happening between us, I said to her, in my most sincere words, "I just want a home."

As we started growing closer, she expressed her excitement about having children. So that's the path I thought we were on, until about three days after the wedding when I found out that this intention was never there, sorry you feel misled, and I never want to speak about this topic again. I quickly began to discover that most of the qualities I had seen in her before we got married seemed to have evaporated after the wedding vows were exchanged.

I could go through my journal and dig up all the painful details, but I don't really want to do that. I don't want to do that to me, and I don't want to do that to her. I'd prefer to remember that I got to spend a number of years with the most unconditional, loving, faithful companion that I could ever hope for. And that was a German Shepherd named Dragon. Oh, and he also came with a human being.

But I don't know that I remember her.

After Mary and I divorced, I moved out of the house that I had purchased when I was twenty-six years old and bought a condominium in Marina del Rey. I purchased it from a seller who was desperate to unload it, so I got a good deal. It had floor-to-ceiling views of the Pacific Ocean on the left and Hollywood to the right, but its interior made a used double-wide in an Alabama trailer park look like Trump Towers. Which is to say that it required an expensive and lengthy renovation. So, while the construction project was going on, with nowhere else to sleep, I spent many lonely nights in my sailboat, often sobbing.

I no longer had Pictage to run, I no longer had weddings to shoot, and I really had nothing to do but spend six weeks crying my brains out. When I was done, I remembered that giving up hope was how I would find ultimate peace and contentment. I had given up hope once before, when I dropped out and went to the Bahamas to teach tennis, but I had gotten caught up in the foolish ambition game again.

This time, the universe would not be ignored. As a child, I had written in my journal, "I think most people are too busy mowing the lawn to hear the wisdom of the universe." I'd known since childhood that in silence I would find my guidance. But I had forgotten. Now, having lost everything again, being forced to sleep on the still, dark waters of a boat harbor, I heard the voice of silence again.

I decided to stop working, and to stop searching for a relationship to fill a hole that I really didn't have.

The Art of Retirement

A lot of people don't how to retire. They don't think it through. They imagine that one week they're going to be working seventy hours at a high-pressure corporate ulcer farm, and the next week they're going to be lazing in a hammock, counting the petals on daisies. And that they're going to be fine with this. What actually happens? They go bonkers. You can't step out of a meat grinder into a vacuum. I've known more than a few people who sold their companies for millions in "retirement money," only to start another company a year later. I didn't want to be one of those people. So I made a list of goals I wanted to accomplish with my post-retirement life.

Goal number one: learn a new language. I chose French because I liked the way French women's mouths moved when they talked in movies. I figured I'd enjoy learning a new tongue because I'd had a lot of fun learning Spanish as a kid.

Goal number two was to improve my tennis game. This was for two reasons. First, I hadn't played much tennis for a while and I missed it. Second, I wanted to get in better shape. It's widely known among tennis aficionados that playing on slow, clay courts is really good for physical conditioning. That's because, due to the high bounce of the ball and its rapid deceleration as soon as it hits the court, the rallies are much longer.

So those were my two goals: learn a language and improve my tennis. Not exactly finding a cure for leukemia, but that was sort of the point. These simple goals would be consuming enough to keep me fully occupied, but not stressful enough to turn me into the shoe-bomber I felt I'd been in danger of becoming if I'd stayed another day at Pictage.

After a bit of research, I concluded that I could work on both goals in Nice, France. There was a school there called Institut de Français, in a beautiful villa overlooking the Côte d'Azur. The Institute offered five days a week of immersion instruction from 9:00 to 5:00, along with excursions on Saturdays. It sounded fabulous. There was also a nearby tennis club that had slow, red clay courts. I was good to go.

In preparation, I purchased some self-study CD courses in French. These turned out not to be enormously helpful unless I really wanted to say, "The boy is underneath the table." So I started doing something much more fun: I watched DVD movies in French.

Most DVDs give you the option, in the setup menu, of changing the audio from English to French, and of adding subtitles in English. So that's what I did. I would watch movies over and over again, listening to the French audio, watching the English subtitles. I started picking up phrases quickly. There is no way a Berlitz or Rosetta Stone course would teach you how to say, "Commander, we're being hit from all sides by crossfire!" or, "I know you have been having an affair with that little hussy and I want you to come clean with me." Good, solid, usable stuff like that you just can't pick up in an audio course.

So, armed with hours of such experience, I felt confident that when I went to the immersion school I would at least be able to hold my ground.

How wrong one can be about even the simplest things.

The first thing I saw upon setting foot on the Institut grounds was a friendly reminder: "French only spoken past these gates." Uh-oh. I felt a mild shiver of terror due the fact that I couldn't even ask where the restroom was, but, hey, I did know how to say, "Commander, we're being hit from all sides by crossfire!" Perhaps that would do in a pinch.

One of the movies I had watched on DVD was Adam Sandler's *50 First Dates*. There's this scene where a guy repeats his name over and over. On the French audio, instead of saying "je suis" (meaning "I am," and pronounced "zhe swee"), he kind of mushes it up and says, "zschwee." So I decided that when I started introducing myself at the Institute, instead of saying, "Je suis Gary," the way those buttoned-down Berlitzers would say it, I would say it in the cool, "real French" way.

When I got to the school, a lady immediately asked my name in French, and I replied, "Zschwee Gary." She gave me a rather pained expression and asked me to confirm. "Is your name really Shui Gary?"

Perhaps French-dubbed DVDs in which the actors' lips were moving in English were not the ideal teaching medium after all.

Next we all sat down to breakfast. Nobody said a thing because, well, we didn't speak French and we were afraid of having our heads lopped off with a baguette if we uttered a word in non-French. So we all chewed wordlessly. Finally I decided it would be a good idea to rupture the silence by catching the eye of a table-mate and booming out cheerfully, "Bon matin!" (My ex-wife Mary, who professed to speak French, had assured me this was a good pre-noontime ice-breaker in the land of Brie and bistros.) My lame outburst was followed by a round of giggles from the more advanced students, then awkward silence. I later learned that this phrase was never used in French and that proper greeting would be the common "bonjour." Using "bon matin," a literal translation of "good morning," is rather like greeting a fellow American on the street with, "A prosperous noon-hour to you."

I was batting a thousand and the school bell hadn't even rung yet.

What I had relied on as a clever primer in the French language—dubbed DVDs—was completely deconstructed within the first five minutes and, after testing into the beginners class, level 2, I humbly accepted my seat. Well, at least it was level 2. (*Zschwee* not a complete idiot.)

Learning a new language is a bit maddening, because teachers tend to teach you to speak they way they *wish* people spoke, rather than the way people really do speak. I'm sure English teachers do this as well. For example, the word "oui," while pronounced "wee" in books and movies, is more often pronounced "way" in French conversation. It's probably like us saying "yeah," instead of "yes." However, in *school* the word "way" doesn't exist. Only in *reality* does one encounter it.

Anyway, we got split up into little classrooms of twelve students, all of the same ability. I happily sat there in my little student desk in this beautiful old mansion overlooking the Côte d'Azur, completely captivated by this middle-aged, long-haired professor named Patrice. He was hilarious. He gestured wildly with every phrase and uttered not a single word that wasn't French. It was entertaining, if not the least bit meaningful.

For example, he would ask our names. If you had no idea what he was asking (as was the case with roughly 100 percent of us), then you had to shrug your shoulders. He would then gesture at his chest with the frantic urgency of a surrendering prisoner of war and say, in French, "My name is Patrice, and you?" Then he would point at you and you would, of course, answer your name. This is the trick of teaching a language without translating it. You use a lot of gestures. I couldn't help but wonder what we were going to do when we got to concepts like "libertarianism," but I appreciated the strategy.

My fellow students were a mixture of idle rich, bored retirees, international executives, and semi-celebrities. We boasted among our ranks a former Miss America and several United Nations representatives.

As the days turned into weeks, a miracle started to occur right before our eyes: We were all getting it. It happened oddly fast. We started speaking in little phrases, which turned into sentences, which turned into paragraphs. And then at lunch, the professor would sit with us and chat. Everyone was extremely patient with whatever mistakes we made. By the third week, with very few exceptions, we were speaking quite comfortably. It was an absolutely transformational experience.

At one point, a social was held in which everyone was free to speak whatever language they wanted. That was an eye-opener, because we soon found out that many of our classmates didn't speak any other common language. For example, one couple I'd chatted with during breaks turned out to speak only Japanese. And so, as a result, we all resorted to our "comfortable" French. That was probably the point, to teach you that you can actually do it. It worked.

I slipped into a wonderful routine of going home to my loft apartment with its private balcony overlooking the harbor of Villefranche, then going down to the local market and buying fresh vegetables, cheeses, fruit, and breads to eat at home. My evenings would be spent with French doors open, gazing at the sparkling lights on the harbor as I diligently did my homework.

I felt like a college student again. No one knew anything about my background, the "big life" I had at home with my personal assistants, luxury cars, and board meetings. Here I had a book bag. I walked to school like a kid. It felt terrific.

Soon I had friends, too. And what was so cool was that we got to know each other in French. The amazement never wore off. Here I was, a resident of Nice, France, reading the national newspaper *Le Figaro* and having political debates, *en Français*, in charming little cafés.

Many people think the French are rude and hate Americans. I found that not to be the case at all. In fact, as soon as I would tell someone I was an American, a look of unbridled sympathy would break out on their faces. It was a look that said, "It must be awful living under George Bush." Disdain? No. Compassion? Yes.

The French aren't rude, it's just that they can't fathom how Americans can stomp into their country and expect it to operate like an American shopping mall. That's the part that makes them crazy. Some Americans really seem to think of foreign countries as extensions of Disneyland. They think it should all be laid out for *their* convenience and amusement. One time my friend Kristen (who's from Atlanta) came to visit me in France, and we sat in one of the sidewalk cafés, playing a little game we invented called "Spot the Americans." It was so easy, there was no challenge. Here's a scene we actually witnessed one day from our table:

A family of five is strutting down the sidewalk, all of them looking confused and pissed off. Dad has a goatee, a huge beer gut, and a permanent scowl on his face. The kids are festooned in undulating orange t-shirts that say France with a stencil of the Eiffel Tower as a background. They all go into a clothing store where the big guy tries to find a size that fits him. He starts bellowing, "Hello? Hello?" Nobody is helping him because he's barking in English and acting inexplicably annoyed. Finally he just blows up and screams, "God damn it, don't nobody speak English around here?" How embarrassing! Can you imagine how this guy would act if someone walked into *his* shop in downtown Poughkeepsie and started bellowing in French in a pissed-off and entitled manner? I'm sure he'd be very understanding.

When I saw this from the French point of view, I was amazed that they even let us out of the airport, never mind tolerating us in their stores and restaurants. One thing I know for sure is that Americans cannot get married in France unless they have been there for at least thirty days. I'm sure they made this rule to prevent the doomsday scenario in which droves of petulant American brides would overrun the gardens of Versailles every Saturday in June.

Living in France never got old. It was as if I had developed a split personality. There was the French Gary, who drove a SMART Car and had a studio apartment up on the hill, and then there was the English-speaking American Gary. He seemed so . . . eighties.

But eventually it was time to go home. This may sound strange, but I actually had to get used to speaking English again. When you form words in French, your tongue lays flatter against your palate and moves farther forward. When I got back to JFK and started speaking English again, the first thing I noticed was my tongue moving back in my mouth and hitting the top of the palate in a much harsher and more percussive way.

Actually, everything about my return to America felt harsh and percussive. I knew it was time to face the rest of my life. Improving my tennis and learning a new language probably weren't going to fill the next forty or fifty years.

In truth, being halfway around the world had not been a *complete* respite from my duties. I still had to attend Pictage board meetings by telephone, and that was always extra crazy. For one thing, they used this annoying little speakerphone on the desk of the boardroom. I couldn't really hear what anybody was saying, and I would nod off in the middle of meetings because they were held in the wee hours of the morning, France time.

Pictage was eventually sold for $30 million, giving a great return to the investors who believed in us. Jason, the CEO, became an instant multimillionaire, and I made close to a million. But the best part of the whole adventure was that we created two hundred jobs out of an idea, and created a business that still provides value to hundreds of thousands of happy wedding couples.

Why Canon Dumped Me

When I came back from France, I found several boxes waiting for me from major camera manufacturers. It was like Christmas! Each of these boxes contained extremely valuable digital cameras. But they weren't just *any* cameras, they were prototypes.

Even though I felt like I had left the photography world behind, it had not left me. Camera manufacturers were eager to get my opinion on the latest in professional equipment because I was that rare breed (in fact, the only specimen) who was both a professional photographer and an owner and founder of an extremely successful digital lab. Yes, I had quit photography, but the world doesn't forget your past as easily as you do. Greg Brady hasn't been Greg Brady for over three decades, but the public hasn't forgotten.

When I first started out, photography magazines were my atlas to what was hot or not in the industry. So it was quite a gas when my work began to appear in ads for the big manufacturers such as Kodak and Hasselblad. As I became a well-known photographer, I would often shoot entire ad campaigns for film or camera companies.

When companies introduce a new camera, they like to have an endorsement and image sample from a famous photographer. That's where I came in. Factories would send me pre-production models, or even prototypes of upcoming cameras, and I would sign a contract that I would never, ever disclose anything about that camera until it was commercially released.

Companies would sometimes send me two versions of the same camera. One of these would be a working model with hand-wired electronics, covered in putty so nobody could see what it looked like. The other would be a plastic, non-working mockup of the camera, which looked and felt exactly like the real thing. The replica mockup was sent to me because they wanted my comments on its look and feel, the placement of the buttons, etc. This one could be oohed and ahhed over but not used. The replica model was never, never, never to see the light of day. It was strictly confidential. I think I had to sign an agreement stating that I would view it only by the light of an infra-red periscope within the confines of Jodie Foster's panic room. I was then to destroy it with C4 in the middle of the New Mexico desert. During a lunar eclipse. So between the two cameras—one covered with putty that *did* work, and one that only *looked* like the real deal but couldn't be unveiled, I would get a good idea of the new camera.

Online photography forums are a huge gossip mill, filled with endless speculation about the next big camera that manufacturers are going to introduce. Literally millions of people join these discussion threads to speculate about the next new camera. It's a guessing game for everybody, though. Nobody really knows a thing.

I would get a kick out of reading these internet discussions because I would actually have the new camera in my hand, but couldn't say a thing about it. It gave me an amazing feeling of power. It was fun.

Until the day I messed up big-time with Canon.

Back in 1979, I got my first ever SLR camera, which was a Canon AE-1. So, being on their rolodex of top photographers was a huge feather in my cap.

Canon was about to release its first-ever digital version of the famous EOS-1. It was to be called, stunningly enough, the EOS-1D, and the photography world was waiting with bated breath. Discussion forums were abuzz with rumors.

Canon decided to pre-send several of these new cameras to a select list of famous photographers. Denis Reggie got his, and I knew Canon was sending me one. I couldn't wait, so I called Canon. They told me there would be two EOS-1Ds coming to me.

Two? Wow! I must be really special. I asked them to double-check this, and the guy on the other end of the line said, "Are you Gary Fong?" I said I was. "Yes, there are two cameras for you, Mr. Fong. They're being sent via FedEx."

Holy crud, Canon was sending me, and me alone, two testing units. I didn't know what I'd done to deserve such an honor, but I wasn't about to complain!

The boxes came and I was floored. This shimmering jewel of a camera—talked about everywhere, available nowhere—was sitting in my hands. And there was another one just like it sitting in the box.

I started shooting with it immediately and couldn't believe how awesome it was. So professional and rugged! Super-fast motor drive! Fantastic!

But no matter how cool it was, I didn't need two of them, so I tried to decide what I should do with the other one.

I did the dumbest thing in history.

I decided to sell it.

On eBay.

A very nice dentist in Arizona bought it for $13,500. Yep, thirteen-five. For a camera. I guess this guy just really, *really* wanted to be the first kid on the block to get his mitts on one of the few EOS-1Ds in the world. After receiving his cashier's check, I shipped it to him. Not a bad day's wages, I thought.

The next morning, I awoke to find a cadre of very brusque emails on my computer from members of the Canon marketing staff. "Urgent—call ASAP regarding EOS-1D." One of my friends who worked for Canon sent me a message that put things even less subtly. "You are in deep shit," was all it said. Uh-oh. What had I done?

My relationship with Canon was a little dicey to begin with. While I did use their cameras and excellent lenses, my opinion at the time was that nobody in the world produced a more beautiful digital image than Fuji. Fuji was in the film business, and they'd made the Fuji Frontier printer that I was using, as well as the paper I was printing my images on. They matched up everything perfectly. Canon was good, but their sensors had this strange bluish tint when shot in open shade, and a weird green halo in some of the highlights. But their lenses were the best.

I have never been shy about making my opinions known, and have turned down endorsement offers from companies I don't like. I was outspoken, for example, about Nikon's digital cameras, which were absolutely awful at the time. Anyway, my public stance was that Fuji had the best image quality, and Canon had the best lenses. So I was in semi-good graces with Canon. That's why they sent me the camera.

Why they had sent me two, though, was still a mystery. One glance at the online forums told me I had done something catastrophically stupid. I don't know how people figured it out so fast, but there were already hundreds of posts from around the world, saying "Gary Fong sells his EOS-1D on eBay!" Under the Comments and Threads, people were speculating that the camera must be shit, because I was the first

gary fong   213

to get it and I'd dumped it overnight on eBay.

I was sunk. I had to call the director of marketing for Canon, the same guy who'd just hired Andre Agassi to be their spokesperson.

There was a pause after he picked up and then a rather understated, "Gary, what were you thinking?" My response was equally inspired. "I don't know, Dave." There was another pause, and then he said, "Well, the good news is, you made a lot of money on that camera." Kind of like those Geico Insurance ads, I guess.

I asked what I could do to make things better. He requested that I simply post a statement on the forums that I sold the camera because Canon had mistakenly sent me two cameras, one of which had been intended for the other Gary Fong.

The other Gary Fong?

Oh, right. Him.

There is another famous Gary Fong who is a photographer. I believe he won a Pulitzer or some such thing. I also believe he was the photo editor for the *San Francisco Chronicle*. I had sold his camera out from under him.

I should have thought of Gary right away. You see, only a short while earlier, Canon had presented me with the idea of doing an ad campaign featuring the two Gary Fongs. Clever stuff. Canon was very excited about it.

Oddly enough, I never did hear back from Canon about the ad campaign. I never heard back from Canon again about anything, in fact, after that debacle. I definitely haven't received any fancy new cameras.

And I guess I haven't felt inclined to break the silence.

But while I have the opportunity, there is one thing I'd like to say publicly to Canon: I'm really sorry about the camera.

Digital Intensive

All of this commotion sounded a siren in my marketing head. If my silly stunt of selling a single camera on eBay could make a serious impact on the initial sales figures of a brand new camera, then it only stood to reason that my opinion on these cameras was being viewed as a forecast of the leading edge in digital photography. I was the guy with the prototypes, the photographer whom the camera companies trusted, so my opinion counted for something, right?

So I began exploiting this digital photography thing. I created a website, with a connected discussion forum, at DigitalPhotographers. net. The traffic was incredible. Almost overnight, we had thousands of members from around the world, all arguing about what might or might not be included in a major manufacturer's newest cameras. And, of course, the one who would settle the score would be me, because I would usually get the prototypes.

Since I was the person with the prototypes *and* the person shooting national ad campaigns for these cameras, it only made sense for me to publish my opinions along with test results of the latest cameras. And with my experience of running a digital photography lab, I had seen countless thousands of bad images where the exposures were off because the cameras were set wrong. I would sometimes wish that I could tell a photographer how to do the most basic things, like reading the histogram. Of course, most people don't even know what a histogram *is*, and that's the reason I decided it was time to go back on tour again. I had to teach people how to read histograms if they were going to produce professionally acceptable digital prints.

I hunkered down in my sailboat and typed out a lesson plan for a two-day Digital Intensive workshop. One day would be dedicated to the "capture" aspect of digital photography, the other to "output." Output included using Photoshop, communicating with your lab (assuming your lab was, of course, Pictage), etc.

As soon as I was done typing my lesson plan and producing the course notebook, I announced the workshops. To my enormous delight, they quickly sold out. Obviously I was on to something. I wound up doing two laps around the country teaching my Digital Intensive workshops. In those classes I taught thousands of photographers how to produce beautiful digital images and extract the highest performance from their equipment.

And one of these thousands of photographers I ended up marrying. We met in Cincinnati, no less. Cincinnati, on the Mississippi River, the town that spawned crazy, unpredictable Alex. The fact that I was openhearted enough to fall for another girl in Cincinnati is proof that

I can weather a brutal end to a relationship, but I am resilient, and with Zen training, I'm good at zoning out and discarding baggage.

Destiny Seems Familiar

There's a spooky déjà-vu thing that sometimes happens when I face a defining moment in my life. Like when I saw Rocky at his studio for the first time—this lucent inner voice whispered, "Replay." That same kind of recognition hit me square in the gut one day when I was teaching one of my Digital Intensive classes in Cincinnati.

It was my first time visiting that city in years, and my very first time teaching the Digital Intensive there. I had been talked into bringing my road show to Ohio by an online acquaintance who promised she would sign up some of her friends. I decided it was worth the risk.

As I was preparing my class materials on day one, in walked Melissa Carl. An electric charge seemed to ignite the air around her. She was gorgeous, but it was more than that. I instantly felt a rush of familiarity (along with a host of other sensations, most of them hormonally induced). I didn't know what to make of it. I quickly shifted my attention back to my notes. I didn't need this kind of distraction, in my class or in my life.

Melissa was in her twenties, with sparkling blue eyes, beautiful dark brown shoulder-length hair, and—I have to say it—an amazing body. I was way too old for her and thirty pounds heavier than I am now. I was wearing a tank top, shorts, old tennis shoes, and my trademark bottle-cap glasses. And my hair was half gray.

In those days I didn't really care about how I looked because I had decided to stay single for the remainder of my natural life. But as I watched Melissa Carl take a seat, then glance up at me, I suddenly cared about how I looked. I suddenly cared a great deal.

I wished I had worn a suit or something cool. I wished I had dyed my hair. I wished I had worn my contact lenses. And I certainly wished I had started that diet I'd been planning for years.

In any disaster-recovery situation, though, one must quickly sort through the rubble and make an assessment of one's remaining assets. I concluded that I still had humor, intellect, and reputation working in my favor.

Oh, and of course, the podium. You know when you go on a blind date and you meet somebody you'd really like to know better, and you secretly wish you could talk about yourself the whole evening, to demonstrate how funny and charming you are? Well, I had that glorious podium. And a golden opportunity to talk for two days straight. Sixteen hours of uninterrupted program time. I had done the show so many times, I knew it inside and out. I didn't have to sweat the course material, which meant I had tons of room to improvise. I was going to be more brilliant than ever. I was going to do a sixteen-hour "audition" that would never be forgotten.

It was my most impassioned performance ever. I am sure that I was wildly impressive to everyone in the room.

Everyone except Melissa Carl. Melissa Carl looked bored. At one point, she began staring cross-eyed at her split ends, twiddling them between her fingers. Not an encouraging sign. I was devastated and didn't know why. It felt as though something important was slipping through my fingers.

To make matters worse, at one point when I was showing students some images on my laptop, she stood next to me, wearing these low-rise jeans that made her hip bone slightly visible underneath her soft black sweater. I remember thinking that this was more than I could possibly bear.

I did have one key ally: Melissa's best friend Jessica Strickland. If there had been a Gary Fong fan club, Jessica would have nominated herself as president. It was Jessica, in fact, who had talked me into coming to Cincinnati in the first place. She knew the names of all of my brides (the ones I'd married *and* the ones I'd photographed). She had read every article I'd ever written and seen every video interview. But she had never seen me in person. To her, this was like being a Trekkie and doing a two-day workshop with Leonard Nimoy in full Vulcan drag. During my entire program I honestly don't remember her even blinking. She thought I was Brad Pitt's cooler brother, even though her achingly beautiful friend wasn't biting.

So at the end of my exhausting first day of lecturing, I invited Jessica and her friends to dinner. How could Jessica say no? She was married, but this was a group dinner. Completely safe and non-threatening. I was so excited to have a chance to get to know the beautiful Miss Carl better.

We all loaded into Jessica's Jeep and headed to Outback Steakhouse. As we piled into the restaurant booth, without any clever maneuvering of my own, Melissa slid in next to me. Voluntarily. I was beyond thrilled. I remember feeling like there was nowhere on Earth I would rather be, ever, than sitting next to her. It was a strange way to feel because I didn't know her yet, and, by all indications, she was totally indifferent to me. But I wanted the experience to last forever.

Most of the evening was spent answering the dozens of well-informed questions that Jessica hurled at me, extending well beyond photography and into my childhood and major life choices. At one point somebody said something funny and I playfully slapped Melissa's thigh, leaving my hand there for an extra millisecond. They say that time is relative. That millisecond swelled into a boundless eternity in which entire star systems were born and died.

We chatted about what motivates a person to do things in their lives. I promulgated the theory that it's your values that determine your destiny. For example, my three most important values at the time were: (1) freedom, (2) change, and (3) learning. The young ladies asked me about relationships and I replied that I didn't have one nor did I want one because, referring to my above list, long-term relationships were not conducive to any of the things I valued most.

After five years of suffocation with my second ex, it was no mystery why I ranked freedom number one. Following my divorce, freedom tasted incredibly fresh and delectable. I could go to Home Depot and buy a hammer any time I wanted, without answering twenty questions. Simple decisions like where to go for dinner no longer required a board meeting. I was on nobody's timeline but my own. If I felt like seeing the Great Wall of China tomorrow, I could hop on a plane and go. I had decided to safeguard that freedom (and protect myself from pain) by making myself completely unavailable. I had erected a huge emotional wall around myself, guarded by armed sentinels.

But something about Melissa was sneaking through my defensive perimeter. The Great Wall of China I had built around my heart was suddenly crumbling. It was troubling, unexpected, and damned exciting.

On the second day of class I pulled out the most stylish clothes I could find: a pair of cool distressed jeans and a fairly decent long-sleeved shirt. I still didn't have any contact lenses with me, but I did put on a perfectly weathered baseball cap. I was ready for the big moment.

It came during one of the breaks. Everybody was running to the restroom, and Melissa and I suddenly found ourselves alone together, without the nonstop chatter of Jessica as a buffer. I was not going to let this "Barbra Streisand" moment slip away.

Before she got a chance to say anything, I blurted out what had been festering in my tiny mind: "You seem so familiar to me. Do I seem familiar to you?" It was an honest question, but, phrased so baldly, it sounded like something that would pop out of a drunken insurance salesman's mouth during Happy Hour at T.G.I. Friday's.

Her eyes quickly scanned the room for the exit. "Um, no," she responded. "Hey, by the way, if I were to get some lenses for my camera, what would you recommend?"

Bam! Door slammed. We were on to lens recommendations.

Class resumed a few minutes later. I still had an eager audience in Jessica, who would perk up whenever I looked in her general direction. So I figured I would maintain eye contact with Jessica in hopes that she would convey to her mysterious friend how cool and smart and funny I was.

Finally, when class ended, my three female dinner-mates hung around to talk to me. I suggested photographing Melissa the next day around downtown Cincinnati (for her website), but she didn't have a place to stay because they had already checked out of their room. At this point I unleashed smooth move number two. I said, "I have an extra bed in my room."

"Uh, gotta go!" And off they went.

Later, I would learn that they hung around in the parking lot for ages talking about how disappointed they were that I turned out to be such a pervy creep.

Time to fire a couple of those sentinels and repair the Great Wall.

chapter ten

Pre-Visualization

I have a technique I call "20/20 Foresight™." It's a pre-visualization technique that I developed while zoning out in the early stages of Zen training. You close your eyes and imagine something you want to have but don't have yet. You see it in all its details, and you make it as virtually real as possible. I remember once, as a kid, imagining myself in a coin-op Laundromat, walking through the entrance and *actually reading* the business cards and ads thumb-tacked to the corkboard.

I never said I was very ambitious.

The more I practiced the technique, the better I got at it. And the amazing thing is, I think this is the reason my life has this fantasy-like quality. It's because I trained myself to daydream with discipline.

I used to do mental tricks a lot when I was poor, because there was nothing else to do while sitting in the van at the swap meet after the TV batteries ran out. I'd daydream about things I wanted as if they were right in front of me. I could see them, feel them, and smell them. My sense of "virtual smell" was sharpened to a razor's edge by having to tune out the unrelenting smell of hair spray and gas fumes for years.

There is a difference between setting goals and pre-visualization. Setting goals is desiring an outcome and making happiness contingent on those expectations being met. Pre-visualizing is picturing a situation vividly in all of its sensory detail. This rehearses your mind so that there are no surprises.

I've always known that surprises are a part of life, so I've made it my habit to prepare for them. Whether it is sleeping under the stairs to simulate homelessness or designing a remote-controlled gun setup at a wig store, by pre-visualizing vividly, I'm able to be more prepared for any situation. That situation can be a disaster or a full-blown miracle. Either way, my little exercise gets me ready.

The Lake House

The town of Kelowna is about five hours east of Vancouver in British Columbia, directly above Spokane, Washington. The best way to describe this town is as a mix between Lake Tahoe and the Napa Valley. There is a gorgeous eighty-eight-mile-long lake, Lake Okanagan, complete with its own version of the Loch Ness monster. There are world-class wineries and championship golf courses. And it's all set within a beautifully arid, temperate climate that offers all four seasons (the best of which is April, when you can ski in the morning, then golf in the afternoon).

I accidentally visited Kelowna's Big White Ski Resort one time while browsing for a mountain with exceptional snow, after having been disappointed in the conditions at Vail in Colorado. That first short weekend trip turned into a multi-week trip, and I ended up purchasing two ski chalets at Big White. There was one that I really wanted, but it had been sold, so I bought a different one that I liked. Then the first one fell out of escrow, and it was too nice, and too good of a deal, to let it go. I couldn't help it—they were just too good to pass up. That was as far as my analysis and due diligence had gone. After winning the lawsuit and purchasing a residence in the village hotel, eventually I would have four properties on the ski resort, but I still had absolutely no idea what that spectacular lake at the bottom of the ski hill was all about.

One day I found out, when my friend Peter took me boating on Lake Okanagan. My mouth gaped at the warm blasts of 83-degree air as we flew around the glassy waters on his speedboat. A full tank wasn't enough to get us to the other side—that's how large this lake is—so we just went around in circles, slicing through the turquoise blue waters and marveling at the view.

One day I was sitting in my ski chalet at Big White, talking to my friend Kristen. I said, "I love this home, but I sure wish it was on the lake." From that moment on I was locked in on a lakefront home. Just like when I was a kid, I would close my eyes and daydream, pretending I could look out the window at the sparkling lake spreading as far as the eye could see. No buildings between the water and me. I made it real in my mind.

I have always found that if you imagine something to be true, it winds up happening because you start shifting your attention in that direction. I started cruising the internet for lakefront homes. Before long I found this beautiful, super-modern house right on the lake, in the same town where my ski properties were.

I contacted the owner. He was asking $495,000 Canadian dollars, which I thought was amazing at the time. The US dollar was worth around 1.6 Canadian dollars then, so $495,000 actually worked out to be $350,000.

I have three rules when it comes to investing in real estate.

Number one: It has to be a good deal. If I get a really good deal, then the property can go down in value and I still won't lose anything.

Number two: It needs to be cash-flow positive. I always try to make sure that anything I buy will have a way to pay its own expenses. It doesn't always work that way, but that's the goal.

Number three: The investment has to be small in the grand scheme of things. I don't want to put everything I own into a particular investment, because if it goes bad I'll be screwed. If I make a relatively small investment and it doesn't work out, hey, at least I'll be okay overall.

I knew that if I snagged a modern beach house for a really low price, then I could rent it out as a vacation rental. It would satisfy my three rules.

I called the owner and, wanting to maximize rule number one, asked him if he would take $395,000 rather than $495,000. He said, "Oh, wow. I'm going to have to ask my wife." Typically I come in with an offer that's quite a bit lower than the asking price. That's not to insult anyone or make them angry, it's just to find out how motivated they are to sell. When buying real estate I usually say, "I can do a cash deal right away, but will you take ____?" Usually the answer is no, but with my Marina City Club condo, for example, it was yes. I got an incredible deal on that one just because I asked.

So I asked the lake-house owner if he would take $395,000. He said, "No, but I will take $450,000, and I'll include all of the furniture and the pontoon boat." I thought that was an amazing deal because to furnish the place would have cost $50,000 and the pontoon boat was worth around $20,000. He'd actually made me a better counter-offer than what I had offered him! I said, "Okay, I'll take it."

There was a moment's pause and he said, "Excuse me?"

the beach house at Woodlake. I bought this house sight-unseen, having found it on the internet

I said, "It's a fair deal. I'll take it. I'll fly up with the funds and we'll close."

He was surprised but happy to go along with me. What I learned later was that his wife thought the offer was way too low. He also didn't tell me that he had listed the place with a real estate agent. (I had found the listing on an online classified ad site.) Because a real estate agent had the listing, he was obligated to pay the realtor a 6 percent commission. The whole thing became a mess and he said, "I'm sorry but the real estate agent said no."

I said, "Well, actually, you made the deal over the phone and I flew up the next day based on that." I wound up having to sue the seller to force him to honor his verbal contract. The real estate agency got their 6 percent and I got the lake house for about $300,000 US dollars.

This place looks like a Malibu beach house—all open windows with an unobstructed view down the length of the lake. The first thing I did was take a cruise all the way around in the pontoon boat. It was like having my own private lake.

Border Blues

The fireplace at Woodlake had a perfect place to put a flat-panel TV . . . but there were no flat-panel TVs in Canada at the time. They were only available in the United States, and for me to ship it into Canada would have been really expensive. So I had my Canadian assistant fly down to Los Angeles with me. We bought the flat-panel TV along with a Tempur-Pedic mattress, another thing you couldn't get in Canada at the time. We loaded up my Range Rover and headed for my new home in Canada. When we got to the border, after thirty-five hours of driving and a stay in a really seedy hotel, I was in an epic bad mood. The excessively cheery border folks said, "Hi. What are you do-ing in Canada—staying or visiting?"

"Visiting," I replied. "I'm going to Kelowna to move into my new house."

"You're going to move into a house in Canada and yet you're just visiting?" Still cheery.

I said, "No, no. I'm not going to move in move in. I'm just fur-nishing it."

"You own a house in Canada?"

"No. Actually I own four."

They said, "You own four houses in Canada?" Less cheery now. "What do you do?"

I didn't know what to say, so I went out on a limb and opted for the truth. "I'm a wedding photographer." Big mistake.

"How long are you planning on staying in Canada?" Not at all cheery now.

"A month."

"You're a wedding photographer? Do you realize that this is the month of June?" I said I did. "Do you have any weddings to shoot in June?" I said I didn't. They said, "Yet you can support yourself for thirty days without having a job?"

Then I did an unfortunate thing. I started to laugh. On top of that, because I was in a really foul mood, I said something smug. I said, "I could support myself forever."

They said something equally smug in return: "Come with us, sir."

I had to go into the office where this young immigration officer who clearly saw me as a major notch on his career pistol grilled me like a portobello mushroom. He said, "I don't know why you're saying you're a wedding photographer when you have a new Range Rover, a flat-panel TV, an expensive mattress, and four homes in Kelowna. I don't know why you're saying you're a wedding photographer when you're spending the entire month of June in Canada. I don't know why you're saying you're a wedding photographer . . . " Suddenly I was back in my first Mercedes again, being pulled over by the L.A. cops at every third red light.

The Canadian border patrol suspected I was a drug dealer, too. Sigh. I was never going to tell the truth about my career again.

The next thing I knew, dogs were sniffing wildly through my car. The officers took everything out, disassembled the back seat, the trunk, all of the side and floor panels. They were obviously experienced at this. Or at least very thorough. They had these power screwdrivers that were super fast, and before I knew it my car looked like a swap meet, with all its parts on display.

Eddie Murphy once had this bit where he said he got pulled over by cops and they were so certain that he had stolen his own car that after a while he began to believe it as well. I was questioned with such intensity and skepticism by the border patrol that for a moment I was even wondering if I was telling the truth.

Finally, after reassembling my vehicle, they said to me, "There are no drugs in your car."

"I know that," I replied as pleasantly as I could.

"But your story sounds very fishy to us. We need to see proof that you can support yourself for thirty days in Canada without working."

I had to drive back a couple of hours, nearly to Seattle, in my incredibly bad mood, find a Kinko's, and fax the border guys a bank statement that showed I had sufficient funds in the bank. Then I had to drive all the way back to Canada. Only then did they let me cross the border.

Because they put me down as "turned back at the border," for the next two years, every time I went to Canada, I was detained at the border and interviewed.

All for the crime of being a wedding photographer.

How I Accidentally Created a Multimillion-Dollar Plastics Enterprise

One day I was on a Horizon Air flight from Seattle to Kelowna when my life took another left turn.

My flight to Kelowna was unremarkable except for one extremely thrilling event: the in-flight magazine had changed. Yay! Trust me, when you fly as often as I do, you learn to appreciate the small things: A new brand of peanut. A new style of European breakfast cookie. And most of all, a crisp new in-flight magazine, unsullied by dozens of faceless travelers' palm-prints.

There it sat in the seat pocket: pages un-smudged, corners un-trammeled, crossword puzzle undone. I tore into my virginal literary adventure with an elevated heart rate.

The first thing that caught my eye was an ad for a plastics man-ufacturer, proclaiming: "We make plastic parts out of your idea!" O-o-o-kay. Now, I can understand ads for top ten steakhouses, or destination resorts, or airport shuttles, but a plastics manufacturer? Advertising in an airline magazine? How many people, on an aver-age day, climb aboard a jetliner tortured by the dilemma, "I have this amazing new idea—if only I could find someone to make a plastic part out of it"?

It seemed about as cogent a marketing strategy as selling industrial real estate at a flea market. My first thought was, "Good luck finding customers this way, buddy."

But then I started getting crazy ideas. The more I thought about it, the sillier my thoughts became. Maybe I should make a plastic model of my hand! Or my foot! Or my elbow! Yes, that's it, I will have a mold made of my elbow, and then I will have a plastic elbow! Hey, they said they'd make plastic parts out of any idea. Weird thoughts invaded my mind, one after another. How about the idea of personal liberty? We could make a plastic mold of that. Or maybe a vomit spill? No wait, someone had already done that.

Then it dawned on me. I should invent the light bulb.

Or at least re-invent it.

See, I had been selling a plastic light diffuser to photographers for a few years now. It had been selling very well, even though it left a lot to be desired. Maybe the time had come to make myself a brand-new toy.

What is a light diffuser? Well, let me explain a couple of things about flash lighting.

In photography, there is a gloriously uninteresting maxim that proclaims: "The specularity of the lighting is in inverse proportion to the size of the light source, particularly at close distances." What does that mean? It means that if you are using a flash, the larger the light source, the less "specular," or harsh, the lighting is. This is why when you see a photo shoot with professional photographers, you'll often see large white umbrellas bouncing the light from the flash strobes. It's a technique for diffusing light.

In digital photography, the need for soft lighting is essential. Digital photography tends to be very contrast-y. A typical flash unit has a little parabolic reflector that shines on the subject with the same effect as pointing a flashlight at a person in the dark. (It gives you that "deer in the headlights" look so cherished in high-end portraiture.)

As a professional photographer, therefore, I avoided flash whenever possible. If I did have to rely on flash, I would try to soften it using any diffuser on the market. All of them were too small and too short.

So, a few years back, I'd decided to market my own. I asked the manufacturer if he could make an extended "tab" to give the light source much more height than the standard model. Having the flash source higher above the camera lens reduces red-eye and gives a much more flattering jaw-line.

I sold a lot of my product. As soon as I announced it on my website, we got over a thousand orders. I had to fly my assistant Nicole down from Canada to bring my dad out of retirement, and we started shipping boxes in my L.A. condo in a wave of madness.

But I was far from satisfied with it. It didn't have a removable top, so you couldn't change the ratio of flash to the ceiling. Plus, I wanted a diffuser that was much larger and completely round so that it would radiate light in a spherical pattern (i.e., "Lightsphere II®").

Nobody made a larger model. The manufacturer I spoke to, one of the leading flash attachment brands at the time, said, "Maybe next year." He explained that the mold for a large diffuser would be too expensive. I must have bugged him for two years running to make this diffuser—I didn't even want a royalty on it, I just thought it was something cool that needed to be made.

"Hey, how's it going on that large diffuser?"

"Maybe next year." I'd heard that phrase constantly growing up, and I was sick of hearing it.

So, spurred by that absurd in-flight ad—"We make plastic parts out of your idea!"—I looked into the possibilities. I learned that there was a new technology in plastic mold-making that was just about as revolutionary to manufacturing as desktop publishing was to the printing business. Using sophisticated CAD software, you could simply give some rough drawings to a CAD engineer, and this dude could quickly work up a virtual model,

the first day after I announced the Lightsphere II on my blog, we had 300 orders to fulfill right away

then basically sit back in his chair, click "print," and a mold would be cut. Presto! Done. At a fraction of the cost of the old technology.

So, with my new idea and about $16,000 that I was willing to risk, I decided to make a prototype.

I really just wanted to make one for myself, so the original Lightsphere II was made for one camera flash only, the one I happened to be using at the time. I figured if I could get the mold costs back from selling other copies, I'd have myself a free flash diffuser. I never dreamed I would sell millions of dollars' worth of this thing!

The prototype was sent to me from the factory. The first Lightsphere II actually did look like a light bulb. Well, in truth, it looked like a penis. So much so, it got the nickname "The Fong Dong." (If I'd known "my" private parts were going to be immortalized this way, I would have made a slightly more flattering design.) When I tested the Lightsphere II, I was delighted. It worked! It made the flash look like available light! The goofy mental hiccup I'd gotten on a plane had given birth to something useful! Once again, my spectacular lack of forethought was bearing fruit where careful business planning could not.

We played around with different colorants and found one that made flesh tones look beautiful. We knew we had something that photographers would want.

I began expanding my model line to fit lots of different flashes. I've now sold hundreds of thousands of Lightspheres. I could live comfortably for the rest of my life on the profits from this one business alone.

But come on, what fun would that be? There are entire new industries to screw up.

The Rotation

The year after I met Melissa, I went through what she calls my "rotation" period. I had a bunch of fun friends whom I traveled with, mostly females who had careers (such as flight attendant or self-employed photographer) that allowed them to just hop on a plane and show up at some fun destination. I was truthful and honest and told them that I was not looking for a soul mate, just warm friendship, a lot of laughs, and adventures in faraway places.

I started to get lonely again.

So I began dating my assistant Dominique. She was an articulate, well-read, engaging, and socially alert person who spoke three languages and had lived abroad. Of course, being an actress in her thirties, she was also . . . er, *concerned* about any changes in her physical appearance, and made great efforts to stay slim, fit, and youthful-looking.

There is a fine line, I've discovered, between healthy concern and pathological obsession.

When we traveled to Venice, the extent of her self-preservation rituals became startlingly clear. It began by covering herself with gigantic hats, oversized shirts, Elton John–sized sunglasses, and SPF 300 sun-block. She would then carefully chart a walking course for herself that led only through caves, wine cellars, and catacombs, in order to avoid direct sunlight. I'd be sitting in a breathtaking infinity pool overlooking the sea, and she'd be crouching in the shade, covered from head to toe in cloth and chemicals, reading a magazine and smiling at me.

She was not only afraid of the sun, she was also afraid of fried food, refined sugars, fats, cholesterol, carbohydrates, and pretty much everything else that wasn't romaine lettuce. So we would go through this maddening routine of hopping from restaurant to restaurant through Europe, trying to find the one with the "healthiest" menu. Have you ever tried to find a restaurant in France that doesn't cook with butter? It makes for a fun afternoon, let me tell you. Almost as amusing as stabbing yourself in the eye, over and over, with a fork.

One evening she ordered fish and asked for extra napkins. The napkins were for blotting all of the cooking oil that had somehow gotten onto the fish during the frying process. She went through this entire thick stack of paper, dabbing both sides of the fish repeatedly until she was left with a bland, white, flavorless piece of protein. Ah, European cuisine!

When I looked at her strangely, she said, "Who wants to drink a cup of oil?" Well, when you put it that way . . .

The final insult came when we were in Spain and she ordered a salad. Knowing that she hated onions (and tomatoes and peppers and bacon and croutons and . . .), I reached over to pluck a little onion slice for my very own. She blew a gasket and slapped my hand—hard. She shrieked, "Your hands are filthy! Don't touch my food!" Everyone turned to look.

In a blazing montage I flashed back on all the little rituals I had tried to ignore throughout the trip. The sun-block indoors. The constant shading of her head with a travel map. The wild swishing and gargling with lukewarm water right after eating. The flossing at the dinner table, propelling bits of chewed food all over the place. This was not just a *Seinfeld*-esque realization. This woman was terrified of everything! Cavities, weight gain, sun exposure, germs. I was with somebody who was seriously obsessive-compulsive, and I no longer wished to be. So I told her that when we returned to the States, we would be finished.

When we got back to California and to my condo in Marina del Rey, I expected an awkward goodbye, like the scene with the party planner before she walked through my screen door. But Dominique began getting ready for bed.

"Umm . . . aren't you going home?" I asked.

"No, it's far too late for me to drive. I'm staying here."

So I said okay and told her that she could stay in the condo and I would sleep in my sailboat in the harbor. The next morning I expected her to be gone. She would still work for me, of course, but I expected her to vacate my condo and do her internet work from her own place from now on.

How wrong I was! Late morning came, which turned into early afternoon, and she was still there, comfortably spread out as if everything were the same. I finally left to run some errands, too exhausted to engage in a confrontation.

One of the things I love most about my condo in Marina del Rey is the floor-to-ceiling view of the Pacific Ocean from Venice to Malibu to the west, and the Hollywood sign to the east. A panoramic, unobstructed view.

Except when the place is occupied by a solarphobe. Dominique had once told another of my assistants, Leslie, that she had experienced third-degree burns on her legs despite wearing jeans. Apparently sunlight had snuck through the window of her car and scorched her between the threads of her Levis.

Dominique kept coming to my Marina condo to work, laden with more and more sun protection every day. One day I came home to my condo to find all the shades drawn across the big window, with newspapers taped to the sides to block any leakage of light through the cracks. Dominique was wearing aluminum foil on her legs and arms, along with sunglasses and a hat. *Indoors*. She looked like something from the souvenir shop at Roswell.

I stopped speaking to her at this point, because, after all, what do you say to someone attired in Reynolds Wrap? Our silent charade lasted quite a while. We never spoke on the phone, only through e-mail. One day I had to take a trip. She was doing valuable work on my e-store, so I left the situation alone as I headed off to my lake house in Canada.

I had met a photographer named Kelly. We were good friends, and sometimes she would travel with me. She was a makeup artist as well, so I hired her to do a national ad campaign shoot. Since we had been to Europe together, though we weren't a sexual couple, we were comfortable sharing a bed. So I emailed Dominique and said that even though I usually slept on the sailboat, my friend was coming into town and we were going to be staying in the condo, so could she please go back to her place in Hollywood?

Dominique kept referring to Kelly as "it"—as if confused by her unisex name. Which had the intended effect of pissing me off. Finally I said, "Kelly is a she, and we are staying in the condo together, so please make yourself scarce."

"Fine, I know how to take a hint," she said.

I didn't realize I had been hinting.

Kelly and I arrived at the condo and out strutted Dominique, made up like a *Cosmo* cover, wearing just-stepped-out-of-a-salon hair, nano-shorts, high heels, and body makeup to make her appear more tan. She was bounding along in large strides, speaking German on the phone, and laughing loudly. Apparently her witty German friend had a crush on her, and she was gently letting him down.

She hung up and gave Kelly the super-courteous ladies-who-lunch greeting, asking all the proper questions and exuding enough sweetness to give the entire 90295 zip code tooth decay. I half-expected the phone to ring, so that she could launch into a one-sided conversation in French. It was a performance worthy of the stage (the dinner theater stage), including the dramatic makeup and the large gestures. When Dominique left for her hot "date," Kelly looked at me and said, "Oh my God, that poor girl . . ."

I once heard a quote by singer/songwriter John Mayer: "Sometimes the relationship you're in is training for the real deal."

My Dominique experience made me *really* give up on the idea of having a woman in my life. I decided I liked who I was. I was okay with the fact that I liked cooking oil on my fish. I didn't need to floss after every bite, and I loved to lie in the sun. All of these *Is* made me realize that I treasured my independence and alone-time way too much to share my life with someone else permanently.

So I rededicated myself to staying permanently single and carefree.

Melissa and I reconnected when Dominique and I broke up. She called with a tech support question about some of my software, and we began to stay in touch through MSN Messenger, emails, and phone calls. I would tell her my crazy single-guy stories, and she would tell me her dating nightmares. Her sense of humor was refreshing and adorably blunt. Since we had given up on trying to impress each other, we began to really enjoy chatting. She had an uncanny memory. She could recall every detail of every story I told her, plus she followed my blog, so she knew what I was doing on a daily basis and seemed vicariously involved in my life.

When I was in Nice, photographing the large river rocks, I posted one of the images online and she begged me to bring that rock to her, "because it was so pretty." Hmmm—did that mean maybe I would be seeing her again?

When I got back to North America, I still had my rotation of female friends who would visit my lake house for a few days or come to one of the ski chalets. Online I'd post snaps of me and whoever I was with. Everybody knew about everybody else, and everybody was okay with it. Melissa thought I was going through some weird phase, but she didn't judge me because she wasn't interested in me in that way.

So, as friends, we would talk daily on the phone. Not too much—just, you know, four or five hours a day. She was funny, and her girly laugh would always make me laugh too.

Little did I know, the rotation was about to come to an end.

Something About New York City

Melissa and I started hinting back and forth about seeing each other in person. We considered meeting in Marina del Rey, but that was a long trip for a girl who had only been on a plane a handful of times. Since I was planning on speaking in New York at an upcoming convention, we agreed that seeing each other in the Big Apple would be a great opportunity.

She had never flown by herself, nor had she ever been to New York City. While she was excited (and nervous) to see me in person, she told nobody about her plans except her mom. She just wasn't ready to confess to friends and family that she was flying to New York to meet a dude eighteen years her senior.

Her mom took her to the Akron/Canton airport, and with her newly purchased bright red suitcase in tow, Melissa departed her hometown (of "Football Hall of Fame" fame) for the big city. While her mom had some trepidation, she knew that her twenty-five-year-old daughter had a great head on her shoulders. She waved her daughter off at the airport, no doubt resisting the urge to stash a GPS tracking device in her luggage.

Knowing what a zoo JFK was, I sent a town car to pick her up. I directed her to go straight to baggage claim and to find the driver holding up the card with her name on it. I wanted the whole thing to be as smooth as possible, but what I didn't count on was that on the way from the airport to the hotel, gazing out the window, she would see more Asian men than she'd ever seen in her entire life growing up in Ohio.

That presented a problem when it came time to meet me in the hotel lobby. Her mind flooded with recent images of Asian men, she could no longer remember what I looked like, other than that I was Asian, wore thick glasses, and had grayish hair. That matched the description of about three dozen of the men she saw in the hotel lobby. There must have been a fortune-cookie manufacturer's convention going on that weekend or something.

She smiled at everyone. Noncommittally, but with a hint of warmth. No responses. She finally called me to get my room number, but got stopped at the elevator since she didn't have a room key.

"I'll be right down," I assured her. I rode the elevator down twenty-three stories and spotted her in the crowded lobby.

I walked up behind her and re-introduced myself. She stared first at my neck, then up at my eyes, and said, "You're taller than I remembered." Great, her lasting impression of me had been that I was short, in addition to being an emotionally stunted horn-dog.

She couldn't get over our age difference, and it really consumed her mind throughout our first lunch date. She was self-conscious about how we looked together, not realizing that such a thing is commonplace in New York City.

For lunch, I selected my favorite sushi place in New York. My favorite little morsel on the sushi menu is a fine set of sea urchin gonads. Known on the menu as *uni*, sea urchin genitalia is what one might call an acquired taste. It has the rich, gooey texture of egg yolk. Not very fishy, maybe a little gritty. And sometimes there's this chewy membrane and a slight vinyl taste. But that's all part of the culinary adventure! I've heard some say that *uni* resembles a tiny teaspoon of barf. Despite the critics, I love the stuff. Puts hair on a man's chest.

In restaurants, they put it on a little bed of rice and wrap it in yummy roasted seaweed paper.

"What's that?" Melissa asked, pointing at the urchin on my plate. (I hadn't dared order it for her because the sushi menu had an asterisk next it denoting the item as "challenging.") Unfortunately, the only language I had to describe *uni* to her consisted of *words*. And there just aren't any words on Earth, in any combination, that can make *uni* sound like something you would want to place in your mouth.

"Nasty," she said. I had to admit, that had a certain poetry.

For her, I had the waiter bring that definitive selection for all sushi virgins: the California roll. I guess naming it after the most All-American–sounding of states makes it more appealing to people not sure about eating uncooked wildlife from the bottom of Tokyo Harbor.

She stared at it. "What's this black stuff?" she asked, referring to the seaweed. "Is it the same as what's on your dish?"

There are no subtle ways to say yes, so I went with the direct route.

Her response: "I'll *never* eat that stuff!" Then I heard her murmuring something about wishing she'd brought a sack lunch. (Years later, the "Crispy/Crispy" Roll at Momo's Sushi Bar in Kelowna is her favorite thing to eat in the whole world—there is a happy ending to this story.)

And so, on an empty stomach, we left the restaurant to explore New York City.

Melissa found New York to be rather a culture shock compared to the family farm in Minerva, Ohio. Though a few years later we would find ourselves clopping around Manhattan in a horse-driven carriage, snuggling cozily under a warm blanket as we gazed in wonder at the shops and lights, initially New York proved to be about as inviting to her as a 3:00 A.M. carjacking.

Walking around Times Square, we passed Madame Tussaud's Wax Museum. I pointed it out to her and suggested it as a good place to visit. No interest. (Months later, during a visit to Las Vegas, we found ourselves in front of a wax museum again. This time there was a vaguely creepy replica of Princess Diana guarding the front entrance. Suddenly Melissa blurted out, "Oh!" This was an epiphany—she'd always thought a wax museum was a place where you saw science exhibits on honeybees. That's why she had been so quick to pass on Madame Tussaud's in New York. We joined Princess Di inside and had a great time.)

Recalling the first New York trip, Melissa describes herself as shell-shocked, disoriented, and homesick. We were not emotionally close enough for me to comfort her—or to cuddle with her as we always do now. She felt terribly alone and out of sorts and was eager to return home.

We both went home and I feared that I'd never hear from her again.

Pretty soon, though, intermittent text messages started coming through on my cell phone. "Hey I got a speeding ticket." "Hey did you see Denis on *The Today Show*?" One day I was in Denver giving one of my classes. It was the after lunch break on the second day and I was exhausted. It's always hard to rev up after lunch. I was thinking I'd better put my game face on when, right on cue, a text message appeared on my screen.

"You are not truly free—ha ha!"

I laughed out loud and texted back: "I'll call you after class."

We started talking again, and laughing. She was so proud of her timing, and for throwing in my face that the top item on my value list, freedom, was not really true all the time. Because I had at least another half day of focused work to do, I couldn't just up and leave, and for that reason I wasn't truly free. She was right!

We were back to our six-hour phone calls, sometimes talking until the sun rose on the West Coast. I was traveling a lot at the time, and would figure my sleeping schedule around Akron/Canton's Eastern Standard Time so I could get my daily fix of the Carl Daily News.

With a little bit of my advice and a lot of encouragement, Melissa started her own successful photography business, and within a short time she was watching the numbers build in her first savings account. I became her biggest fan, and loved hearing about how great her referral business was growing in her home town.

One night (chiming in from Ohio on Instant Messenger to me in France), she said, "There's a movie you *have to* see—it is so you!" The movie was *The Family Man* with Nicolas Cage. In the movie, the lead character gets a glimpse of his life in a parallel universe, where he had made the choice of love over a career. He sees that if he had made the love decision, it would have led him to an anonymous-seeming but happy domestic life raising kids in the 'burbs, whereas the career decision he actually made had rewarded him with a fancy New York apartment, a screaming red Ferrari, and a walk-in closet filled with custom-tailored suits.

Melissa has this voodoo way of making me see things her way. I used to joke that she had some kind of "girly Jedi mind-control technique," because the more we talked, the more I would start seeing things her way. I once joked that someday I would wake up wondering what I was doing running an orphanage in Uganda. So I watched the movie.

She asked me what I thought of it, and I said, "I just loved his apartment, the walk-in closet, and the Ferrari. Is that why you wanted me to see the movie?" She said no, she saw me more in the domestic story. She even went so far as to suggest that the entire point of the movie was that the flashy single guy discovers that he feels empty because he doesn't have the loving wife and kids. I don't know what movie *she* was watching.

"Never!" I proclaimed.

When she first met me at that workshop in Ohio, her overall impression of me had been that something was missing. Not mentally—she didn't mean I was one tater tot short of a Fisherman's Combo. She meant that my infomercial-like enthusiasm when I described myself as "so happy being single" made her a bit skeptical. She didn't suggest that she knew what the missing link to my happiness was, she just thought something was lacking in my life.

She knew about my eccentric bachelor/renegade/commitment-phobic bravado and chuckled about it. She knew my ideal day was waking up alone in the harbor in my sailboat, with the Sunday paper strewn all about my bedroom. She knew I loved my Porsche, a car that had no room for a child seat.

Well, on my next birthday, I told her I wasn't celebrating because I was feeling pretty lonely. Though a few friends and my assistant Nicole came over, that birthday felt empty. I began to realize that the person I was really lonely for was Melissa.

Melissa kept insisting that I go out and do something. I said I didn't feel like it, and she said, "If I were there, I'd drag you out of the house. I don't know what we would do next, but I would drag you out." I pictured her with a playful smile, both of her hands wrapped around my forearm, dragging me out of my chalet with her beautiful brunette hair bouncing.

I took her up on the offer and had her meet me up at my hotel suite at the Big White Ski Resort. I explained to her in full disclosure that my place had only one bed, and that the other chalets were all rented out.

She said, "Well, just stay on your side of the bed and there won't be any problems."

Big White Ski Resort Village

When we got to the resort, everything had returned to normal with us. We were great at communicating by phone, and we clearly had feelings for each other, but what was untested was how that would play out in person.

To my enormous delight, it actually worked this time. In fact, we didn't leave the room for five whole days—laughing, cuddling, napping, sharing.

One of the things I love about owning a residence within a hotel is the room service. I knew the waitresses, and they knew that I always left the door unlocked in the morning so they could just come right in and put breakfast on the counter and quietly leave. They're incredibly good at spoiling the guests, and they all knew my breakfast ritual.

They also knew that I had a rotation.

So when they delivered breakfast to our room, with Melissa being the newest (and now permanent) guest in the bed, the servers quietly brought the food to the kitchen counter and discreetly left. There was kind of a "What happens in Vegas, stays in Vegas" feeling about the whole situation. *No need to explain, Mr. Fong.*

"I wonder if they think we're all stupid," Melissa mused.

Say again?

"They always deliver breakfast, right? And you have different girls here, right? I wonder if they think we don't know about each other, that you're playing all of us for fools."

Good question!

By the fifth day of not leaving the room, things started to get a little claustrophobic and we got into a little tiff over something minor. It was our first disagreement in person, and we didn't know how to handle it. Melissa and I (now) agree that during a dispute there has to be a "safe" forum whereby each partner can discuss the issue free of interruptions or distractions. These days, we will convene a "family meeting" (though it's just the two of us for now, we're in training for a brood). But back then, we reverted to our most comfortable way of arguing. We opened our laptops and started Instant Messaging each other.

We were sitting so close that we could hear each other's messages chiming on our buddy windows.

Once we got it all out, we felt better. We were respectful of each other's feelings, we were receptive to what we heard, and we made each other feel safe saying it. I don't know if I taught her this or she taught it to me, but I sure am glad we can do this. It makes all the difference.

I wrapped my arms around her and the two of us spooned in the most entwined way that two people can without the involvement of Jell-O. I felt her feet rubbing the tops of mine, and our fingers interlaced as we gazed out at the magnificent view, watching the skiers racing toward us. My heart began to cover with velvet.

We became a couple. And we became as inseparable as two people can be while living in separate countries. Seeing each other always meant a flight, but we still managed to do it a lot. Her socks filled one of my sock drawers. Every morning became breakfast, newspapers, and laughter.

One evening, on our way to a hockey game in Kelowna, I held her hand. And she held mine back. And whatever it was that she'd known I was missing just clicked into place. That "something missing," unbeknownst to either of us when we first met, had been her.

I had been in love with her for a while, but there was also the matter of the impenetrable shield I'd built to protect myself. As I've no doubt made abundantly clear, I am all about self-preservation (e.g., my childhood Declaration of Independence, my Desert Survival Kit, my radiation-suit, etc.). Puncturing my rapture of goofy love was this looming fear of getting hurt. So it took me a little while to say those three little words.

We were in the spectacular pool at the Grand Wailea resort in Maui, next to a roaring waterfall, and I was ensconced in a book. She was teasing me because I speed-read, making sound effects to accompany my rapidly darting eyes. "Zoop! Zoop!" I would grin back and keep reading. She wanted more attention from me.

As I continued reading, Melissa began swimming laps back and forth in front of me, like a target in a shooting arcade. Then a great pair of legs went hand-standing past my eyes. She dangled her upside-down feet just past the view of my captivating book. She was feeling a little ignored, and this was her way of attracting my attention. I laughed because it was adorable.

I was laughing so hard she could hear my laughter underwater.

When she surfaced, the words came flying out of my mouth: "I love you."

Her reply? "You're so cute."

Ouch.

Later she explained that though she knew that she loved me too, it took her another eight months to be ready to say it. Melissa doesn't say things she doesn't absolutely mean, and it took her that long to be totally sure that her feelings were real.

Abandoning Ship

Once I deserted her on a sinking ship, yet we still managed to survive as a couple.

We were in my speedboat, in a boat lock. A lock is like a water elevator for boats. The Panama Canal is a series of boat locks. You go in, they raise or lower the water level, then they open a retractable seawall so you can enter the lake or marina at a different level.

On this particular trip, we were going down. Lowering the water level takes about five minutes, and meanwhile, you have to grab on to something to keep from banging into the other boats in the lock. My job was to work the motor, hers was to hang on to a rail for as long as possible. But then she got one of history's most inspired ideas: She decided to tie the nose of the boat to the rail.

Even if you've only seen a few *Looney Tunes* episodes, you can picture what happened next. As the water went down, the nose of the boat started to tip upward toward the sky. Soon a crowd formed. The nylon rope got so tight that she couldn't untie it. Helpful Canadians could be heard shouting things like, "Oh boy, they're in a pickle, 'ey?"

Finally someone said something that had survival value: "Does anyone have a knife?!"

With the boat nose now nearly straight up, looking like a missile ready to launch, I bailed. I jumped out onto the dock, leaving her straddling the vertical boat. It probably looked bad that the captain of the boat jumped off first, but I figured I could be more help on land than at sea. Why have *two* people suspended in space, when one of them could be trying to locate a knife? Also, wouldn't my presence on the boat make it heavier, and therefore harder to cut loose?

I had a list of excuses about why I bailed. That list has grown much longer since the actual incident.

If I were lying on a couch in a therapist's office, a potent combination of hypnosis and sodium pentothal could probably get me to admit that I was actually thinking, "Girl, you're the dumb-ass who got us into this situation, you deal with it."

Finally, somebody found a knife. Melissa shimmied down to the rear of the boat and huddled in the stern while the speedboat made a resounding crash into the water.

We had an appointment to go trail riding at a stable across the lake. It took about fifteen minutes to get there, and neither of us said a word the whole way. I would glance at her, and she would have the same look a golden retriever wears after being yelled at for eating the wedding cake. I'm sure she felt stupid enough all by herself, so I wasn't going to say anything to make her feel worse.

But finally I couldn't help it. "What the hell were you thinking?" I asked, very quietly. She burst out laughing, and so did I. She then began bearing the brunt of my endless teasing. Each time we passed the dockmaster, I would yell out, "Remember her?" and point at my beloved with a giant grin on my face. She hated it, but also loved it.

We were soul mates. And shortly thereafter, she said that she loved me too.

chapter eleven

Never Say Never

The first moment we stood on the sagging deck of the dilapidated house overlooking that spectacular lake, neither of us said anything, but we knew we had found the spot to have our wedding. We weren't even engaged yet, but we knew.

When it came to horse ranch ownership, the idea sounded about as appealing to me as owning a slaughterhouse. I just couldn't understand for the life of me why people would choose to hang out with horses, unless they were trying to win a dare or something. I thought saying "I love horses" was about as genuine as writing "I love long walks on the beach in the rain" in a dating agency questionnaire. No one likes long walks on the beach in the rain. You get soaked.

Nor, I thought, could anyone really *like* horses.

If you'd asked me for all the reasons to *not* like horses a few years ago, my list would have read like the side effects warnings in a drug ad. First of all, they smell like horseshit. Second, they draw flies. (Probably has something to do with all that horseshit.) Third, they are not at all like dogs. They don't cuddle up in your lap during *American Idol* and look into your eyes like you are the Son of God reborn. They are aloof, completely uninterested in you, and dumb as a bag of horseshoes. They are so dumb, in fact, that they can stand in a field for an entire day not doing anything, just staring at nothing. I have yet to see a horse play fetch. Or roll over on command. Or sniff

245

out a smuggled banana at international customs.

I have seen a polar bear riding a tricycle, but I don't think you could get a horse to do that.

So I've always thought that horses were the dumbest and most ridiculous "passion" one could have. Well, and collecting clown paintings. That was my opinion until I became the owner of a horse and joyfully discovered that these are the sweetest, most magnificent creatures ever created.

And I became the owner of a horse because, well, I had purchased a giant horse ranch and had no horses.

Like most things in my life, I bought the ranch on a whim. Walking through a restaurant at the ski resort, I picked up a free real estate magazine lying next to the gumball machine. I flipped through it, and something caught my eye: "Horse ranch, panoramic view, 5,500 sq ft home, 12.5 acres, $1.15 million."

I could never have imagined myself owning a horse ranch. Ever. And I never *ever* would have imagined paying seven figures for a house. I'm just way too cautious with my real estate bucks to buy a home for over a million dollars.

Needless to say, I called the realtor.

She gave me the address, and Melissa, my assistant Nicole, and I drove to the property. Those two extraordinarily persistent women had been bugging me for months to buy a ranch, and they knew I was always on the lookout for good deals in real estate. Every time they mentioned the idea of a ranch, though, I would brush them off with the same word: "Never."

With fifteen minutes to spare before we had to catch a flight, the three of us ran wildly over the property. I could hear the girls yelping from different corners—we were too excited to stay together. It's like the moment you pass through the amusement park gates as a kid. You instantly forget about the parents who brought you there and scatter like caffeinated hummingbirds.

The stupendous beauty of the view was evenly matched by the dilapidated state of the house. The land was the most incredible I had ever seen. The house was a catastrophe. They told me that it was a mess, and my response was, "Look at that view!"

Included in the house, I was told, was a $140,000 allowance to bring the place to "pre-loss condition." O-o-o-okay.

I stepped out onto the hill one last time and took in the view. This prompted me to trot out my keenest negotiation tactic. I called my realtor on my cell phone and said, "I must have this house—whatever it takes!" Yup, I made the deadly full-price offer. Take *that*, small-timer.

I won't bore you with the stupendously, astoundingly, mind-bogglingly painful frustration I experienced in turning this house into a home. I will share with you this, though—anybody who says that buying foreclosures is a good idea is probably also trying to get you to purchase a set of books and videos for an amazing low, low price. Every single negative experience you can possibly have in the foreclosure process, from pre-foreclosure to buying the mortgage to actually foreclosing on the owner, came into play in my getting the keys to the money pit.

First I bought the mortgage from the bank and was out nearly a million bucks. This step, I naturally assumed, entitled me to a set of house keys. But no. I didn't own a ranch, I only owned a mortgage! I didn't get the keys until I foreclosed on the house in court. This process took months of negotiation around the numerous Bugs Bunny–like obstacles that people who wanted more of my money kept throwing in my path.

But it wasn't until I actually *got* the house that the *really* idiotic part started. It took nineteen months (three was the estimate) and nearly $2 million in reconstruction costs to fix it up. That's *over* the purchase price. In case you're not a whiz with math, that works out to fourteen *times* the estimated $140,000 cost.

What happens is, cost overruns spread incrementally, like a tumor. Why, for instance, would I spend a ton of money on propane when I could have an environmentally conscious geothermal system, whereby they pipe the house's intravenous heating and cooling system 1,500 feet into the ground (the height of three Seattle Space Needles) to equalize it to a constant 69 degrees? It's only $200,000, and it will pay for itself in about, oh, about fifty years!

The best/worst thing was the pool. This was a property screaming for a pool. Knowing that this home would also be rented out as a wedding facility made investment decisions feel more justified. And for only five times the original estimate for a rectangular, vinyl, pre-fab pool I could get a ridiculously beautiful pool with the two infinity edges, a swim-up bar with an opposing dry bar, and a six-inch water-depth tanning bay for chaise lounges. I *could* have gotten the cheaper pool, but then I'd just want to rip it out later. Doing it now would save all that waste. By jiminy, I couldn't afford *not* to go with the infinity pool!

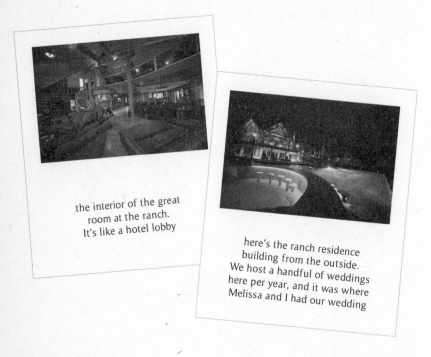

the interior of the great room at the ranch. It's like a hotel lobby

here's the ranch residence building from the outside. We host a handful of weddings here per year, and it was where Melissa and I had our wedding

See what happens? This is how you go fourteen times over budget.

Doubling your budget is scary. Tripling it is *terrifying*. Then you just stop caring. You get that look in your eye like Christopher Walken when he's aiming the pistol at his head in *The Deer Hunter*. And when the contractors tell you the quote, you find yourself covering your ears with the palms of your hands and chanting, "Blah blah blah blah blah blah" until noise stops coming out of their mouths.

This is why I call this little tale "Never Say Never." If someone had told me a few years prior that I would spend nearly $3 million to live in a freaking horse ranch, I would've said absolutely never. And now, I absolutely love it. I even get the horse thing! In fact, I've got to go feed my four-legged friends now. Weeds. They eat weeds. So I pull weeds from my garden by hand! Who would have guessed?

My Last Lap Around the Globe

One thing I loved from the start about my relationship with Melissa was that she knew and accepted every unusual thing about me.

She knew that by nature I was restless and fidgety. If two weeks went by without flying somewhere, I would get antsy. So one summer, while we were together in the Midwest, I just had to go back to France. She understood, because I usually spend two months a year there.

I met up with my friend Denis Reggie, his two kids, and his uncle in Paris. While we had a great time, Denis' kids started to observe that their "uncle" Gary was getting a little testy. I would be restless during the waking hours because I couldn't talk to Melissa (it was the middle of the night in the Midwest).

Paris got old fast. I had been there so often in the last few years, it felt like my sixteenth trip to Disneyland—it just wasn't amusing anymore. When the Reggie family returned to the states, I decided to leave for Barcelona.

I'd never been there, so I was excited. My travel agent set everything up. I was stoked to play tennis on the slow, red clay courts.

The trip was miserable. While I have often traveled alone and am comfortable doing so, I just wasn't feeling it this time. One night I was having the renowned paella at the world-famous 7 Portes restaurant and it hit me. I had traveled the world. I'd been almost everywhere, and it just wasn't for me anymore. I wanted to be home.

I knew that home would be wherever Melissa was, so I called my jeweler in New York. I was back in L.A., but since I was planning to go to Ohio to be with Melissa, and then two weeks later we were both going to Hawaii, I didn't have time to go to New York to pick out the ring in person. So I told him exactly what I wanted.

He sent it to me UPS Next Day Air. I bolted to the Mailboxes Plus store in Marina del Rey and ripped open the box to find a beautiful six-carat F-colored brilliant cut with two ¾-ct trapezoids in F color, VSI. (Yes, I knew a bit about diamonds, this being my third purchase of this kind.) I stuck the ring in my pocket and hopped on a plane toward the rest of my life.

I carried that ring inside my computer bag for two weeks, waiting for our trip to Hawaii. Hawaii was where I had taken Melissa for her twenty-sixth birthday, and it was the first place that I told her I loved her. Maui was very special to us, so I planned a perfect engagement, right on the same beach where I had spent the evening watching her prance around in the surf like a silly ballerina.

We got to the island around 7:00 P.M., which is 1:00 A.M. Ohio time. She was sleepy, but I was nervously excited because I was about to propose. And it was going to be perfect!

Next thing I knew she was in her pajamas crawling into bed. "I'm exhausted," she declared.

This was not going according to plan!

"No! Let's go for a walk on the beach!" I cheerily announced.

She looked at me doubtfully, and with some resignation said, "Okay, but if we're going to go do this now, let's get dressed up."

Bingo. She obviously knew what was going down, so there was no need for a big charade. She knew that she was too tired right now to fully appreciate the big moment of our engagement, so she'd unilaterally decided (by proxy of pajamas) to crawl into bed and continue the matter on the next, well-rested evening. But the problem was, friends were arriving the next day, and we wouldn't be alone. So it needed to be tonight.

Telling me to dress up was so classical Melissa. She wanted to remember the moment forever, and she didn't want to remember it with me wearing a tank-top and baseball cap. So I changed into something nice, and I assumed that both of us were now partners in this "surprise" unveiling of the ring.

But since I have an awful poker face, I couldn't keep up the charade.

When we got out to the beach, I said, "So, do you want to see it?"

I remember thinking it was a shame that this couldn't be more romantic. After all, we were sitting in a pair of beach loungers under a spectacular canopy of stars and a crescent moon, and the surf was washing warm foam on our feet.

"See what?" she asked.

"You know what. The ring. Do you want to see it now?"

"What ring?" was her reply.

I rolled my eyes. Very funny. Come on, must we do this? "The ring. Do you want to see it or not?"

"I don't know. Is it in your hat?" she shrugged, as if she had no idea what I was talking about.

I rolled my eyes again (like she taught me to), pulled the ring out of my pocket, and said "Here" with a note of comical resignation.

Under the moonlight I could see her mouth drop open. Her next words were not what I expected. She said, "Is this a joke?"

Getting engaged isn't usually a joke, and that ring was certainly no joke. What was I to make of a question like that? Did she think the ring was funny? I was so confused.

She kept repeating it over and over again. "Is this a joke? Wait. Is this a joke?"

At that point it dawned on me that she really didn't know. She was totally surprised. My assumption that she did know had made me turn the whole thing into an eye-rolling charade. I desperately tried to salvage whatever romance I could from the moment. I got down on my knee in the moist sand. I started to cry as I slipped the ring on her finger.

I could see that her mind was racing, thinking thoughts I couldn't imagine. So, to get my emotional bearings, I made the rather colossally inappropriate declaration: "We're engaged."

"Aren't you going to *ask* me first?" she pleaded.

Uh, yes, that would be a good first step. So I did. I asked in the most heartfelt, sincere way I could.

"Who else knows?" she yelled out.

Then her wheels started spinning again. She looked me up and down and said, "Okay, you're wearing the khaki shorts and that white shirt, I'm wearing the . . ." as if she wanted to store in her memory everything about the moment.

I said, "Aren't you going to answer me first?"

She said, "You'll have to call my father and ask for his permission."

Ohio was six hours ahead of us. We rushed back to the room and sat staring at the ring, trying to decide whether we should call her dad and wake him up or wait until a decent hour.

Finally, at breakfast, I called him. I wasn't expecting any surprises, because from the first time I'd met him, he had treated me like family. When I called, he had one question for me: "Do you love her?"

My response: "More than life itself."

With his blessings, I then asked my wonderful Melissa to be my wife. She said yes!

We hugged and kissed and held each other, taking in the beauty of the island as we shared a breakfast of pancakes and eggs.

Though I'd been married twice before, each time I'd had strong second thoughts shortly before the wedding. The first time I actually canceled it. The second time, I freaked out a few nights before.

But this time there was only a giddy sense of joy, underlain by a deep pool of inner peace. I can honestly say there was not a single moment of doubt or uncertainty about getting married to Melissa. Though I swore I would never get married again, I am absolutely in love with her. I was never in a hurry to have children, and now I can't wait.

While the proposal didn't go at all according to plan, just like my life, it wound up being perfect. So finally, on my wedding day, as I absorbed the rapture of hosting so many of my wonderful, loving friends and family at our newly finished ranch, watching the love of my life emerge through the theater doors, beaming at me with her sparkling blue, teary eyes, I lost it. I thought I'd known happiness before, but this was so overwhelming. That "something missing" that Melissa sensed when she first met me was no longer there. I was complete.

An Unexpectedly Wonderful Life

My business life today is about as atypical as the circumstances that brought me here. GFI (Gary Fong, Inc.) is a multimillion-dollar corporation with an international reach. Yet I have no office building. Instead, everybody in my organization works off of laptop computers, communicating via the internet. I have only a few employees—in

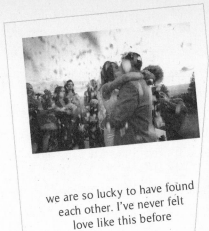

we are so lucky to have found each other. I've never felt love like this before

Melissa is my best friend, who knows me better than I know myself, my trusted advisor with sound judgment, and the most beautiful girl in the world

Washington, Ohio, Florida, and California.

Products are manufactured in Madison, Wisconsin, and loaded onto pallets to be shipped to ports worldwide. I design all of our products—by using my experience as a photographer but also by visiting camera stores and talking to fellow photographers and camera salespeople. Everybody tells me what they wish they had to help them with their photography, and I sit down with designers who use CAD software to create new designs.

Starting with the Lightsphere, I've created numerous lighting solutions for various purposes. The fold-flat Origami is a fantastic softening diffuser that fits in your pocket for travel. The Puffer is a parachute-looking device that fits in the flash-attachment shoe of a camera and softens the harsh light remarkably.

After I sketch out a new design, I fax the scribbles to my patent attorney for review. It normally takes a couple of years and costs between $50,000 and $100,000 for a utility patent, but it's a necessary expense because these little plastic pieces, left unprotected by patent law, could easily be knocked off.

Once the patent attorney begins taking steps to protect my designs, the CAD specifications go to the factory in Wisconsin for mold production. The prototypes get sent to me for testing, then we begin box design and shooting sample images of models. I also record video instruction for my websites on how to use the new products, as I've always found that having really clear, concise instructions is crucial for word-of-mouth referrals. These referrals are the lifeblood of my business; we do hardly any advertising. This is a lesson I learned from my wedding photography days—try to get the consumer to tell a friend how great the product is. To me, that's the only sure-fire guarantee of business success.

I also have my hospitality business, which offers lakefront and ski destination rentals in California, Washington, and British Columbia. I have twelve properties, plus a yacht, which is available for charter. Bookings, marketing, and reservations are all done online. The fear of having to sleep under the stairs again will never escape me, and I make it a point to try to rent out whatever assets I can, whenever I am not using them.

Our ranch has become a wedding destination, and we host about six high-end weddings per year, which, after expenses, covers the mortgage.

My staff usually meets remotely every morning via Instant Messenger. Though we're separated by thousands of miles, I would say that our team spends more time working together than any other organization I've ever run. The employees all work from their homes, including me. And for me, that home is wherever Melissa is.

We basically live in three cities: Seattle, Kelowna, and Marina del Rey. In Seattle and L.A., we live on the waterfront, and most of the time we're in California we sleep on my yacht. In Kelowna, we spend the summer at our horse ranch and the weekends at our place in the nearby Big White Ski Resort.

A typical day in what some may consider an "upscale" life is not that different from a typical day when I had less stuff. I've noticed that no matter how large your home is, you pretty much hang out in just a few key areas. The rest of the space is just used for throwing parties.

Most of my time is spent watching financial charts, reading the international news, and monitoring investment strategies. I spend an awful lot of time on Facebook, Twitter, and on my blog, which probably has more updates than any other blog I know of. I even have a little area on the left side of the web page I call the "Where I Am CAM," which uploads iPhone images from wherever I am in the world.

The website gets hundreds of thousands of hits a month from around the world, and on it I share a lot of my investment advice. Most of that advice is very traditional and non-earth-shattering. I explain that what has worked for me has been to save as much as possible, risk only small amounts that I can afford to lose, and invest very, very conservatively.

If I've discovered anything, it's that each day is perfect if there is no true agenda. Both my wife and I love to nap, and our timing is often in sync—we'll just dive under the covers midday, snuggle into dozing off, and waking up hours later to watch the beautiful sunset from our mountain.

Tonight, as the sun set over the beautiful Okanagan Valley, a dramatic splash of purple clouds covered the spectacular mountains. I gave my wife a piggy-back ride around the pool, and we leaned over the edge, watching the city lights begin to flicker on. My beautiful but goofy Friesian Warmblood horse (a creature that was never intended to be part of my life's plans) gazed curiously at us from behind a young willow tree. I locked into her eyes for a timeless moment, soaking in the simple wisdom I saw there.

And I realized that my life is absolutely perfect.

But not at all like I had originally planned.

If you ask me—and I guess you sort of did by buying this book—making plans is highly overrated.

My Approach

I am often asked for advice on how to become successful. For me, it certainly wasn't by following The Plan. All I can do is liken my approach to photography.

Let's say I set out to photograph a cheetah running at full speed. I would prepare for this shoot by making sure that I had space on my memory cards and that my camera batteries were fully charged. I'd carefully select a long telephoto lens and a camera with a high-speed motor drive. I would consult nature experts for the best place to find a cheetah hunting for prey. Then I would go to that spot, fully prepared for the moment.

If I was successful—and there's a sizeable chance I wouldn't be—I would credit 90 percent of it to preparation and 10 percent to luck. Most of the effort is getting ready, so when the shot appears, it is all just a matter of reflex. It's where preparation meets chance.

But now imagine that while I was waiting for the cheetah, a spaceship landed in front of me, and out stepped Elvis. Would I ignore that moment and *not* take the photo, even though it wasn't part of The Plan?

I think you know the answer to that.

So the ability to change course at the drop of a hat is also an integral part of my success formula.

Notice I haven't said anything about hard work.

"Work hard and never give up." "Make a goal and stick to it." "Stay on course and don't waver." This is the advice that fills bookshelves in the self-help, biography, and business aisles. (One former president that comes to mind even ran his administration this way.)

I've read many of these books, and, at least for me, the advice just doesn't stack up.

Let's take the ubiquitous "hard work" message. In photography, we rarely credit a stunning image to hard work. You can struggle up the longest hill, carry the bulkiest equipment, and take the longest path to the mountaintop, yet your shot may not be as good as that of the nearby tourist who took his photo from the clearly marked "Scenic Vista" right next to the highway.

Those who say that the only path to success is hard work evidently define success as working hard. I don't.

What about persistence? Being stubbornly persistent won't serve me very well if I'm a thousand miles from the nearest cheetah. I'd be wasting a lot of precious time in a futile situation.

Staying on course? Good idea, I guess, but not if you are on the wrong course! For example, I knew I was not in love with my first wife, so I cancelled the wedding. Then, in a stupefying snap back to conformity, I agreed to go back to her and set a new wedding date five months later. We both should have known better, and because we didn't, we lost several good years by "staying on course."

This begs the question, so when do you know you're on the wrong course? The answer to that is uniquely personal and can't come from a book. But I do know that as a photographer, if I think a shot is not going to present itself where I'm standing, I get fidgety pretty soon and start looking around. And if another spot—or another photo subject entirely—looks more promising, I move there. Experienced lake fishermen do the same thing.

Setting concrete goals and sticking to The Plan can be foolish. What if my do-or-die goal was to capture an image of Santa Claus landing on a rooftop? Yes, that would be a remarkable image. But in all likelihood, trying to get it would be a tragic waste of time, no matter how persistent I was or how clearly I envisioned the goal.

The world is constantly shuffling its deck. What worked yesterday probably won't work tomorrow, despite all the "good" advice out there about hard work, persistence, and staying on course. As an inventor, entrepreneur, or investor, my successful moments have come not through holding on to goals, but through trying to guess where the trend is going next, so I can be there when the crowd arrives. It's like being a photographer and waiting for the cheetah. You don't *cause* the cheetah to come, you just make your best guess about when and where it's going to show up, and prepare for it.

I did that successfully with wedding photography, by making my albums tell a story. I did it with Montage software, by knowing that the photography industry was going to become computerized, and that photographers would need specialized software. And with digital photography, I knew that photographers would eventually need a dedicated lab connected to their online viewing, so I started Pictage's lab. I also felt that the harsh contrast of digital photography was going to create a lot of blown-out images, so I invented the Lightsphere II. Nobody knew about the sleepy little town of Kelowna when I bought my first property there, but with the new international airport and those incredible views, I knew it was just a matter of time before the crowd arrived. And arrive it did, driving the value of my investments way up.

So there have been many times when I've been well prepared and have bagged the cheetah. Being prepared, though, is not the same thing as having a plan. Not at all. The fact is, whenever I made a plan with narrowly defined goals and pursued it with focused attention, I failed miserably. That is partially due to a little principle I call the Law of Repulsion.

The Law of Repulsion

The Law of Attraction gets a lot of press these days. What you never hear about is its lesser-known corollary, the Law of Repulsion, which is every bit as powerful. Its job is to deliver to you the exact opposite of whatever it is you are fervidly seeking.

When a well-meaning New Ager attempts to explain the Law of Attraction to you, s/he will often use a magnet as an example: "Your thoughts are like a magnet, pulling your desires to you like another magnet. When you put happy thoughts out there, happy things are drawn to you." What the earnest New Ager fails to tell you, though, is that a magnet has two poles, and you never know which end is coming at you. Your happy magnet can just as easily send that other happy magnet skittering across the floor in retreat, never to be grasped by you in a zillion years, just like those little black-and-white magnetic dogs they used to sell in joke shops when I was a kid.

I often think my life has been governed more by the Law of Repulsion than the Law of Attraction. Over and over, I've gotten the precise opposite of whatever goal I've striven most intensely for. The harder I tried to make money, for example, the more money problems I had. The harder I tried to get work, the harder the work was to find. Whenever I sought love in a needy way, I only brought myself loneliness and misery. The more I sought guidance from others, the more confused I became.

The list goes on. But here's what I finally realized: the Law of Repulsion is neither good nor bad. It just *is*, like electricity or, well, the Law of Attraction. The Law of Repulsion can just as easily deliver surprising benefits as it can bring bad news. The more I retreated from working as a professional photographer, for example, the more famous I became. When I decided to shoot fewer weddings, the demand for my services skyrocketed—and so did my prices. When I gave up hope, happiness snuck in through my back door.

There's an old Greek saying: "The Gods ask little but that they be remembered." I think maybe the Law of Repulsion is "the Gods'" way of reminding us that we are not in charge.

And that, it turns out, is a very good thing.

You see, the Law of Repulsion often serves to smash our nearsighted plans to bits so that something even better can occur. As a law, it is every bit as helpful and "on our side" as its sexier counterpart, the Law of Attraction. But instead of delivering what our warped little minds *think* they want, it opens up the space for something even better. It opens up the space for magic.

What if I had *loved* my life at UCLA, rather than finding it potentially deadly? Maybe I would be a physician today, working long hours at some HMO, pulling down maybe $150,000 a year and spending half of it on malpractice insurance and repaying student loans. Yay, plan realized.

If UCLA had given me what I wanted, I wouldn't have ended up at Santa Barbara. I wouldn't have seen that *Life* magazine article, I wouldn't have gone to Rocky Gunn's studio, and I wouldn't have gotten into wedding photography. Which, in turn, means that I wouldn't have created Montage software, co-founded Pictage, or invented the Lightsphere. I would never have gone on that speaking tour, I wouldn't have met Melissa Carl, and I wouldn't be happily married or starting a family or sitting here on this beautiful ranch.

The point I'm trying to make is that hammering away at The Plan is as likely to cause you to miss greater opportunities, or to bring about the *exact opposite* of your goal, as it is to bring about success. So I don't put much stock in it as a success strategy.

Being prepared, though, that's different. As Louis Pasteur said, "Chance favors the prepared mind."

So *that's* my great success advice, after all these pages? The corny old Boy Scout motto, "Be prepared"? Well, yeah. Except with a little twist. My motto is actually, "Be prepar*ing*."

Preparing for *what*, though?

It almost doesn't matter. For whatever cheetah you're hot to photograph. Using your own personal blend of imagination, research, foresight, and creative visualization, you work up an intelligent guess about when and where your particular cheetah is heading, and you start preparing yourself to shoot it when it gets there.

Does that mean you're going to be right? No. But again, it almost doesn't matter. As long as you're fully engaged in the process of preparing for *something*, that means you're learning and growing, you're stretching and adjusting, you're adapting to a changing world, you're learning to read the landscape, you're throwing out old maps. And that alone is preparing you for *some* next stage, even if the cheetah you were hoping for doesn't show up.

with my dad and my wife Melissa

I learned karate so I could kick more schoolyard ass, but what it really did was prepare me to be calm in times of business turmoil. I bought my Desert Survival Kit to prepare me for homelessness. Homelessness never came, but the self-reliance I learned in that adventure has served me over and over. When you're passionately preparing for one thing, the universe may be preparing you for something else. As long as you're actively and creatively preparing for *something*, you're usually on the right track.

It's the times when everything is going according to plan, you're meeting your goals, and you're not making any real demands on yourself that you've got to worry about. The process of getting ready for what's around the corner is what makes life so much fun. Your preparation may not pay off when or how you think it will, but it *will* pay off eventually. How this happens is the grand mystery.

I can't control fuel prices or the economy or the job market or the costs of war. But I can control my patience. I can control my fears. I can face those fears and prepare myself for a changing world, rather than freaking out and running around in circles. Beyond that, all I can do is find some new cheetah to chase, prepare to shoot it, detach from the results, and let whatever happens happen.

When I snag my shot, I celebrate. And when I don't, instead of being disappointed that The Plan fell through, I recognize that in some mysterious way, I've been preparing myself for this magical new moment for years.

about the author

GARY FONG is a globally renowned photographer, inventor, and entrepreneur. He is the father of "storybooking," now the industry standard in wedding photography, in which candid shots are arranged in real time to tell a story, as opposed to the archaic method of taking posed, stilted shots. He is also the inventor of the Lightsphere, a specially colored dome that is held in place over the flash unit of a camera. Before long, more than 200,000 units were sold worldwide, thus creating a multimillion-dollar plastics business. Since inventing the Lightsphere, Fong has built a veritable cottage industry around variations on the popular product, including The Origami and The Puffer, all of which have become standard equipment used by most wedding photographers worldwide. He is considered one of the most influential photographers and inventors of his generation.

Lauren A. Chapman, openField photography

acknowledgments

This book started with me talking into an iPod. In three and a half weeks, the manuscript was done, or so I thought. Two years later, it hit the bookshelves and there are a lot of people who got involved after the original manuscript was done. I wish to thank all those who helped me. Without them, I could not have completed this project.

This book wouldn't have gotten published without the help and encouragement from our dear friend Jodee Blanco. After reading her book *Please Stop Laughing at Me* (a *New York Times* bestseller), I took it upon myself to send her some clips from my original book, *SNAPS*. Much to my amazement, she wrote me back. Then to further that high, she brought her editor, the legendary Kent Carroll (founder of the elite publishing house, Carroll & Graf), to add his immeasurable skills to my rough words, and we had the refined book. I knew we might have something when Kent said he liked it.

My sincere appreciation to Andy Wolfendon, my extremely talented editing partner who gets all of my jokes and makes them funnier. To Shelley Surpin, my entertainment lawyer (and producer for one of my favorite movies ever, *Grace Of My Heart*), for hovering over this project with her watchful eye. And of course, to Glenn Yeffeth, my publisher and his enthusiastic staff at BenBella Books, for believing in this project enough to put it on their roster of quality books.

So many of the lessons I've learned in life I can credit to two key mentors. My father, Chek Fong, for teaching me the importance of saving and living below your means, and Rocky Gunn, who taught me that "nobody needs a salesman knocking on their door, but everybody could use a new friend."

Most of all, to my best friend and wife, Melissa Carl, for her love, constant support, and encouragement in all of my pre-visualizations. It is wonderful to live a life where you daydream together with someone you love.